GUILTY UNTIL PROVEN INNOCENT

THE CRISIS IN OUR
JUSTICE SYSTEM

GUILTY UNTIL PROVEN INNOCENT

JON ROBINS

FOREWORD BY MICHAEL MANSFIELD QC

Biteback Publishing

First published in Great Britain in 2018 by
Biteback Publishing Ltd
Westminster Tower
3 Albert Embankment
London SE1 7SP
Copyright © Jon Robins 2018

Jon Robins has asserted his right under the Copyright, Designs and Patents Act 1988 to be identified as the author of this work.

All rights reserved. No part of this publication may be reproduced, stored in a retrieval system or transmitted, in any form or by any means, without the publisher's prior permission in writing.

This book is sold subject to the condition that it shall not, by way of trade or otherwise, be lent, resold, hired out or otherwise circulated without the publisher's prior consent in any form of binding or cover other than that in which it is published and without a similar condition, including this condition, being imposed on the subsequent purchaser.

Every reasonable effort has been made to trace copyright holders of material reproduced in this book, but if any have been inadvertently overlooked the publisher would be glad to hear from them.

ISBN 978-1-78590-369-4

10 9 8 7 6 5 4 3 2 1

A CIP catalogue record for this book is available from the British Library.

Set in Minion Pro and Knockout

Printed and bound in Great Britain by
CPI Group (UK) Ltd, Croydon CR0 4YY

CONTENTS

Foreword *by Michael Mansfield QC* — vii
Preface — xi
Introduction — xiii

1. The Waiting Game — 1
2. Full Disclosure — 39
3. From One Fix to the Next — 73
4. Defying Gravity — 107
5. Salem Comes to Salisbury — 143
6. Staring into the Abyss — 177
7. Collateral Damage — 203
8. A Medical Diagnosis of Murder — 221
9. Making a Murderer — 247
10. Caught in the Dragnet — 271
11. Innocent – But Not Innocent Enough — 295

Acknowledgements — 325
About the Author — 329
Index — 331

FOREWORD

I am reminded of the famous Monty Python sketch in which four Yorkshiremen competitively gripe about just how 'bad' the bad old days were: 'There were 150 of us living in a shoebox in the middle of the road,' says one. 'Cardboard box?' replies his friend. 'You were lucky...'

However, having just completed my fiftieth year of practice at the Bar, I reckon I am well placed to compare the state of the legal world as it is now, relative to my early years of legal practice.

It's not that nothing has changed; it has got worse. The need for active vigilance is now more imperative than ever. Once again, Jon Robins, in his groundbreaking and persistent work, has performed the vital task of pinpointing where the justice system is continuing to fail.

Those who cannot remember the past are condemned to repeat it. As I write this, I look back over the past six months. In 2016, Labour MP David Lammy was asked by the then Prime Minister David Cameron to conduct an investigation into the over-representation of black and minority ethic people in the criminal justice system.

You would think from the results of his review that the lessons contained in the landmark Macpherson Report, which was published almost twenty years ago after the racially motivated killing of Stephen Lawrence, was merely a straw in the judicial wind.

In his report, David Lammy describes prejudice, bias and discrimination in the justice system as a 'social time bomb' that requires urgent action. He has called for a review of the common law doctrine of joint enterprise, which has disproportionately targeted young black people in our cities (see Chapter 10).

It was the authorities' attitude to black youth, and its impact on the investigation, that lay at the heart of the grotesque mishandling of Stephen Lawrence's murder case, as well as the appalling treatment of his family. A matter still to be scrutinised by the undercover policing inquiry, which was established by Theresa May amid cries of horror at the idea of an unaccountable police state within a state. There has been an unexplained and inexcusable delay since the inquiry was launched in July 2015. Nearly three years on and still no evidence has been heard. Maybe the inquiry itself will be undercover?

Two cases were dropped in the space of a week in December 2017, due to shocking failures to disclose by the police and Crown Prosecution Service. There have been further collapses in the new year. In one case (Liam Allan, see Chapter 6), the withheld material, communications between complainant and defendant, could not have been more obviously vital. The prosecution acted like another of John Cleese's best-known creations – *Fawlty Towers*' Spanish waiter, Manuel: 'I know nothing'.

For those of us who practise in the criminal courts, such

disclosure failures are an all too common experience. They are certainly not limited to sexual offences. Figures show that, in 2016, 900 cases were dropped due to issues with disclosure, up from 732 the previous year and 537 in 2014.

For the Director of Public Prosecutions, Alison Saunders, to attempt to assure us that there have been no miscarriages as a result, as she did earlier this year, is an extraordinary claim. Tell that to the young student, Liam Allan, who was very nearly convicted and his life almost ruined.

What is going on? We went through this in the 1980s with the 'Irish' cases – the Birmingham Six and Judith Ward – discussed in this book. The judges hoped such gross non-disclosure would not be repeated. Subsequently, various safeguards were put in place, but, apparently, to little avail. At the end of the day, it depends on the quality of the personnel charged with the duty of disclosure as well as a conscientious judiciary.

Within a few days of such revelations, the forensic science regulator, Dr Gillian Tully, issued a stark warning that 'without urgent action there would inevitably be miscarriages of justice'.

Wait a minute. We've been here too. Forensics, like vast areas of the justice system and the health service, have been deregulated and fragmented in the private sector. In 2012, the government abolished the Forensic Science Service, which, despite its failings, tried to set basic benchmarks.

There is, of course, another agenda at play here. Austerity. There have been huge cuts across the board. By the end of the decade, the Ministry of Justice's budget (which covers prisons, probation and the legal aid system) will have been slashed by 40 per cent since the coalition government came to power in 2010.

Such cuts are already impacting on the availability of quality lawyers, police and prison officers and even judges.

When I started out, British justice was held up as an example to the rest of the world. It has been diminished and demoralised. I write this without accounting for changes to legal procedure that have changed the landscape: the abolition of the right to silence; the relaxation of rules relating to the admission of hearsay and previous convictions; the abolition of the need for corroboration; and the pressure for early pleas. It's not so much convicting the guilty, but putting the innocent at risk.

You are guilty until you prove you are not.

Michael Mansfield QC
May 2018

PREFACE

The front door crashes open. It's just gone 5 a.m. There are feet pounding up the stairs. As you stumble out of bed, you're taken aside. You hear the words that you have heard so many times before on TV: 'You don't have to say anything…'. The neighbours' curtains twitch as, head bowed, you're placed in the backseat of a police car. You have nothing to hide. You have faith in the criminal justice system – but your nightmare is only just beginning.

As a lawyer specialising in criminal defence for twenty years, I have news for you: many of the people I represent are not guilty. How sure can any of us be that the police will realise when they have taken a wrong turn? That the CPS will decide not to take the matter any further? That the jury will find sufficient doubt to outweigh their 'no smoke without fire' prejudice?

It has been more than a quarter of a century since scandalous miscarriages of justice – such as the Guildford Four and the Birmingham Six – shocked the public out of its complacency about the supposed infallibility of our courts. Widespread concern led to a royal commission and fundamental reforms. Such reforms never fixed the problem, and it would be naive to think that they ever could.

As practitioners in our criminal courts, we witness at first hand the frailties of the justice system. This book is being published at a time when an underfunded system is creaking. Unprecedented pressures on the police and prosecution, swingeing cuts to the Ministry of Justice's budget, not to mention two decades of frozen legal aid rates for defence lawyers have all contributed to a growing crisis.

Should the aim of the criminal justice system be to ensure that all guilty people are convicted, even if that means a few innocent ones go down? Or should it strive to protect the innocent at all costs, even if that means letting a few that are guilty slip away? Both options involve 'miscarriages of justice', but the presumption of innocence favours the latter over the former.

Sadly, that presumption has been under heavy fire over the last two decades from ambitious politicians and a press quick to be outraged, but reluctant to understand.

The cases that feature in this book should send shivers down the spines of every law-abiding citizen. The increasing focus on convicting the guilty instead of protecting the innocent means that we may soon all have cause to fear the dawn raid.

Rod Hayler
Old Bailey Solicitors

INTRODUCTION

When a miscarriage of justice case hits the headlines, it is easy to dismiss it as a shocking one-off aberration – a minor hiccup in a system that otherwise functions in an exemplary fashion. After all, we are told by politicians and lawyers that our criminal justice system is the finest in the world.

In reality, our justice system is in a state of permanent crisis. Our dilapidated courts are falling apart. It's not just that paint peels off the courtroom walls and the roofs leak; inefficiency has become endemic. More than half of criminal trials in this country have to be called off or rescheduled. In 2015, some 1,200 Crown Court trials were unable to start as scheduled because the private companies contracted to escort prisoners to court failed to deliver the defendants on time. According to the spending watchdog, the National Audit Office, the Crown Prosecution Service spent £21.5 million that year on preparing for cases that were never heard.

Austerity has hit the criminal justice system hard. The Ministry of Justice's budget, which covers prisons, probation and the legal aid system, will have been slashed by 40 per cent since the coalition government came to power in 2010 by the end of the decade. That is a cut from £9.3 billion in 2010/11 to a predicted £5.6 billion by 2019/20.

Legal aid lawyers, derided in the press as 'fat cats', have not had an increase in their fees for twenty years. It is a measure of the disdain in which the rights of defendants are held that the coalition government threatened to impose a 17.5 per cent cut in legal aid rates. Where else do we see cuts on that scale?*

Our courts operate on a 'two-nation' system. There is 'the wealthy, international class' who opt to settle their cases in London with its 'gold standard of British justice'. And then there is everyone else. The rest of us have to put up with 'a creaking, outdated system'.

That is not the confected outrage of some vested interest with an axe to grind. It is the assessment of a recent Lord Chancellor. 'I have heard too many accounts of cases derailed by the late arrival of prisoners, broken video links or missing paperwork,' said Michael Gove in 2015, in his first speech as Lord Chancellor. The politician observed for himself lawyers arriving in court with their huge bundles of paper, describing the large stacks with typical flourish as 'snowdrifts of paper held in place by delicate pink ribbons', and wondered what century our courts were living in.†

Gove did not last long in the post. Lord Chancellors don't these days. There have been six in the past six years. The problems that he rightly identified, however, have only got worse.

---

* In 2014, a cut of 8.75 per cent was imposed on the legal aid fees for criminal defence solicitors and a second equal-sized cut was put on hold.
† Michael Gove gave his first speech as Lord Chancellor at the Legatum Institute on 25 June 2015. He said: 'I have seen both prosecution and defence barristers in a case that touched on an individual's most precious rights acknowledge that each had only received the massive bundles in front of them hours before and – through no fault of their own – were very far from being able to make the best case possible.' He was sacked from the post by Prime Minister Theresa May in July the following year.

At the same time as this impoverishment, the criminal justice pendulum has swung dramatically in the direction of victims' rights and away from the rights of defendants. Successive governments have bought into Tony Blair's 'tough on crime, tough on the causes of crime' mantra.

'Some of our reforms will be controversial,' Tony Blair told Labour Party conference delegates in 2002, ahead of the launch of his criminal justice White Paper. The then Prime Minister promised to 'rebalance' our justice system, so that the rights of suspects did not outweigh the rights of 'the law-abiding majority'.

In his conference speech, Blair sought to redefine what we understand by 'miscarriages of justice'. Perhaps, he suggested to the party faithful, 'the biggest miscarriage of justice' in today's system is 'when the guilty walk away unpunished'.

Of course, Tony Blair's speech was not controversial in the slightest. It now takes a brave politician to speak out in defence of the rights of defendants in this climate. At the start of 2018, a series of high-profile rape cases collapsed over a two-month period because of failures to disclose evidence. In the high-profile case of Liam Allan, the police had downloaded 40,000 text and WhatsApp messages from the woman's phone. Allan's lawyers had repeatedly asked for the data to be handed over to them before the trial. Instead, they were assured there was nothing to disclose. The messages were finally released three days into Allan's trial. This wealth of evidence revealed that his accuser had pursued the 22-year-old psychology student for (her words) 'casual sex'.

A miscarriage of justice was narrowly avoided. Allan had

been on bail for nearly two years. It was the prosecution counsel who insisted on the defence seeing all the evidence three days into the trial at Croydon Crown Court. 'The system nearly failed,' the barrister said. 'This is a criminal justice system which is not just creaking, it's about to croak.'

As a result of this and a run of similarly collapsed cases, the Metropolitan Police drafted in more than 100 officers to review 600 rape and sexual assault cases. An unreserved apology has been extended to Allan.

This is not a one-off.* The number of prosecutions in England and Wales that have collapsed due to a failure by police or prosecutors to disclose evidence has increased by 70 per cent in the past two years. Meanwhile, the miscarriage of justice watchdog reports that failures in disclosure are the biggest cause of wrongful convictions.

The Director of Public Prosecutions, Alison Saunders, was asked if it was possible that there were people in prison today because of failures of disclosures. Apparently, there is nothing to worry about.†

• • •

On 14 March 1991, Paddy Hill, Hugh Callaghan, Richard McIlkenny, Gerry Hunter, Billy Power and Johnny Walker left the Old Bailey. They were finally free, having spent sixteen years behind

---

* The Liam Allan case is uncannily similar to the case of Elgan Varney (see Chapter Six).
† When asked on BBC Radio 4's *Today* programme on 18 January 2018, the DPP Alison Saunders said: 'I don't think so because what these cases show is that when we take a case through to trial there are various safeguards in place, not least of which is the defence indicating what their defence is going to be.'

bars after their convictions for the murder of twenty-one people, as a result of bombs placed in two Birmingham pubs in November 1974, were overturned.

Set up on the very day that the so-called Birmingham Six were released, a royal commission was tasked with repairing the battered reputation of British justice. That scandal had exposed a mindset at the top of the judiciary that valued maintaining the appearance of integrity over the lives of individuals destroyed in the rush to judgment.

It was a view most infamously articulated by Lord Denning. Then Master of the Rolls, Denning ruled in 1980 that there would be no further appeals in the Birmingham Six case. 'If they won,' he said,

> it would mean that the police were guilty of perjury; that they were guilty of violence and threats; that the confessions were involuntary and improperly admitted in evidence; and that the convictions were erroneous. That was such an appalling vista that every sensible person would say: 'It cannot be right that these actions should go any further.'

It was a position that Denning did not resile from even in retirement. Historian A. N. Wilson asked him in 1990 whether he was glad that the death penalty had been scrapped. 'Not really,' the esteemed judge replied. 'It ought to be retained for murder most foul. We shouldn't have all these campaigns to get the Birmingham Six released if they'd been hanged. They'd have been forgotten, and the whole community would have been satisfied.'

All 'systems' make mistakes. No sensible person would be

surprised that one so complex, chronically underfunded and dependent on other autonomous but similarly cash-starved agencies as British justice would from time to time err. A willingness to acknowledge fallibility, as well as being the decent and humane thing to do, is the right thing to do.

From the Birmingham Six to the 1989 Hillsborough football stadium tragedy, extreme institutional denial of the justice system has done more to undermine public confidence than the begrudging confirmation that the police really did beat confessions out of innocent Irish men or, in the case of Hillsborough, falsely made out grieving football fans to be drunken, ticketless louts who invited tragedy upon themselves.

It took the Hillsborough families twenty-eight years to get their measure of justice in the form of the 2016 inquests, which ruled that the ninety-six fans were 'unlawfully killed'.

Like many people, all these years later, I can still recall the moment I first saw those distressing television images of Hillsborough stadium on the afternoon of Saturday 15 April 1989. I come from a family of Liverpool FC fans. My father and brother were both at the match. My mother and I endured a long wait before discovering that they were OK. Then there was further anxiety until we heard news about my brother's friend, who had travelled with them. Ray was one of the lucky ones. He managed to extricate himself from the Lepping Lane stand and climbed over the fencing to the adjoining pens.

On 29 September 2016, I interviewed Margaret Aspinall, chair of the Hillsborough family support group at Liverpool FC's ground. Her eighteen-year-old son James died in the stadium disaster. 'Even now it feels raw,' she told me. 'He goes off to a football game and he comes back five days later in a coffin. You need answers.'

In the background as we spoke, the Kop boomed out 'You'll Never Walk Alone'. It was playing on a fifteen-minute loop over the Anfield speaker system, for the benefit of fans from all over the world who were touring the hallowed ground.

The Hillsborough families had a community behind them. 'That is why we have to try and change things,' Margaret Aspinall told me. 'No parent should have to go through what we did alone.'

There are many families out there fighting for justice on behalf of loved ones. Their campaigns do not have the critical mass of the Hillsborough campaign – they go it alone.

• • •

Much of this book was written in the year of the twentieth anniversary of the Criminal Cases Review Commission (CCRC). The most concrete of 350-plus recommendations of the royal commission, set up on the day the Birmingham Six were released, was its proposal to create the first state-funded miscarriage of justice watchdog.

If you are in prison for a crime you have not committed, and you have unsuccessfully appealed, then your one and only chance of clearing your name resides with the Birmingham-based CCRC. It alone has the power to refer your case back to the Court of Appeal.

On average the CCRC receives 1,500 applications a year, mainly from prisoners. In the year of writing, the miscarriage watchdog referred just twelve cases back to the Court of Appeal.

The commission, oversubscribed and understaffed, is just another symptom of a failing criminal justice system. It is no coincidence that the system's so-called safety net mechanism has suffered more under austerity than any other agency.

In 2016, the CCRC's chair, Richard Foster, told MPs that for every £10 that his predecessor had to spend on a case a decade ago, he now had just £4. That represented the deepest cut that had taken place anywhere in the justice budget.

Almost as soon as the CCRC was set up, it was undermined: first by politicians and then by the Court of Appeal.

Many lawyers and academics would say that the Court of Appeal has changed little since those bad old days.

• • •

Guilty Until Proven Innocent is about miscarriages of justice (but not of Tony Blair's kind). Each chapter starts with a different case of alleged wrongful conviction. The purpose of the book is to explore the common ground between the cases, all quite different and unique, in an attempt to shine light on why the criminal justice system keeps failing us.

This book is the work of a journalist, not an academic or a lawyer, although it is influenced by the debate in legal and academic circles. There is a small constituency of concern comprising lawyers, academics, journalists and campaigners that has mobilised around miscarriages of justice.

Many of them have written for the Justice Gap website, taken part in the House of Commons' justice committee 2015 investigation into the CCRC, and are currently involved in the formation of the all-party parliamentary group on miscarriages of justice. I have been influenced by their work in writing this book (but the book is an entirely independent enterprise).

The book is not arranged thematically, but I examine the following big issues:

- There is no adequate safety net. The Court of Appeal continues to fail to get to grips with miscarriages of justice.
- There is no effective watchdog. The CCRC is so chronically underfunded and overwhelmed that it fails to do the job it was set up to do.
- These are hidden problems. The creation of the commission has usurped the role of others who previously investigated miscarriages of justice and, as a result, this failure of our justice system has gone largely unreported. As a result of a two-decade pay freeze on legal aid, very few lawyers are willing to undertake appeal work. Similarly, the media (with honourable exceptions) have largely given up on miscarriage cases. I began this introduction by saying: 'Whenever a miscarriage of justice case hits the headlines…' The reality is that they very rarely do.
- We have little meaningful 'open justice'. There remain huge problems with disclosure and access to evidence, and more generally a lack of accountability on the parts of the courts and legal profession.
- Failures in policing persist. Tunnel vision, police misconduct and allegations of corruption feature in many of the cases included in this book.

- Poor legal defence. The inevitable consequence of the crisis in legal aid is that many defendants suffer as a result of incompetent legal representation.
- Inexpert evidence. Courts are often over-reliant and misled by flawed expert evidence.

Prior to the CCRC, there were clear types of cases (terrorism, unreliable identifications, police misconduct etc.) that came to redefine in people's minds what a 'miscarriage of justice' was.

Over the past twenty years there have been clear categories of miscarriages of justice ('joint enterprise' convictions, especially in the context of gang and knife crime, junk science cases and historical sexual abuse cases). But they are less well understood by the public.

As I said, each chapter features a different case. Each one is complex. They are not black and white. I attempt to write about the cases in a way that is fair to all sides. It does not help anyone to embellish the facts of a case and present it in a more positive light.

• • •

One day in March 2015, I found myself sitting in the lounge of a married couple. They had been through a hellish experience. The husband had spent twenty months in prison for crimes he always insisted he had never committed. He was convicted of offences relating to historical sexual abuse allegations. Miraculously, the couple had come out the other side intact.

On his first night in prison, the husband had contemplated taking his own life. He had a heart condition and had recently had a stent fitted in his upper thigh to regulate the flow of blood. He planned to take the plug out and 'lie there; quietly bleeding to death'.

But, he insisted, he had had it easy compared to his wife. One day she was sitting outside school in her car, having just picked up their seven-year-old son. She was about to pull away from the kerb when the mother of one of her son's friends came over. Her window was open and the woman punched her in the face. As she walked away, she keyed the side of her car. All the time, their son sat behind his mother with his seatbelt on.

Her husband is now a free man because of the hard work of a loving wife, who refused to give up despite what must have seemed an impossible fight. His conviction was quashed in the Court of Appeal.

As I sat down on their sofa, I placed my iPhone on the table ready to record. The interview had been cancelled and then rescheduled. The husband didn't want to talk to the press. His wife believed it was important that they did. She wanted to tell other people in their position that they weren't alone.

So I hit 'record'. I sense there is something he wants to say before we start. There is. 'As a society, we accept that there are miscarriages of justice and that there has to be collateral damage,' he tells me. 'For every eight people who get sent to prison in relation to these types of allegations, two might be innocent. *They* are the collateral damage.'

• • •

Over the past couple of years, there has been a surge of interest in the topic of miscarriages of justice. Curiously, this renewed interest has had nothing to do with the deepening crisis in the justice system, and everything to do with the success of American documentaries into cases of alleged wrongful conviction.

The best of these programmes was the Netflix hit *Making a Murderer*, which documented the plight of Steven Avery of Manitowoc County, Wisconsin, who spent eighteen years in prison for a sexual assault that he did not commit.* Two years after Avery's release, and having just filed a $36 million lawsuit, he was arrested for murder. What followed over ten episodes was an unsparing dissection of what looks like some pretty rough justice. The two film-makers, Laura Ricciardi and Moira Demos, spent ten years working on the series.

As you reach the climax of Avery's story, one of his lawyers, the wise and eloquent Dean Strang, using words that resonate on this side of the Atlantic, delivers the following impromptu soliloquy on the limits of American justice:

> Most of what ails our criminal justice system lies in an unwarranted certitude on the part of police officers, and prosecutors and defence lawyers, and judges and jurors, that they're getting it right. That they're simply right. It is just a tragic lack of humility.

This book is dedicated to our justice system's collateral damage.

---

* The US podcast *Serial*, which narrated an unfolding investigation into the case of Adnan Syed, who was convicted of killing his ex-girlfriend, is the most popular podcast ever and is reckoned to have been downloaded 68 million times.

CHAPTER ONE

THE WAITING GAME

In the early evening of 4 June 1992, off-duty police officer Paul Caddick opened the garage door at No. 6, Grafton Drive in Upton, on the Wirral peninsula not far from Liverpool, and made a gruesome discovery. His sister-in-law, eight and a half months pregnant, was hanging by the neck from a rope that had been suspended from a ceiling beam.

The death of Paula Gilfoyle continues to cast a long shadow over the lives of family and friends more than a quarter of a century later. When Paul Caddick, then a 34-year-old police sergeant based down the road in Upton village, arrived at No. 6, he still had a bright career ahead of him. Paula's death would change his life irrevocably.

The nightmare began when Caddick's father-in-law rang him at 7 p.m. that evening; Norman Gilfoyle wanted him to come to his son's house. When Caddick arrived, he found his brother-in-law, Eddie Gilfoyle, distraught. Norman passed over a handwritten note from Paula, as if it would explain everything.

Dear Eddie,

I've decided to put an end to everything and in doing so end a chapter in my life that I can't face up to any longer. I don't want to have this baby that I'm carrying. I wish now that I'd got rid of it. When I was thinking about it, I wouldn't be hurting the way I am now...

The couple both worked shifts and had picked up the habit of leaving notes on the kitchen work surface for each other. Gilfoyle claimed to have only read the opening lines when he returned from work earlier that afternoon. Convinced that he was reading a 'Dear John' letter – and that his wife had walked out on him – Gilfoyle said he had driven directly to his parents' house ten minutes away.

Paul Caddick kept reading:

Don't blame yourself, Eddie, it's not your fault. I've caused all your pain and heartache. I've destroyed you and your life. I just hope you can rebuild everything and realise your goals and dreams.

I am sorry for hurting my family, your family and my friends, but most of all hurting you. I never meant to. Don't be afraid to tell people the truth, they can't hurt me because I'm not there to face up to them all. I loved you in my own way but I destroyed it all through my own stupidity. All my moaning and nagging at you wouldn't have helped us to rebuild things between us.

Eddie, I've done some things in my life that I am not proud of but I got through somehow but this is just too much. I can't face up to my problems any more. I had packed a bag and even moved some of my clothes already but I can't run any more, it is the end of the line for me on this earth.

Give my mum and dad a keepsake for me, explain things as best as you can, tell them I love them and that I'm sorry for everything.

Eddie, I hope you will find it in your heart to forgive me and that one day we will meet again until that day, take care of yourself, don't be afraid in life, I will watch over you and protect you from harm. I've ruined your life, it is the best I can do maybe it will be the one thing I can do right in life.

I can't change or alter what I've done but if I could, I would. They say time heals a broken heart, I hope your heart heals pretty quick. I don't want you to waste any more of your life. It's time to turn the clock forward instead of backwards and go forward.

Good night and God bless.

Love,

Paula

PS: I apologise for all the pain and suffering I have caused by taking my own life. I don't mean to cause any problems for anyone, no one is to blame except myself.

The due date for Eddie and Paula's baby was in two weeks: 18 June.

While Paul Caddick read the note, Norman Gilfoyle rang around family and friends who might know of his daughter-in-law's whereabouts. Caddick called Upton Police Station, requesting that a colleague come over and make a missing person's report. Caddick asked if Norman and his wife Jessie had looked upstairs. They had. What about outside? No.

Caddick asked Eddie Gilfoyle for the keys to the garage. While Caddick was trying, but failing, to open the garage door, a uniformed colleague arrived. Gilfoyle directed Caddick to a spare key kept underneath the porch mat. There were two Yale keys there.

No. 6 was a semi-detached house, with a lean-to garage at one side. Caddick peered through the frosted glass of the garage doors and glimpsed a blue outline, but he could not make it out, and opened the door to make his grim discovery. He was immediately confronted by Paula's suspended body. Beneath it was a small aluminium stepladder. Paula's feet trailed from the ladder's lower step, her knees some fifteen inches from the garage floor.

The second police officer on the scene was PC Brian Jones. He arrived at 8 p.m. As coroner's officer for the Wirral, PC Jones reported unnatural and suspicious deaths.

During the course of his ten years in the job as coroner's officer, Jones had made many visits like this, and had seen the aftermath of countless suicides. He saw Paula's suspended body and drew the obvious conclusion. He cut the body down to, as he later put it, 'preserve her dignity'. Jones took Paula's weight by holding her under the armpits, while his uniformed colleague severed the rope. The pair then laid the body of Paula Gilfoyle on the floor.

As coroner's officer, PC Jones assumed control of what, in his view, was evidently a case of suicide. When the scene of crime officer arrived at Grafton Drive at 8.18 p.m., Paula's body had already been laid out on the garage's cold, concrete floor. Jones informed the scene of crime officer that photographs were not necessary. Two CID officers soon arrived. 'There's nothing for you,' Jones told them.

Two minutes later, the police surgeon turned up. He detected early signs of rigor mortis. Some seven officers were called to the garage that day.

Out of respect for a grieving family, PC Jones climbed up the stepladder, removed the rope from the beam and put it in his pocket. The following day, a post-mortem was held at nearby Arrowe Park Hospital. Nothing was recorded that suggested anything other than suicide. A mortuary worker threw the rope that Jones had removed from Paula's neck into the waste bin.

• • •

The year before Paula Gilfoyle died, there was such a crisis of confidence in the criminal justice system that the public was promised a royal commission. On 14 March 1991, Paddy Hill, Hugh Callaghan, Richard McIlkenny, Gerry Hunter, Billy Power and Johnny Walker stood outside the Old Bailey, free after sixteen years, having had their convictions overturned for the murder of twenty-one people as a result of bombs placed in two Birmingham pubs in November 1974.

The Birmingham Six, as they were known, were completely innocent. The royal commission was announced on the same day as they were freed.

On 21 November 1974, the men had been drinking in a pub at New Street Station in Birmingham, before boarding a train to catch a ferry to Belfast. Within six minutes of their departure, the bombs exploded.

A bomb concealed in a duffel bag exploded at the Mulberry Bush pub in central Birmingham, and ten minutes later a second bomb ripped apart the Tavern in the Town. Twenty-one people died, thirteen of whom were under thirty, and a further 182 were injured.

It was the worst mainland attack in Britain since the war. The IRA bombing campaign unleashed a vicious backlash in Great Britain, and in its wake there followed a series of wrongful convictions. In the case of the Birmingham Six, false confessions were secured through police beatings and bolstered by dubious forensic evidence. Dr Frank Skuse conducted a series of Griess tests on the hands, fingernails and belongings of the men, and concluded with '99 per cent certainty' that Hill and Power had handled explosives. In the autumn of 1985, an investigation by ITV's *World in Action* revealed how shuffling an old pack of playing cards could score a positive result. The men had been playing cards on the train.

The Birmingham Six scandal did more to undermine public confidence in the justice system and damage the reputations of the police and judiciary than any other case in living memory.

It led to the 1993 Runciman Commission, which promised fundamental structural reforms. This book is about the justice system that came out of those reforms, and its willingness to recognise wrongful convictions.

The scandal of the Birmingham Six exposed a view on the part of the senior judiciary that public confidence in the system was more important than justice being done in individual cases. At the Court of Appeal in 1980, the Master of the Rolls Lord Denning spoke of the 'appalling vista' that would arise were it ever to be demonstrated that the six men were telling the truth about being beaten up in police custody. This was no one-off throwaway comment. In 1988, Denning said (again in relation to the Birmingham Six): 'It is better that some innocent men remain in jail than the integrity of the English judicial system should be impugned.'

Nor was the Birmingham Six miscarriage of justice case a one-off. The release of the six men came hard on the heels of a series of scandals: the convictions of the Guildford Four and the Maguire Seven, in 1975 and 1976 respectively, for the Guildford pub bombings of October 1974, were quashed in 1989 and 1991. In Guildford, the IRA had detonated two six-pound gelignite bombs at two pubs popular with troops stationed at the local barracks. Four soldiers and one civilian were killed. A further sixty-five people were wounded.

• • •

Four days after Paula Gilfoyle's death, a tragic but otherwise unremarkable suicide became a murder investigation. Paula died on the Thursday; Paula's old friends visited her sister, Margaret Glover, on the Sunday. They did so, according to Glover's recollection, because they wanted 'to help us clear Paula's name'. The following day, two of Paula's co-workers gave statements to the police. They had a shocking and quite extraordinary story to relate.

Eddie Gilfoyle worked as an orderly at a private hospital. Gilfoyle, the two co-workers said, had got Paula to write fake suicide notes as part of a work assignment. They recalled a conversation with Paula in the staff canteen. 'We were sat at a table having a normal conversation when Paula said: "You'll never guess what I had to do last night", one of the women told the police. 'We both asked her and she said: "A suicide note..."'

A third work colleague, again a close friend of Paula's, also went to the police and recounted a separate conversation.

> Her pregnancy was showing by now, and I passed a remark to this effect. She seemed quite normal, but then said to me that she was 'a bit worried, Eddie is frightening me'. I asked her what she meant. And then she told me that Eddie was doing a suicide course at work.

Meanwhile, on the Saturday night, the men from the two families, plus friends, met for Paula's wake at the Farmers Arms in Moreton, a local pub where Paula and Eddie used to drink in their courting days. It was, unsurprisingly, a subdued evening. Eddie Gilfoyle remained devastated, apparently incapable of processing Thursday's tragic events.

The evening ended on a sour note when Paula's brother-in-law, Peter Glover, and Gilfoyle's father, Norman, clashed. Glover had broken down, only to be told by Gilfoyle Sr that he must 'be strong for Eddie'. Glover, on his own recollection, responded: 'You have only known her four years. I have known her for twenty-six years. If anyone has got a perfect right to be upset, it's me.'

On the Monday, a murder investigation began.

• • •

Merseyside Police detectives began to think that they might have a cold-blooded killer on their hands. An idea began to take shape: Eddie Gilfoyle had coaxed his heavily pregnant wife to put her head into a noose on her own volition. It seemed far-fetched, but perhaps no more so than a woman taking her own life just weeks before the birth of her child.

Yet the 'murder' scene suggested no struggle had taken place. The testimony of Paula's friends was likely to be of limited evidential value; hearsay generally isn't admissible in the criminal courts.

Four days after Paula's death, a Home Office pathologist conducted a second post-mortem. This revealed two tiny suspicious scratches on Paula's neck that had previously gone unnoticed – evidence, it was suggested, of her struggle. Gilfoyle's play-acting suddenly seemed much more sinister. The pathologist also noted the distance from the top of the ladder to the upside of the beam: 7ft 10in. How could Paula, 5ft 8in. and eight and a half months' pregnant, have wrapped the rope around the beam and tied the knot unaided?

On 8 June, Eddie Gilfoyle was arrested on suspicion of murdering his wife. Shortly afterwards, the police searched No. 6 Grafton Drive. Inside a footstool, they found a partially completed suicide note. 'To whom it may concern I, Paula Gilfoyle, have taken my life and I'm doing...' it read.

They also found a notebook, bearing the impressions of an earlier draft of a suicide note in a handwritten set of Paula's accounts. The sheet of paper itself had been ripped out, but her writing had left its indentation on the pad.

I am sorry for what I am about to tell you. I feel that I must put things right before I end my life which was turned on its head.

> *I don't want to go on any longer. I have cheated everyone for so long and now the truth will be out I don't think I will be a popular person.*

Were these notes evidence of Eddie Gilfoyle's practice runs? The pad, where one note had been written and torn out, had a list of accounts. If the writing of that suicide note predated the first entry on Paula's written accounts, then Gilfoyle could have been planning the murder since as early as March.

A second search of the garage was carried out. The police discovered a rope tied in a slip knot: a practice noose.

• • •

It had all started to go wrong for Eddie and Paula Gilfoyle when they moved to Grafton Drive in 1991. They had met in the summer of 1988 at the wedding of Gilfoyle's sister, who married the brother of one of Paula's friends. Eddie and Paula quickly became an item. They were engaged by Christmas and got married at Moreton Presbyterian Church. Paula's funeral would be held there four years later.

Eddie Gilfoyle had previously been in the army, serving in Northern Ireland and completing two tours of the Falklands. During his seven-year army career, he had worked pretty much exclusively with trauma patients. He was posted on HMS *Sir Tristram*, one of two British warships, the other being HMS *Sir Galahad*, that were bombed by Argentine aircraft in the Bluff Cove attack. Fifty-six soldiers died in the attack, and a further 150 were wounded, many of them colleagues of Gilfoyle.

For much of his time in Northern Ireland, Gilfoyle was not in uniform – other than when he was ordered into Londonderry on riot patrol after Bobby Sands, an IRA hunger striker, died in prison. His patrol was petrol-bombed and his clothes set on fire.

Gilfoyle had signed up for nine years, but ultimately left the army two years early in an attempt to save his first marriage. Initially, he tried to buy his way out, but in the end he went AWOL. The marriage failed anyway. When he left the army he looked for work in hospitals, where he could use his medical experience, and ended up as an orderly at Spire Murrayfield Hospital.

I know the area well. I grew up a couple of miles away from Upton, in a house similar in both period and style to No. 6 Grafton Drive. In my early teens I would cycle from Meols, a small village on the north coast of the Wirral peninsula, over the fields towards Moreton. I would cut down Pump Lane across more fields, these ones home to an old Second World War American Air Force base, cycle through Greasby and head towards Upton.

The M53 motorway runs down the Wirral and splits the peninsula that lies between Liverpool and north Wales. To the north, there is Birkenhead, which looks over the River Mersey towards Liverpool and is blighted by many of the same post-industrial economic problems. In the late 1980s, the Wirral's unemployment rate was twice the national average, and it had the highest rate of heroin use in the country.

To the south, looking over the River Dee towards Wales, lie affluent towns like West Kirby, home to the Royal Liverpool golf club. A little further south is Caldy, which, with its millionaire mansions, has become a retirement community for ex-Liverpool footballers.

Class runs through the Eddie Gilfoyle story. Although both families were firmly working class, Paula's parents felt she was too good for Eddie, who they saw as a bit of 'scallie'. To swap the Gilfoyle's marital home – a terrace in Wallasey, a short distance from the entrance of the Liverpool tunnel and known locally as 'debtor's retreat' – for Upton was a big deal. The couple were moving up in the world.

But it was not easy. Eddie and Paula overstretched themselves on the mortgage for their three-bed semi. It would also need a major overhaul before it could be considered habitable by house-proud Paula.

All of this placed a huge amount of stress on a young couple in love. Gilfoyle, whose job mainly consisted of washing and sterilising medical instruments, earned £540 a month. Paula made about £600 a month at the Champion Spark Plugs factory. It was Paula who looked after and fretted over their finances. She topped up their income by working for the Freemans catalogue company, selling to workmates, friends and family.

Paula moved back in with her parents while Gilfoyle worked on the house at Grafton Drive. It was supposed to be only a temporary move, but months went by without any change in their situation. In Paula's view, the house at Grafton Drive was never quite ready.

During his wife's continued absence, Eddie Gilfoyle grew close to a work colleague, Sandra Davies, and, with no sign of Paula joining him at Grafton Drive, Gilfoyle ran out of patience. He decided that his marriage had run its course.

The relationship with Sandra Davies was never physical. On both their accounts, they never kissed or saw each other outside of work – but they grew close. By July 1991, they thought that they were in love.

In October, Gilfoyle invited Davies to 'pack her bags' and move into Grafton Drive. He told her that he intended to file for divorce. She agreed to move in. Sandra Davies was prepared to leave a husband and young son; she would give it all up for Eddie Gilfoyle. She told her husband that she was leaving him.

But it wasn't to be.

Gilfoyle told his wife that their marriage was over. It was then that Paula dropped the first of a series of bombshells: she was pregnant. The baby had been conceived on one of the rare nights the couple had spent together. Realising that she was about to lose her husband, Paula moved into No. 6. She rang Sandra and warned her to stay clear of Eddie.

It wasn't necessary. Sandra Davies no longer wanted anything to do with Gilfoyle. She shunned him at work, and when he sent her cards, via a friend, to celebrate both her birthday and Valentine's Day – her birthday was on 11 February – she tore them up in front of a work colleague.

In April, according to Gilfoyle, Paula dropped the second bombshell. In a letter left for him in the kitchen, she wrote:

Dear Eddie,

I'm sorry for what I am about to write, but I can't go on living a lie any more, I've cheated and lied to you, I just can't carry on any more, I am having to write it down on paper as I can't tell you face to face. The baby I'm carrying is not yours. I have been having an affair for the last fourteen months with a guy called Nigel. The baby is his. If you work it out the baby could not possibly be yours. I was living at mums [sic] at the time, we hardly seen [sic] each other, never mind sleeping together. I tricked you into thinking the baby was yours by the dates I gave you, in fact the baby is due three to four weeks before that.

I know I have messed your life up. I can't apologise enough. No one knows, not even Julie, about Nigel but they will soon. Nigel has asked me to go and live with him abroad. I have said yes. You can have the house and furniture. I will only be taking a few small items. You can divorce on adultery, send the papers to mum and dad for me to sign as when I have told them what is really going on, I will give them my forwarding address.

I would like you to try and pick up the pieces with Sandra, as I know she really loves you, you deserve better than me. Don't do anything stupid, I'm not worth it. Hopefully by the weekend I'll be out of your life for good and I'll be starting my new life with Nigel.

Eddie Gilfoyle seemed to take even this revelation in his stride. 'True there is no love left between us, but then again there is no hate,' he wrote in a response to what later became known as the 'Nigel letter'. 'We are parting on good terms and that can only be good for us both as we start to re-build our lives, you with Nigel and the baby and me on my own.'

Gilfoyle attempted to show Sandra Davies the 'Nigel' letter, but Sandra had no intention of being dragged into his marital problems, although she did show the letter to a colleague. Gilfoyle also confided his domestic troubles to his line manager, who sent him home to sort things out.

Despite the apparent breakdown in their marriage, Gilfoyle and Paula had not reached a point of no return. Kitchen notes between the couple explained that 'Nigel' had gone abroad, leaving Paula 'in the lurch'. Eddie wanted nothing more than to be father of the child, irrespective of who the 'real' father might be.

So what happened to Paula Gilfoyle? Was it murder or suicide?

• • •

Merseyside's two main newspapers, the *Liverpool Echo* and *Daily Post*, competed on a daily basis to get the scoop on the unfolding drama of the murder investigation.

'DID MUM-TO-BE REALLY KILL HERSELF?' asked the *Echo* two weeks after Paula's death, in a typical front-page article headlined 'BODY IN GARAGE MYSTERY'. 'I am not satisfied at this stage that there are no suspicious circumstances surrounding Paula's death,' Detective Chief Inspector Baines told the paper.

'I DIDN'T MURDER MY LOVELY PAULA', was the headline from the *Daily Express* after the police completed the second post-mortem. 'I've lost the best thing any man could ever wish for,' Gilfoyle told the media. 'We loved and adored each other. I've lost my wife and baby. I can't describe how distraught I am.' Gilfoyle revealed that the baby would have been called Olivia.

Whenever a development in the case occurred, it seemed that the press was on hand to report it. For example, journalists were there when Gilfoyle was arrested. Suffering from a nervous breakdown, he ended up in the psychiatric ward at

Clatterbridge Hospital. 'Three detectives arrived at the hospital just after one o'clock,' reported the *Liverpool Echo*. 'They emerged fifteen minutes later. One was carrying a shoulder bag and two full carrier bags, while the other two escorted Mr Gilfoyle to the car.' The article was accompanied by a photograph of Gilfoyle, handcuffed to two officers. When the police staged a reconstruction of the suicide/murder, with an eight-and-a-half-month pregnant officer from Liverpool standing in as Paula, photographers managed to capture the scene on camera. 'PAULA'S FINAL HOURS', read the headline.*

The media frenzy heightened the anger of Paula's family and friends towards Eddie Gilfoyle and his family. Their outrage was not helped by Gilfoyle's father, Norman, telling anyone who would listen that Paula had killed herself because she was having an affair, and that Eddie was not the father of her child.

Such was the animosity that a noose was thrown at Norman Gilfoyle's living room window.

• • •

It was in this overheated atmosphere that the trial of Eddie Gilfoyle began, on Wednesday 9 June 1993, at Liverpool Crown Court – just a year after Paula's death. Mr Justice McCullough presided.

Over the opening two days of the trial, no fewer than seventeen witnesses who claimed to have seen Paula Gilfoyle in the days leading up to her death took the witness stand to attest to her cheerful and uncomplicated joy at the prospect of

---

* The Gilfoyle family later complained to the Police Complaints Authority that the police were tipping off reporters. Their complaint was not upheld.

motherhood. 'She was a lovely person, very bubbly, full of life. She would do anything for anyone,' said the opening witness on day one, a female machine operator at the Champion Spark Plugs factory. A male colleague described Paula as 'bubbly, done [sic] anything for anyone, just friendly to everyone, happy'. 'Bubbly ... a bundle of fun,' her brother told the jury.

The jury learned how Paula had prepared a nursery for the baby; purchased a complete spare set of baby gear, so that one could be left with her mother while she worked; twice asked the vicar to christen the baby; and, just two days before her death, visited the library, returning with six baby books, including one on baby names. The question for the jury was straightforward: why would a happy mother-to-be take her own life?

In striking contrast, Eddie Gilfoyle, the man accused of murder, was strangely absent from his own trial. He did not give evidence, nor was evidence called on his behalf. No witnesses spoke for Eddie Gilfoyle.

Mr Justice McCullough explained to the jury that it was up to the prosecution to prove that Gilfoyle was the murderer, and not for the defence to prove his innocence. 'From first to last, the burden of proof rests on the prosecution, and you will not convict him unless you are sure that the charge of murder is proved against him in all its essential elements,' he said. 'If you are left in any reasonable doubt – in other words, if you are less than sure that any essential element of murder has been proved against him – then you must find him not guilty.'

Before the jury could convict, they had to be sure of four facts. 'First, that she died from acts which he did to her, not acts which anybody else did,' the judge continued to tell the jury.

Second, that he did those acts deliberately, in other words, not accidentally. Third, that those acts were unlawful. No lawful justification for doing them has been, or could be, suggested. Fourth, that when he did those acts he intended to kill her or to cause her some really serious bodily harm.

In short, the Crown had to prove that a murder had actually taken place. If the prosecuting barristers could not establish murder by fake suicide – the mechanics of it and the opportunity for Gilfoyle to execute it – then there was no case to answer.

So when could Eddie Gilfoyle have killed his wife? On the day of Paula's death, he went to work late in the morning. A market researcher called at Grafton Drive and spoke to Paula and Eddie at around 11 a.m.; Gilfoyle invited her in. The couple completed a survey on their wine-drinking habits and chatted for fifteen to twenty minutes. Sandra Davies and a colleague saw Gilfoyle at work reading the *Auto Mart* magazine in the staff canteen at 11.30 a.m., ahead of his shift, which started at 12.30 p.m.

At 11.50 a.m., a courier from a catalogue company called with a package for Paula. No one answered the door. The parcel was delivered to her mother. Paula then missed her antenatal appointment at 2 p.m. This was the first time she had ever done this, and it was suggested by the prosecution that she was dead by that time.

Based on this account, there was therefore a window of opportunity in the morning between the wine survey and Gilfoyle being seen at work – albeit a slender one – for Gilfoyle to execute a meticulously planned murder.

It was never the prosecution's case that Gilfoyle murdered Paula after he returned from work. Gilfoyle was due to finish work at 8.30 p.m. that evening, but he asked if he could leave at 4.30 p.m. instead. He claims to have arrived home at around 4.50 p.m., finding the suicide note, reading the opening lines and driving to his parents' house, where he waited with his mother for his father to return home at 6 p.m.

However, three witnesses put Gilfoyle back at No. 6 at about 5:30 p.m., including the woman from the courier company, who returned to attempt to deliver another parcel, and a neighbour who saw him leave noisily in his car. This, it was suggested, revealed that Gilfoyle had lied about his movements.

But how had he murdered his wife? There were no signs of a struggle in the garage. Dr James Burns, the Home Office pathologist who conducted the second post-mortem, told the court that Paula had been 'a willing victim'. She had placed her head in the noose of her own free will because she was under the impression it was all part of her husband's 'suicide project'.

Burns had detected the two small scratches on Paula's neck, close to where the rope had been. Burns claimed to have seen at least ten cases of suicidal hanging a year for the past twelve years. 'And I can find not a single case of true suicide by hanging in which there is even one scratch mark on the neck,' he told the jury.

Video footage was played of the police reconstructions, including a scene of a female police officer at a similar stage of pregnancy to Paula struggling to throw the rope over the beam. Burns sought to offer his expert opinion on that point as well.

Dr Burns was 5ft 10in. He reported on his own attempts to throw the rope over the beam – he managed it once, but he told the jury that, in his view, a pregnant woman would not have been able to manage it. The judge expressed concern that the pathologist was straying from his areas of expertise to questions about (in his words) 'chucking ropes over beams'.

The testimony of the three co-workers, who claimed to have spoken to Paula about the fake suicide notes, was not allowed to be heard as it was considered to be hearsay. Ordinarily, witnesses can only give first-hand evidence – the three women were repeating what they claimed Paula had told them.

The defendant struck a pathetic figure. Eddie Gilfoyle had left Clatterbridge Hospital's psychiatric ward to be held on remand at HMP Liverpool ahead of the trial.

At Liverpool Crown Court, he appeared a broken man. At an early stage, Mr Justice McCullough stopped proceedings to ask if the defendant was capable of following what was going on. Gilfoyle and his family became targets for abuse, and there was a bitter and highly unusual legal battle when Paula's family challenged Eddie's right, as husband, to bury his wife and also for his share in the house. Paula's body remained in the mortuary for ten months as the two families battled it out in the High Court in London to resolve these issues. Gilfoyle lost. No. 6 was sold some years later and the proceeds went to Paula's family.

Weeks before Gilfoyle's criminal trial started in Liverpool, hundreds of mourners crowded into Moreton Presbyterian Church to say farewell to Paula. Eddie Gilfoyle was not allowed to attend. He received death threats. It was reported that the couple's child would have been named Natasha (not Olivia).

• • •

Gilfoyle's legal team were pinning their hopes on Mr Justice McCullough throwing out the case, since the Crown had failed to establish that a murder had taken place. It proved a disastrous miscalculation. The defendant was told that the prosecution case had been made and that he was expected to stand trial.

Eddie Gilfoyle refused.

Two detectives from Merseyside Police interviewed him on twenty-three occasions over the course of five separate days for almost fourteen hours. At the very end of the trial, the jury heard sections of those interviews read out by the officers who conducted them.

Eddie Gilfoyle presented a version of Paula totally at odds with the 'bubbly' mother offered to the jury over the preceding three weeks by a parade of Crown witnesses. Asked about Paula's state of mind, Eddie responded: 'When you say "depressed", she was shitting herself, literally. She was petrified of the birth.'

The jury heard him telling the officers of his love for Paula, how she refused to move in with him, and how he came to the conclusion that the relationship was over. What did he make of the 'Nigel letter'? 'I didn't really believe her about it because there wasn't really the opportunities for her to go and see this fellow Nigel,' he said.

'Nigel' had been an invention created by his wife, Gilfoyle claimed. She wanted to 'have a dig' in revenge for his dalliance with Sandra Davies. According to Gilfoyle, despite Paula's bombshells, there was neither acrimony nor anger on his part – when she wanted to leave him, his response was to go along with it. When she wanted to move back to No. 6, Eddie claimed to accept that too, irrespective of the child's paternity.

And there was one more bombshell. According to Gilfoyle, two days before Paula took her life, the couple talked into the early hours and she revealed the identity of 'Nigel'. 'On the Tuesday night before [the Thursday she took her life], she asked me to sit down. She told me that the man who was the best man at the wedding, her brother-in-law, was possibly father of the baby. His name is Peter Glover.'

Paula, Gilfoyle said, had claimed that it was 'hard for her to tell me because she knew that my dad had two children to my auntie, and I knew the shame that brought on us and our mother'.

According to Eddie Gilfoyle's account, Paula took her own life because 'she couldn't live with the shame of telling her mum and dad'. This revelation came in the eleventh interview, days after Gilfoyle was first interviewed by the police.

No one spoke up for Gilfoyle except his brother-in-law, the police officer Paul Caddick. He told the court of a conversation between the two of them, a week after Paula's death. Gilfoyle confided in Caddick about Peter Glover being the possible father of the child. The following day, Caddick went to the police station and made a statement, and Gilfoyle went voluntarily to be interviewed.

According to Caddick, Paula made Gilfoyle swear not to tell anyone about her relationship with her brother-in-law. Paula was terrified that the baby would look like her brother-in-law. He dutifully promised. 'Did you ask him why he had given that promise?' Mr Justice McCullough asked. 'The situation was such, my Lord, that I did not want to push him too hard,' Caddick replied. 'I wanted what he was telling me to be told to the police by him.'

This, Paul Caddick told the court, was why Eddie Gilfoyle had gone to the Farmers Arms for the wake: he wanted to hear from Glover himself whether he was the baby's father. The evening ended in a stand-off between Glover and Gilfoyle's father.

• • •

On 24 June, the jury visited Grafton Drive. They arrived escorted by police motorcyclists and, as ever, the media. Eddie Gilfoyle came separately, accompanied by three prison officers, and remained in his minibus as the judge and jury inspected the small garage. Some jurors climbed a ladder to better inspect the beam.

After a trial lasting seventeen days, the verdict was announced on a Saturday afternoon, after a jury of six men and five women had deliberated for three days. The twelfth jury member had been discharged because of illness.

Members of Paula's family cheered as the jury at Liverpool Crown Court returned its verdict. Eddie Gilfoyle was found guilty and sentenced to twenty-five years in prison. As he was led from the dock, Eddie turned to his family and shouted: 'I am still innocent.'

• • •

Eddie Gilfoyle's first nights in prison as a convicted murderer happened to coincide with the start of the most fundamental structural reform of our criminal justice system in living memory.

The Runciman Commission published its recommendations on 6 July 1993. It had been established, with Lord Garry Runciman at its head, to restore public confidence in the criminal justice system.

'That need has not diminished since we were appointed,' the report noted. The guilty verdict in another Irish terrorism-related case (Judith Ward) was quashed in 1992, alongside guilty verdicts in the Stefan Kiszko, Tottenham Three, and Cardiff Three cases. Runciman's report made 352 recommendations. Its big idea was to create the first-ever state-funded miscarriage of justice watchdog, an independent body with wide-ranging and unprecedented powers to investigate cases. That body was to become the Criminal Cases Review Commission.

The proposals largely left the Court of Appeal untouched. The court had been established in 1907, in response to another crisis in confidence, following cases such as George Edalji, who was wrongly convicted on the bizarre charge of disembowelling a horse, and Adolph Beck, an innocent Norwegian.*

The court was established as the justice system's safety net: an opportunity to provide one final re-examination of the facts of a case, impartial and comprehensive. It was a role that the court neither wanted, nor lived up to. 'The Court of Criminal Appeal was a compromise and a misnomer,' said Labour peer Lord Reginald Paget QC in a House of Lords debate in 1996. 'It has never been the Court of Appeal. Under a series of Lord Chief Justices, its original function was forgotten. The court confined

---

* Sir Arthur Conan Doyle, the creator of Sherlock Holmes, had championed both men as victims of miscarriages of justice.

itself to points of law. Unfortunately, guilt or innocence is not a point of law.'

* * *

With Gilfoyle behind bars, the media was free to go to town with lurid tales about 'Evil Eddie'. 'GILFOYLE IS GUILTY', screamed the headline in one local paper. 'Two-timing husband hanged his nine months pregnant wife and tried to make it look like suicide,' began one report. 'The husband of a heavily pregnant woman found hanging in garage told one of her friends that he used to be a backing guitarist for Eric Clapton, a court heard yesterday,' was another. 'Norman Edward Gilfoyle weaved an intricate web of deceit to escape punishment for the murder of his pregnant wife, Paula,' wrote the *Daily Post*. 'He hatched a plot too far-fetched even if conjured up for the twilight world in paperback detectives. But the hospital technician – described as a Walter Mitty character – tried to be too clever.'

The newspaper claimed that the evidence against him had been 'overwhelming'. 'If she had taken her own life, Paula would have been the first heavily pregnant woman ever to do so,' it said. Detective Chief Inspector Baines explained how the murder was committed.

> We think she really did believe he was doing this course. Initially, Paula feels all right with a rope around her. It is not tight. She is standing on the floor. She feels safe. Suddenly, he just lifts her feet up, holds them and then puts them on the stepladder. We think he was holding her feet until she went unconscious.

But death was not instantaneous because later we found the fingermarks around her neck where she tried to pull the rope off.

Baines described Eddie Gilfoyle as 'a real cool cucumber', refusing to be rattled during the interviews. 'It was not a crime of passion. He just wanted Paula out of his life. He wanted Sandra Davies in. We were putting some very strong allegations to him about killing his wife and child, but he never moved. He was a complete Walter Mitty character.'

'BEAUTY'S KISS LED TO WIFE'S MURDER', ran the headline in the *Sunday Mirror* with a striking picture of a laughing, seemingly carefree Sandra Davies. 'This is the woman whose kiss on the cheek drove an obsessed admirer to murder his pregnant wife,' began the article. Davies told the court that their physical contact had only ever been a kiss on the cheek.

Detective Chief Inspector Baines called for a change in the law to allow hearsay evidence, such as the testimony of Paula's three co-workers. 'If the jury had been aware of this and other vital information it would have made their deliberations easier,' he told the press.

As ever, Baines was on hand with a succinct but memorable quote. 'He is an absolute bastard,' he said.

Two themes dominated the media's coverage: first, Eddie Gilfoyle was 'a Walter Mitty' – as one newspaper put it, 'a Romeo who bragged and lied his way through life' and who once claimed to have played guitar with Eric Clapton; and, secondly, the media was obsessed with the statistical improbability of a pregnant woman taking her own life.

'The Million-to-One Murder' was the headline in one Sunday supplement. 'Dr Sheila Rossan of Brunel University revealed that out of more than 3 million full-term pregnancies in England and Wales since 1982, only three women had committed suicide before the birth. This put the chances of Paula killing herself at one in a million.' It is the kind of eye-catching statistic that sticks in the mind of a jury. Simple – yet misleading.

The idea that a pregnant woman would never commit suicide was a myth. Earlier that year, John Rainey had returned to his house in Bangor, Co. Down, in Northern Ireland, to discover that his wife, Carolaine, had taken her life. There were even eerie similarities between the two women's deaths. Carolaine had ended her life by throwing a rope over a beam in the garage and hanging herself two weeks before her due date.

Within days of Eddie Gilfoyle being sent to prison, a pregnant woman in Oldham took her own life less than an hour's drive away from the Wirral. 'A young mother-to-be who had "much to live for" hanged herself days after discussing wedding plans,' the *Oldham Evening Chronicle* reported. She was found in her bedroom, having attached a rope to scaffolding in place for the installation of a suspended ceiling. Noting that it was odd that she had tied a rope to the frame, the coroner said: 'I would have thought it wiser for the rope to be removed out of the way of temptation.'

The notion of a 'bubbly' expectant mum was, no doubt, easier to sell to a jury twenty-five years ago when suicide was more readily regarded as a 'taboo' subject.

There is now a body of empirical literature on antenatal depression and suicide. One 2015 study concluded that suicide was one of the leading causes of death in pregnant women.* It accounted for one in ten of the women who died during pregnancy, or up to a year after giving birth.

• • •

The CCRC opened its doors in April 1997. It was the first publicly funded organisation in the world set up to investigate wrongful convictions. Anyone claiming to be the victim of a miscarriage of justice now has to apply to the CCRC to have their case referred to the Court of Appeal. In the case of Eddie Gilfoyle, two appeals – in 1995 and 2000 respectively – came in quick succession, straddling the old and new regimes.

When Gilfoyle took his first trip to the Royal Courts of Justice for the 1995 appeal, Michael Mansfield QC represented him. In the early 1990s, Mansfield was becoming synonymous with miscarriages of justice and acted in landmark cases including the Birmingham Six and the Guildford Four. He had set up his barristers' chambers, Tooks, ten years earlier at the height of the 1984 miners' strike. Much of the chambers' early work involved defending miners accused of riot and affray.

Impressed by Mansfield's growing reputation from the so-called Irish cases, Paul Caddick was keen to get the barrister on board, and decided to contact the barrister's chambers. Mansfield's clerk explained that it did not work like that. Instead, he needed a solicitor to instruct a barrister. The clerk suggested he try a Salford-based lawyer, Campbell Malone.

---

* 'Perinatal Mortality Surveillance Report' – UK Perinatal Deaths for Births from January to December 2015

Malone had represented Stefan Kiszko, jailed on Christmas Eve in 1975 for killing an eleven-year-old girl. Kiszko was a gentle character who suffered from a condition called hypogonadism, which meant his sexual organs were underdeveloped. He served sixteen years in prison for the murder and sexual assault of schoolgirl Lesley Molseed.

Kiszko had been prescribed testosterone which, it was claimed, made him prey to uncontrollable sexual urges. He was freed on appeal in 1992, but died the following year from a heart attack, aged forty-one. In 2006, a DNA match led to the arrest of Ronald Castree for Lesley Molseed's murder.

• • •

The short period of time immediately after a murder is critical to the later investigation. According to the police's 'Murder Investigation Manual', it is the 'golden hour'. Decisions made in that period, good or bad, impact whether or not police are likely to catch the killer.

It quickly became apparent that Merseyside Police's response to Paula Gilfoyle's death had been a complete shambles. The police guidelines in situations like the one discovered in the garage of No. 6 could not be clearer: 'In every case of a sudden death, the CID must be informed as soon as possible and the divisional CID informed immediately. There may be good reason for treating a suspected suicide as murder, but there is no excuse for treating a suspected murder as suicide.'

Those guidelines were set out in an internal review conducted by Detective Superintendent Humphreys of Merseyside

Police in August 1992. At the time, Eddie Gilfoyle was still on bail. If there was anything suspicious about the death, 'everyone present should be excluded from the room or place, but kept at the scene pending the arrival of CID officers'. No one should have gone into the garage before the CID officers arrived.*

That Paula Gilfoyle was thirty-eight weeks pregnant should have been 'sufficiently suspicious in itself to cause a full inquiry to be made', Humphreys stated in his review. Instead, officers who turned up at No. 6 felt that they were faced with a fait accompli. It was, they were told, a suicide. No attempt was made to secure the scene of the crime or preserve evidence. In total, seven police officers traipsed in and out of the garage.

Gilfoyle had been flagging the drive at the time, and there was a pile of builder's sand in front of the garage. The sand was, as DS Humphreys noted, 'well trampled ... thereby destroying any possible footprint evidence'.

The disposal of the noose following the post-mortem was described as 'inexplicable' by Humphreys. Jones, as coroner's officer, should have been present at the mortuary at the time of the examination the following day. The officer was 'suddenly taken ill' and admitted to hospital suffering from 'a severe migraine, which resulted in a blackout'. 'It may well be that the onset of the illness had commenced the previous evening, and that contributed to his lack of judgement,' Humphreys noted.

The initial police response to Paula's death may have been a farce, but what happened next was more disturbing. Before the

---

* Paul Caddick did not go into the garage. He told me he did not go in for this reason.

end of the year, the Police Complaints Authority had begun an independent investigation into the conduct of the Merseyside Police. It was led by Detective Superintendent Graham Gooch from Lancashire Police.

In July 1994, a twenty-volume report comprising 6,000 pages was handed to the Crown Prosecution Service. It urged the CPS to consider prosecuting four of sixteen officers involved in the original investigation. 'Supt Graham Gooch lists a catalogue of alleged blunders,' the *Sunday Times* reported. Gilfoyle claimed to be at work at the time Paula was said to have been murdered. Gooch's team found that of the twenty-nine people who worked with Gilfoyle, twenty-two had not been approached by the police. Of that number, three testified to working with Gilfoyle all day. No one was prosecuted, but three officers ended up facing disciplinary charges.

• • •

When the case came before the Court of Appeal for three days in September 1995, Michael Mansfield attacked the Crown's 'speculative' case, arguing that the court had been wrong to reject the defence's argument of 'no case to answer'. In other words, he argued that prosecuting counsel had not made out its case that a murder had actually taken place. Gilfoyle's lawyers claimed to have new evidence that completely undermined what was left of the prosecution's case.

Maureen Piper went to Moreton Post Office every Thursday to cash her mother's pension. On hearing of Paula's death from a friend the day after, she apparently replied: 'I only just spoke to her yesterday. I'd seen her at the post office. I'd seen her about 12.40 or 12.45.'

If true, this meant that Paula had been alive after Eddie Gilfoyle was seen at work – he could not have murdered his wife. What made Piper's account all the more convincing was that she had recounted this directly to Paula's sister, Susan Dubost, who immediately grasped the significance of what she had been told and urged Piper to go immediately to the police.

Piper recalled Paula wearing floral dungarees. The appeal judges heard that Piper never gave evidence because Gilfoyle's own lawyer was under the impression that she had changed her mind about her recollection. This was incorrect. The lawyer never actually interviewed her.

Gilfoyle's new legal team wanted to introduce the evidence of Professor Bernard Knight, who had served as a Home Office pathologist for thirty-one years, and had worked on countless high-profile cases including those of Fred and Rose West and child-killer Mary Bell. He had been prepared to give evidence at the original trial, but was never called – apparently another error by Gilfoyle's original legal team.

Murder by hanging was 'extremely rare to the point of being almost unknown', Professor Knight wrote in a report prepared ahead of the appeal. 'I haven't seen a genuine case in thirty-seven years of pathology practice and would be hard pushed to recall any reports of one in Britain or similar countries.'

Professor Knight saw no significance in the two small scratches on her neck. 'My thirty-seven years as a pathologist, thirty-three of them in full-time forensic work, have led me to believe almost anything as regards to the unexpected and sometimes bizarre behaviour of persons intent on self-destruction,' he stated. 'Time after time I have heard, from relatives and in coroner's inquests, strident claims that the deceased would never have killed themselves. A number of obvious suicides are never accepted by the families and spurious murder investigations begun.'

The pathologist illustrated his point by referencing a colleague who looked into an undoubted suicide. A young woman had killed herself with a shotgun. As a result of the gun's recoil, the weapon had ended up standing upright against the wall, as if placed there by her attacker.

The Court of Appeal brusquely rejected all the arguments. Lord Justice Beldam refused Professor Knight's evidence on the grounds that his arguments could have been heard at the original trial.

Maureen Piper's evidence, briefly considered, was also not accepted. The appeal judges took the view that it was highly unlikely Paula would have returned home, changed out of her dungarees and then taken her own life. It was far more likely that Piper, who went to the post office every week, had simply mixed up the dates.

While the Court of Appeal on the one hand gave short shrift to new evidence capable of overturning the conviction (it was dealt with in less than a page), it had no problem accepting testimony that had been rejected by the trial judge.

Lord Justice Beldam quoted extensively from witness statements provided by the three work colleagues of Paula (the hearsay witnesses) about her writing fake suicide notes at Eddie Gilfoyle's behest. Their evidence was explicitly excluded by the trial judge. This was evidence never challenged in court, and given in the heated aftermath of Paula's death by friends wanting to help a grieving family. It was Eddie Gilfoyle's argument that a fatal mix of work gossip, and a misguided but understandable desire to clear Paula's name, sent the police galloping off in the wrong direction. Their case, it was argued, was built on an edifice of conjecture and canteen speculation. The evidence also ran at odds with the prosecution's case: if Paula was so alarmed by Eddie's fake suicide notes – as the three friends of Paula's claimed – why put her head in a noose at his invitation?

This untested evidence was front and centre of the Court of Appeal's 1995 judgment. Despite acknowledging that it was within their powers to do so, the appeal judges didn't compel the three women to come to court. Their testimony was included in unedited form.

Lord Justice Beldam made clear that this was to serve as a warning to those who might take up the Gilfoyle cause. He said: 'We mention it here lest public credence of the apparent insistence that he is the victim of a miscarriage of justice based upon an insupportable and far-fetched theory conjured up by the Crown gains unmerited support.'

• • •

That warning went unheeded. In 1996, the Channel Four series *Trial and Error* aired a one-off documentary that featured Eddie Gilfoyle's case. Presenter David Jessel called Merseyside Police's investigation 'a Keystone Cops comedy of errors: shoddy, idle and just plain wrong'.

The documentary included the video footage played to the jury of the reconstructions staged by Merseyside Police showing two women officers similar in size and height to Paula, one of them thirty-eight weeks pregnant, struggling to throw the rope over the beam. It also included one sequence not shown to the court in which the coroner's officer, PC Jones, snapped the very rope used in Paula's hanging. 'I've broken the evidence,' he laughed.

Both women officers actually managed to pass the rope over the beam.

An expert in knots – from the International Guild of Knot Tyers, no less – demonstrated that a brief application of common sense meant that the task was easily achievable. Doubling the rope gave it the required stiffness, allowing it to be fed over the beam in one easy motion. Nor did the rope have to be knotted at the beam height, which would have required Paula to have been at full stretch, but could have been tied lower down and within easy reach.

Of course, Merseyside Police would not have been left to such speculations had they not lost the rope that had been around Paula's neck in the first place. If it had been preserved, how the knot was tied would most likely have revealed whether or not Paula could have killed herself.

The documentary shone light on the late and highly convenient appearance of the practice noose. What kind of impact must that discovery have made on the jury, reasoned Jessel. 'And imagine the impact on the jury if they had known a later police inquiry would have cast serious doubts as to whether that noose was there at all.' *Trial and Error* revealed that the practice noose had been discovered as late as 23 June and only after a forensic scientist directed officers to keep an eye out as to the possibility of 'finding other significant items such as other ropes'.

In other words, the rope appeared three weeks after an earlier search by Merseyside Police's specialist search team. The small garage had one item of furniture in it: a chest of drawers. The rope had been discovered in one of three drawers. The original officers who searched the garage were incredulous at the rope's appearance.*

James Burns, the pathologist who had conducted the second damning post-mortem, was interviewed. He retreated from his trenchantly expressed position at trial that he had never seen a true suicide where there had been scratches to the neck. In fact, he conceded that scratch marks in genuine suicides were 'well documented'.

Professor Bernard Knight, the man who was never called by Gilfoyle's original legal team at trial, and whose testimony was rejected by the Court of Appeal, told Jessel that if Gilfoyle had killed his wife then he would have made a unique but grim bit of British criminal history.

Although people do get murdered by hanging, they either have to be drunk, drugged or forcibly restrained, which would leave bruises or scratches, he said. 'Nobody wants to be hung, for God's sake. I have never seen a proven case in forty years of this job.'

---

* The officer who conducted the search was interviewed by Detective Superintendent Graham Gooch in his later investigation. 'He recalls looking in the drawer in which the rope was found and it was not there,' the report said.

According to Professor Knight, the only case of a fake suicide by hanging was Roberto Calvi, the Vatican banker found hanging under Blackfriars Bridge. 'His death is known to have involved international freemasonry, political corruption at the highest level, a banking scandal and the Vatican,' said David Jessel. 'Resources somewhat beyond Eddie Gilfoyle – a washer-up of surgical instruments from the Wirral.'

• • •

Prisoner DX1827, otherwise known as Eddie Gilfoyle, watched *Trial and Error* from prison. 'We didn't have a TV in our cells,' he told me. 'The only way you could watch anything was if the screws put a video on for you on the landings.'

In the 1990s, when there were only four television channels to choose from, *Trial and Error* commanded a huge prime-time audience. It transformed the Gilfoyle saga from a rather tawdry murder story into a potential miscarriage of justice.

The documentary was played during dinner time, when Gilfoyle's fellow inmates were in their cells. 'The lads on the landing wanted to watch it as well – so the cleaners lifted the flaps on the doors so they could see it,' he said.

The change in the prison officers' attitude towards Gilfoyle was immediate. 'Before they had been dead chatty and suddenly they didn't know how to talk to me,' he said. Shortly afterwards, Gilfoyle was taken to the wing office. He recalled ten prison officers there. 'I just thought: "What the fuck have I done now?" I was told by the governor that the officers didn't know how to deal with me.' Did it make a difference to how he was treated?

'No, my life was shit in prison. They continued to treat me like shit – the same as everyone else.'

I first wrote about the Eddie Gilfoyle case in 1999 for the *Big Issue*. The CCRC had just referred his case back to the Court of Appeal. 'Gilfoyle is only one of 2,500 applicants that the CCRC has received in its short two-year life,' I wrote. 'He is one of the lucky few and only the forty-second to be referred. To date only nine convictions have been quashed. Underfunded and understaffed, the commission has been swamped.'

The title of the article was 'The Waiting Game'. Little did any of Eddie Gilfoyle's supporters know quite how long he would have to wait.

CHAPTER TWO

FULL DISCLOSURE

Just before 3 a.m. one Saturday morning in September 2003, three police community support officers found Sean Rimington in the entrance to the lost property store at Millgarth Police Station in central Leeds. He was crashed out drunk, fast asleep. The eighteen-year-old was arrested at Millgarth at around 4:30 a.m. and then taken to the cells at the Leeds Bridewell custody suite. Shortly afterwards, Rimington left in an ambulance for Leeds General Infirmary, badly beaten and bleeding profusely from a head wound.

Police constable Danny Major was alleged to have repeatedly attacked Rimington as he hauled him out of a police van and, again, later, when he was in the cells. Rimington was left in a pool of his own blood. Earlier in the evening it was Rimington who had assaulted Major, a uniformed patrol officer, punching him twice in the face. It was claimed that this was what had caused Major to later lose his temper.

How could someone detained in a police station in one of our major cities on a typically busy weekend wind up in such a state? On the night in question the station was full of police officers dealing with the constant stream of typical weekend casualties: the inebriated, the drugged-up and the unlucky. CCTV cameras were positioned at every corner of the building recording the goings-on.

For example, one camera was fixed outside the Bridewell on top of a lamp-post-high pole that pointed directly at the dock where the police vans and cars arrived. It was alleged by a fellow officer that Major had pulled the 6ft 4in. boy out of the van head first, smashing his face into the concrete before kneeing him in the head and punching him three times in the face. This had apparently taken place in direct view of the camera.

Major then took Rimington to cell number nine.

All the time, other officers were going about their business: two cameras were fixed on the charge desk; one camera was directed at the desk of the custody sergeant's clerk; and all the corridors were covered.

Before Major left Rimington in the cell, it was alleged he dropped down to one knee and punched him in the face four or five times for good measure. Allegedly, Major then removed the young man's handcuffs and left him bleeding heavily on the floor.

Danny Major has always insisted that the accusations against him were a pack of lies. He claims he was framed by colleagues trying to cover up the actions of another officer. After Sean Rimington had been rushed to hospital, Danny Major believes that the guilty officer panicked and thought that Rimington might be about to die. So he decided to pin the blame on an expendable younger officer: Danny Major. According to Major, multiple officers lied on oath, fabricated and suppressed evidence – and then their superiors covered the whole thing up.

• • •

Danny Major always planned for a career in the force. 'Dad was a police officer for thirty-two years,' Major told me. 'Like any child, you see what your parents are doing and you want to be like them.'

PC Danny Major's six-year career in the force came to an abrupt end on 1 November 2006 at Bradford Crown Court, when he was found guilty of assaulting Sean Rimington. Major was sacked in June the following year and jailed. It took two trials to bring him down. The first resulted in a hung jury and at the second he was sentenced to fifteen months in prison. He served four.

On sentencing Major in November 2006, Judge Roger Scott told the court that Sean Rimington had become a 'non-person' for about forty minutes. 'Police officers are not to take revenge on their prisoners,' Scott said.

> This case has demonstrated that it is possibly very difficult for a police officer to keep his cool. Many would not keep their cool in the circumstances demonstrated in this case, but as an officer you are expected to keep your cool and you did not. The message obviously has to go out that police officers have to obey the law. They cannot assault their prisoners and therefore I would be failing in my duty if I did not lock you up.

• • •

On the night of 5 September 2003, Sean Rimington was out on a bender. In his statement, he recalls his evening starting with five quadruple vodka and cokes in the first pub, followed by two pints at a second, before then hitting a student bar.

The teenager first came to the attention of the police in the early hours of the morning when a community support officer watched him get thrown out of the Merrion Shopping Centre on the edge of the city centre opposite Leeds Metropolitan University. She tracked Rimington's progress on the centre's CCTV as he approached two girls. His hands were down his trousers 'massaging his genitalia in a manner suggestive of masturbation'.

It took twelve years for the truth to start to emerge about how Sean Rimington came to end up in Leeds General Infirmary. In November 2013, Greater Manchester Police started a review called Operation Lamp, promising (as its name suggested) to shine much-needed light onto the murky goings-on in their neighbouring force.

Towards the end of 2014, I was made aware that the publication of the Operation Lamp report was imminent. I approached West Yorkshire's Police and Crime Commissioner Mark Burns-Williamson, who originally commissioned the report. He offered a measured but intriguing response. 'The evidence supports the premise that there may have been a miscarriage of justice and that there is sufficient "fresh evidence" to support the case being referred back to the Criminal Case Review Commission,' he said.

To refer a case back to the Court of Appeal, the watchdog needs to identify fresh evidence not produced at the time of trial that might provide grounds for a fresh appeal. It can then refer a case if there is a 'real possibility' that the conviction would not have been upheld.

When the full Operation Lamp report was published in early 2016, it did not pull any punches. 'In thirty years in the police service I have never seen a report as critical of one police force by another force,' said Chief Inspector Ian Hanson, chairman of the Greater Manchester Police Federation. 'The report vindicates Danny Major and what he has been saying for twelve years.' Hanson described the report as 'explosive'.

How could it be possible for police officers to frame one of their own for a series of assaults that took place within the precincts of a police station where there were, on Danny Major's reckoning, in the region of thirteen CCTV cameras?

The official line was that a freak serial malfunction of technology had taken place at the Bridewell, preventing the footage from being retrieved. The lead investigating officer, Inspector Michael Green, failed to recover four of six videotapes that covered the alleged assaults. The 500-page dossier compiled by the Operation Lamp review team found that of the two tapes that were recovered, eight hours of footage on each tape was condensed to just ninety minutes. According to the Lamp review, the abridged version 'excluded evidence that undermined the prosecution and would have assisted the defence'.

'There were so many cameras in the Bridewell, all on the same system,' Major explained. 'But, apparently, none were working. Five tape machines should've been running, but only two tapes were ever seized – all the others were broken or not recording.'

According to Major, an alarm would sound when the tapes needed changing. 'It was not possible not to have the tapes recording. The system was set up for that not to happen,' he said. 'It's quite clear what was going on.'

Danny Major's solicitor had requested all the CCTV footage when his client was first interviewed under caution on 29 October 2003. He had been assured that he had received all the relevant video.

But it was not just a failure to recover CCTV footage: Operation Lamp identified five 'potentially key' witnesses never interviewed in West Yorkshire Police's own investigation. This included some obvious candidates, including the two custody officers and the control room operator manning the CCTV cameras. The latter told the review that he saw 'nothing untoward' that evening.

He also failed to speak to a pair of officers from Pudsey where they were based who buzzed into the Bridewell just twenty-six seconds ahead of Major. They were 'more likely than not' in the van dock when Major was allegedly manhandling a reluctant Rimington out of the van. According to the officer who made the allegations, there was no other van. Major always insisted that there was.

Operation Lamp refused to accept the allegation that PC Major 'speared' Rimington – deliberately ejecting the young man from the van head first into the concrete. Rimington was 6ft 4in., lying prone in the van's cage with his head facing the front windscreen. According to Operation Lamp, there was 'insufficient room' for him to be turned 180 degrees. Nor were there injuries consistent with such a claim.

The officer who made the allegations had 'more than likely' visited Rimington in the cell despite his denials, according to Operation Lamp. The report also recorded that the same officer had a 23-minute meeting with a superior immediately after Rimington went to the hospital. It is not clear what they discussed.

The report's authors accepted Danny Major's version of events as 'factually more accurate' and 'overall more plausible' than the evidence that had originally been accepted by the jury. The report found that the other officer 'either deliberately or inadvertently' misled the court.

The carefully worded Operation Lamp report avoids using words such as 'cover-up' and 'whitewash'. Instead, it records that the officer who led West Yorkshire Police's investigation, Inspector Green, displayed 'poor investigative rigour' and 'a mindset that could be described as "verification bias"'. In other words, the investigators settled on their suspect and focused only on evidence that supported their view. It is a criticism made of Merseyside Police in relation to Eddie Gilfoyle (for example, in relation to the evidence of Maureen Piper, who said she had seen Paula after the time that he was supposed to have murdered her).

In the case of Danny Major, inconvenient evidence was pushed to one side. For example, scene-of-crime photographs taken on the day of the incident identified bloodstains but were never exhibited. Those taken almost a fortnight later (described in the report as 'markedly different') were used instead.

Inspector Green headed up not one but three investigations into the incident: a criminal investigation against Major; a misconduct investigation into the performance of West Yorkshire Police; and a criminal investigation into allegations made by Major against Rimington. This, Operation Lamp noted, presumably with understatement, placed the inspector in 'a difficult position'.

Some eighteen months after the alleged assault, Sean Rimington went to see a doctor who told him that his nose had been broken. The diagnosis was sought in support of his compensation claim. As a result, the Crown amended their indictment to upgrade one of the counts against Major to the offence of assault occasioning actual bodily harm. An earlier assessment by a better-qualified, specialist ear, nose and throat consultant at Leeds General Infirmary, made only six days after the incident, recorded that Rimington's nose had not, in fact, been broken at all. Operation Lamp noted that it was inexplicable that both prosecution and defence had 'either missed or ignored' the earlier assessment. None of this stopped West Yorkshire Police's lawyers from relying on the Leeds General Infirmary's evidence to mitigate their own liability in relation to Rimington's civil claim.

• • •

'In my view, the West Yorkshire Police station at the Bridewell in September 2003 was not fit for purpose,' said Judge Roger Scott when he sentenced Danny Major.

Addressing prosecuting counsel, Scott said: 'We saw an unorganised, unsupervised rabble. You described it accurately and very politely as a "shambles". In my view, it requires further investigation and possible charges against a large number of police officers.'

Danny Major lost his liberty, his job and his reputation on the evidence of three officers. Meanwhile, the apparently 'lost' CCTV recordings showed Rimington talking to paramedics.

In the course of the conversation, Rimington pointed to five officers who were present, including at least two of the officers who made allegations against Major (Major himself was not there), and recalled waking up and saying 'these bastards did this to me'. Major claimed only to have gone into the cell once with Rimington – again this is confirmed by the CCTV evidence.

During the course of Danny Major's retrial, one of his three accusers – a female civilian detention officer – made serious allegations against one of the other two officers, who happened to be her ex-husband. It is Major's belief that the allegations related to child sexual abuse. The allegations were recorded the very day Danny Major was convicted – 'a coincidence that remains unexplained', Operation Lamp noted. That female officer was also believed to be in a sexual relationship with the third officer.*

The Operation Lamp report blew the Danny Major case wide open.

• • •

In August 2010, Eddie Gilfoyle's new solicitor Matt Foot turned up at Bebington Police Station, near Birkenhead on the Wirral, at the invitation of Merseyside Police. He had been dropped off at the station by Gilfoyle's brother-in-law and former

---

* West Yorkshire Police were invited to comment on the case, specifically about the allegations relating to the three accusers. They said that the case was subject to an ongoing criminal investigation, and pointed out that it would be 'wholly inappropriate' to comment and doing so 'could potentially undermine ongoing enquiries'.

police officer, Paul Caddick. Foot was there to go through the unused exhibits.

Police investigations generate a wealth of material. Some of it proves useful in their preparation of the prosecution case; the rest gathers dust. But what might not be useful to the police might well be useful to the defence. Sometimes such material can be fatal to the prosecution case. Sometimes it never sees the light of day.

Matt Foot was ushered into a room in the back of the station where boxes of copied papers awaited him. But he had not come all this way to collect paperwork that could have been sent to his north London office. Foot had expressly requested sight of the unused exhibits, not the files. Whether this was deliberate game playing or an innocent mistake, the solicitor remains unsure. He recalled challenging the officer who was, as Foot put it, 'very Liverpudlian and gracious about it'.

Foot insisted on coming back. Paul Caddick picked the lawyer up and they returned the next morning. This time when Foot walked into the room, the first thing he spotted was a padlocked metal box, roughly twelve inches by six with a key taped to its top. It was just the kind of place in which a child might hide their keepsakes and secrets away from the prying eyes of the adult world.

Inside the box were two five-year diaries. Each page had five entries for the same date on each of the five years. Paula was experimenting with her handwriting, as children do. In 1972, her thirteen-year-old letters are just about joined up, neat and carefully written to the line; in 1973, she writes in huge loops; in 1974, her writing begins to veer backwards from left to right and becomes spidery. Paula's last entry in a third diary, the only one disclosed ahead of the original trial, was made in the summer of 1986.

When Matt Foot picked up the second diary, it fell open to reveal a cutting from the *Wallasey News* dated 7 February 1977: 'Murder after sex in a park'. It was a yellowing report about a young man called Mark Roberts who had been sentenced to life for killing a teenage girl in a park in Wallasey on the Wirral.

Mark Roberts had been Paula Gilfoyle's first love. He was convicted of the murder of a girl he had never previously met, three days after Paula had broken off their engagement. Earlier that evening, Roberts had dragged another girl down an alley, but she had fought back. When a passer-by heard her screams, he had been forced to run off. 'It must have been the worst thing to have happened in her life at that time. Why would you keep it in your diary as a memento? I found it chilling,' Foot told me. 'It's a macabre fact that she kept hold of that cutting all of her life in that secret place amongst her other secret belongings.'

The diaries revealed a Paula who was at odds with the 'bubbly' character painstakingly constructed and presented to the jury by the prosecution in 1993.

The twin themes of suicide and violence were constants throughout her teenage years. Paula Gilfoyle met Mark Roberts when she was fourteen years of age at her sister Margaret Glover's twenty-first birthday party. Roberts was five years older than Paula. 'This lad Mark walked me home – he slept at Margs,' she wrote. The next night he joined her babysitting. 'Had a good laugh. He has two scars on his waist and stomach,' she wrote.

Their relationship quickly became sexual. Paula's diaries

record her pregnancy scares, her relief when her period would start and trips to the 'FPC' or family planning clinic. There was an early suicide attempt: 'Slept at Marks took some sleeping tablets, 10. Mark went mad but I done it to him [sic].'

On the first anniversary of the relationship, the couple announced they planned to get engaged and their parents met. While the relationship followed the course of a fairly typical teenage romance, there was a disturbing undercurrent. Roberts was a deeply troubled individual. He was in and out of work, regularly appearing in court and was occasionally in custody.

The murder is foreshadowed by random and unexplained bouts of violence recorded without emotion by Paula. On one occasion, Roberts was glassed in a Liverpool bar ('Had eighteen stitches arm and eye. Terrible state.'). He was there with Paula. It is not explained how the fight happened. Another time the couple had an argument. 'He [Mark] smashed bus stop window. Got picked up by police. He had eight stitches in fingers...' Paula recorded Mark hitting her, and being left with a 'bruised mouth'. In March 1976, Roberts was sentenced to six months for stealing cars. 'My God I will crack up,' Paula wrote.

In October that year, Roberts throttled Christine Buckley to death with his belt hours after having sex with her near the park's toilet block. 'Afterwards, a sick feeling came up inside me and I felt disgusted because I had sex with somebody I have never seen before,' he later told the police. 'I don't usually go with just anybody. I took my belt off and put it around her neck. I lost control of myself. I couldn't stop hitting her.' He dragged her dead body over a fence and then dumped it into a lake.

This is how the teenage Paula recorded the arrest. 'Went to

work. Had to go to Manor Road [Police Station in Wallasey] to give a statement on Mark, he has been charged with murder,' she wrote. 'Mum came to pick me up at his house. Nervous wreck.'

Paula expresses no empathy for the victim, no concern at her boyfriend's psychotic behaviour, nor does she even acknowledge the shocking nature of what has happened. 'Went to pick Marks [sic] clothes up at Police Station. I got his wallet too. His belt and jeans had blood on,' she wrote. A couple of months later, Paula had an opportunity to see Mark when there was a court hearing ahead of the trial at Liverpool Crown Court. She recalls having 'a lovely time. We kissed, talked; we are both in love. I want him and I need him.' After another rendezvous, she wrote: 'He gave me a love bite. He is sick but I love him.'

Paula had one other serious relationship; this man threatened to take his own life. 'Please don't blame yourself or anyone else for this,' he wrote to Paula. 'It's me that can't take it so there is only that left to do.' That letter, too, was in the box. In Paula's suicide note, she exhorts Eddie: 'Please don't blame yourself.'

None of this came out at trial, nor was it disclosed to the defence team. Merseyside Police reckoned that they had had the diaries since 1994.

Mark Roberts was barely mentioned at the trial. During cross-examination, Peter Glover was asked about 'an unfortunate experience' Paula had had as a teenager. 'She was heartbroken, but she got over it,' he replied.

In the judge's summing up, more space is devoted to Paula's wheat intolerance than to her formative first love with a convicted rapist and murderer.

• • •

Failure to disclose is 'the single most frequent cause' of miscarriages of justice, noted the Criminal Cases Review Commission in 2016.

It was ever thus. Judith Ward was released from prison having served seventeen years after being wrongly convicted for the M62 coach bombing in the same year that Paula Gilfoyle died. An IRA bomb hidden in the luggage locker blew up a coach carrying off-duty soldiers and their families, killing twelve people including three civilians. Ward was sentenced to twelve life terms and thirty years' imprisonment for that terror attack and two other bombings.

Troubled and sleeping rough at the time of her arrest, Ward was a highly vulnerable person who, mentally ill, signed numerous implausible confessions. 'Judith spilled confessions and admissions like beans,' wrote her barrister Michael Mansfield QC. 'They were all over the place, in every sense of the phrase – bizarre and random.'

At the time she was supposed to have planted the bomb, she was more than 100 miles away at the Blue Boar in Chipping Norton, Oxfordshire, having a drink with a dozen other people.

However, her serial confessions were backed up by overwhelming scientific evidence – or so the court was told. It was the Home Office forensic scientist Dr Frank Skuse (whose reputation was to be destroyed by the Birmingham Six travesty) who found traces of nitroglycerin on her hands and her duffle bag, left in a freight wagon she had been living in. Scientists from the Royal Armaments Research and Development Establishment also testified that traces of nitroglycerin had been found on the floor of the caravan where she had stayed.

Judith Ward's conviction was overturned in 1992. It transpired that West Yorkshire Police had sent the Director of Public Prosecutions just 225 of the 1,700 statements it had acquired. Some sixty-three interviews had taken place with Ward, but only thirty-four were disclosed. Amongst the huge amount of information that the Crown had failed to disclose were three independent reviews of the case that took place in 1985, 1987 and 1989 respectively – all of which found that something had gone seriously wrong. The eminent scientists were discovered to have suppressed evidence that showed that boot polish could test positive (as well as playing cards) on the Griess test.

'Our law does not tolerate a conviction to be secured by ambush,' said Lord Justice Glidewell when giving judgment. The court held that the Crown's disclosure duty was not limited to material it believed might help the defence; it should have the right to examine everything that the prosecution possessed. The Ward case was supposed to herald a new era of openness in disclosure.

The experiences of Eddie Gilfoyle and Danny Major suggest it did not.

• • •

The rule on disclosure is simply stated: every unused item held by the police that is considered relevant to an investigation should be reviewed to see if it is capable of undermining the prosecution or assisting the defence case. If either outcome is satisfied, then the evidence must be disclosed to the defence.

In 2017, two watchdog bodies, Her Majesty's Crown Prosecution Service Inspectorate and Her Majesty's Inspectorate of Constabulary, found that the quality of disclosure by the police was 'poor' in more than four out of ten of cases (42 per cent) and, in relation to the CPS handling, poor in one in three cases. The inspectorates examined 146 Crown Court files. Ninety of these were randomly selected, and fifty-six were identified because of a poor outcome as a direct result of problems with disclosure. They identified eight cases that had (as they put it) 'unresolved disclosure issues'.

One case concerned a defendant in an armed robbery who had protested his innocence from the start. He claimed that the 'victim' was a violent drug dealer who had actually robbed him. Neither the police nor the CPS bothered to check out the defendant's story until his barrister reviewed the case just before trial. He contacted the police and then discovered intelligence that confirmed the defendant's account. The defendant had been remanded in custody for more than six months.

The watchdog's findings were published on the same day as a major report into another infamous miscarriage of justice case: the Cardiff Three. Lynette White had been brutally murdered in a flat in Cardiff in 1988. Five men were prosecuted and, two years later, three of the men – Stephen Miller, Tony Paris and Yusef Abdullahi – were convicted of her murder and sentenced to life imprisonment. In 1992, the Court of Appeal quashed those convictions. Almost a decade later, as a result of advances in DNA techniques, Jeffery Gafoor was arrested and, in 2003, he pleaded guilty. The Cardiff Three were exonerated.

Richard Horwell QC, a prominent criminal barrister, was

instructed to look into the Cardiff Three debacle. In the report he subsequently wrote, he described it as 'one of the worst miscarriages of justice in the history of our criminal justice system'.

That report was prefaced with the prophetic words of the senior investigating officer, Detective Chief Superintendent Christopher Coutts, who had been put in charge of reviewing the case: 'The only way this case will fail is through disclosure.'

So, as Horwell put it, how could five men have been prosecuted for a murder that they had nothing to do with? How could witnesses have placed those men at the scene?

In 2009, three police officers and two members of the public were charged with conspiracy to pervert the course of justice and perjury. The trial of the first eight defendants (R *v.* Mouncher) collapsed when the prosecuting counsel 'lost confidence in the disclosure process'.

There were fears that key documents had been destroyed. Weeks after the Crown withdrew its case, the 'destroyed' documents were discovered at the police headquarters. 'Concerns of "establishment cover up" and "conspiracy" naturally followed,' Horwell noted.

The so-called Mouncher report examined what caused the collapse of the UK's biggest police corruption trial. Richard Horwell concluded that bad faith played no part in mistakes made by both the police and prosecution. 'It is human failings that brought about the collapse of the trial, not wickedness,' he said.

He went on to describe how disclosure problems had 'blighted our criminal justice system for too long'. He noted that the public 'must be utterly bemused' as to why our justice system appears incapable of coping with a principle that was 'long established and central to the tenets of fairness and justice'. But, as Horwell put it, the pendulum has swung both ways. The era of openness in the wake of the Judith Ward case ('...often described as that of the "keys to the warehouse"', he said) had long gone.

Horwell closed his report with the hope that the 'begrudging or reluctant attitude' to disclosure would be consigned to the past and replaced with 'a new spirit of openness'. He was not confident. He urged defence lawyers to play their part and engage properly in the disclosure process. 'Many a cynical, battle-weary practitioner will say that the first and second of those further objectives are unattainable and pure fantasy,' he said. 'I hope they are wrong.'

• • •

In the Danny Major case, alarm bells rang every step of the way. At every stage of the tortuous judicial process, problems over disclosure were raised: at the original trial in April 2006 and retrial in October that year at Bradford Crown Court, in a visit to the Court of Appeal in July 2007 and during a review by the CCRC the following year. It took the investigation by Greater Manchester Police into a neighbouring force to get to the bottom of what happened.

Ahead of a trial, the prosecution picks the material it will use for its case. The remainder is supposed to be retained by the police and all unused material should be recorded in detailed schedules. These schedules, together with the unused material itself, are considered by the prosecution. Operation Lamp identified ten classes of material that should have been on the disclosure schedules but were not, including the videotapes and four scene-of-crime photographs taken of Millgarth's foyer showing a red stain on the wall. A separate issue, but also notably absent, were any details about the disciplinary record of one of the officers making allegations, who will be referred to as Officer X.

> 'It is not possible to convict Mr Major ... unless you accept that the evidence of [Officer X] is accurate and reliable,' Judge Scott warned the jury. 'I repeat in this particular count it is not possible to convict this defendant unless you are sure that [Officer X's] account is accurate and reliable.'

The witness's credibility was key.

The jury did not know that shortly after the alleged assault against Rimington, Officer X had been disciplined for inappropriately touching a female colleague. He initially denied the accusation, but was caught red-handed. 'The incident was captured on CCTV and could easily have been interpreted as sexual assault,' noted Operation Lamp.

A few weeks later, the same officer was accused of misconduct in the way he dealt with an assault outside a Leeds night club. The father of one of two young victims complained that the pair had been forced to make retractions. There was a further complaint relating to the same incident from a fellow police officer.

Danny Major was jailed on the basis of a single police officer's evidence – not only was information withheld by West

Yorkshire Police, but it was also claimed that there were no disciplinary issues relating to Officer X.

There was a first trial at Bradford Crown Court in April 2006 but, because of disclosure concerns, that became an abuse of process hearing. Judge Sutcliffe then highlighted 'a disturbing failure' within West Yorkshire Police's professional standards department over its obligations to disclose. Following a full trial, there was a hung jury and the CPS sought a retrial.

The retrial started in October 2006. Again, disclosure failures dogged proceedings. Judge Scott observed that the investigating officer could be 'described by a lot of adjectives ... incompetent, ineffective, inaccurate'; however, as far as he was aware, he had not been called dishonest.

During cross-examination, it emerged that the investigating officer had not watched the two videos of CCTV footage that were released in heavily edited form. The unedited footage was released in the last week of the retrial – but only after the main prosecution witnesses had given evidence.

Danny Major and his parents were given just one night to sift through thirteen hours of previously unreleased CCTV tapes. The footage directly contradicted the account offered by the officer making the allegations. However, the family was told by their own lawyers that it was too late.

When the case came to the Court of Appeal in July 2007, far from being an obstacle to a fair trial, the chaotic approach to disclosure was deemed to have delivered an unfair advantage to Major. 'We do not understand how the exposure of that material can justify any argument that the trial should be stopped as an abuse of process,' the appeal judges said. 'It was a very substantial benefit to the appellant that the material emerged when and in the way that it did.'

The Operation Lamp team did watch the full videotapes. It took them two months. In their view, the videos had revealed the 'fresh evidence' which is vital to securing a successful appeal. As a consequence, the Operation Lamp team felt that it 'would not have been unreasonable – in fact, it may even be considered to have been fair' to have adjourned the case to allow both the prosecution and defence teams sufficient time to properly evaluate the footage.

The report also noted that the appeal court judges 'lacked a proper understanding' of what the additional footage revealed because they, like everyone else, had not actually taken the time to watch it.

• • •

Shortly after Matt Foot's visit to Bebington Police Station, Eddie Gilfoyle was finally freed after serving seventeen years for the murder of Paula Gilfoyle. 'I've told them year after year I'm not admitting to something I haven't done,' a defiant Gilfoyle told *The Times*' investigations editor Dominic Kennedy in a phone call from prison. 'I don't give a shit what you do to me. I'd sooner die in jail.'*

The campaign to overturn his conviction had been slowly building momentum over the years and finally seemed

---

* When Gilfoyle left prison, a gagging order was imposed that prevented him, his family, campaigners and even sympathetic MPs from talking to the press. It was challenged by his lawyers and subsequently dropped.

unstoppable. His local MP, Lord David Hunt, was a minister in the Thatcher government and had taken up Gilfoyle's case in the 1990s; the former assistant chief constable of Merseyside, Alison Halford, called the case 'a rank injustice' in 2000; and, critically, the forensic psychiatrist Professor David Canter had swapped sides.

Ahead of the trial, Professor Canter had written a report tentatively concluding that Paula had probably not written the suicide note with the intention of killing herself. His report was never part of the prosecution case. Despite this, his name was linked to the case. When he took up the post of chair of psychology at Liverpool University, the local media dubbed him 'the Gilfoyle case criminologist'. *The Sun* ran an interview with the academic, in which he explained how he had used approaches from psycholinguistics to 'crack' the Gilfoyle case by analysis of Paula's suicide note.

The media reported how Professor Canter was setting up a £250,000 unit at the university, comprising a thirty-strong team of researchers, to pioneer criminal profiling techniques. The academic was keen to stress that his approach was nothing like that of Jodie Foster's character in the 1991 serial-killer thriller *The Silence of the Lambs,* or the ITV drama *Cracker*, which featured Robbie Coltrane as criminal psychologist and flawed genius Fitz. 'Investigative psychology is not about an individual genius acting on a hunch – what I call a hit-and-run expert,' he explained.

Around this time, Eddie Gilfoyle's sister, Sue Caddick, happened to be in the Adelphi Hotel in central Liverpool with a journalist, who mentioned that Professor Canter was in one of the lounges. Caddick was furious with the academic. She blamed his report for persuading the police to take her brother seriously as a suspect. She gave the professor a piece of her mind and pointed out that the police had not given him all the documents he needed to make a proper assessment. Apparently, his response was calm, but he seemed surprised that information had been withheld. He agreed to meet Caddick for lunch, and promised to review any paperwork that she had.

He took another look at the case. Reflecting that he might have been 'naive' in accepting the police's version of events, he decided that Paula's suicide note was more than likely genuine and that she had written it unaided. He went public with his concerns.

Despite the fact that the original report had never been used at the trial, Professor Canter agreed with Sue Caddick that it had 'bolstered the determination of the prosecution'. 'I must carry at least some little responsibility for Eddie Gilfoyle being convicted of his wife's murder and being given the inevitable consequence – a life sentence,' he wrote in 2008.

The 'real-life Cracker' Professor Canter met with an editor from *The Times* to talk about cases that troubled him. Inevitably, he mentioned his concerns about Eddie Gilfoyle. As a result of that meeting, the newspaper's investigations editor, Dominic Kennedy, began to look into the circumstances of a death that had taken place sixteen years earlier.

It is now rare for a newspaper to champion a miscarriage of justice case – certainly not in the way that newspapers rallied behind earlier causes célèbres such as the Guildford Four and Birmingham Six. The exception is *The Times*'s support for Eddie Gilfoyle.

Their backing is all the more surprising given what happened in the wake of Channel 4's *Trial and Error*. The Court of Appeal had explicitly warned off journalists and campaigners who might take up Gilfoyle's cause.

When the media focused their energies on exposing police corruption in the 1990s, it often proved to be a risky and expensive business. The Police Federation would automatically sue on behalf of its members.

In an astonishing three-year period leading up to the *Trial and Error* programme, the Federation's lawyers, Russell Jones & Walker, fought and won close to 100 defamation actions, netting £1,567,000 for their members. Police libel claims used to be known in the force as 'garage actions' because, at the end, the police officer could afford to build themselves a new garage or conservatory from the proceeds.

The huge risk of fighting the Police Federation meant most media companies settled out of court. Channel 4 defended their work on *Trial and Error*, and argued that the police investigation was 'fundamentally flawed'. The case was settled out of court. Channel 4 accepted that one of the officers involved had not behaved corruptly.

• • •

'The injustice meted out to Eddie Gilfoyle began as tragedy, sank into scandal but could yet be salvaged from finishing as farce', read a *Times*' editorial in August 2010.

The day before, Matt Foot had submitted a new application on behalf of his client to the CCRC. The newspaper's leader writer, Tory peer Daniel Finkelstein, compared the case of the Falklands veteran from Merseyside to that of Alfred Dreyfus, the Jewish artillery captain convicted of treason in 1894 in France. Dreyfus had been exiled to Devil's Island in French Guiana. His wrongful conviction was a defining moment in the fight against anti-Semitism.

'The tenacity with which the legal system and those responsible for the original case hold to their story and to their insistence that they were not in error is astonishing,' wrote Finkelstein. 'Doubt it? Then read the history of the Birmingham Six or the Guildford Four ... Or read the story of Eddie Gilfoyle.'

Just as with the Dreyfus case, Finkelstein argued, the evidence against Gilfoyle had collapsed. By the time the *Trial and Error* special aired, it was clear the prosecution case was built on sand – but over the next few years it was to be washed away by Dominic Kennedy's investigative work. 'I am only reporting on the story, on the facts and covering that there were holes in the case,' Kennedy told me. 'As a reporter, I am not taking sides. The newspaper absolutely is though.'

Newspaper convention dictates that murderers lose their title – they appear, for example, as 'Gilfoyle', not 'Mr Gilfoyle'. In *The Times*'s leaders, Eddie Gilfoyle was referred to as 'Mr Gilfoyle'. 'The view of the newspaper is that he is innocent,' says Kennedy.

Even after *The Times* chose to champion Eddie Gilfoyle, Merseyside Police still refused to disclose vital information. Kennedy had to invoke Freedom of Information legislation to try to force them to release copies of notes of interviews with officers who were at the garage when Paula Gilfoyle's body was discovered.

Merseyside Police insisted that no such notes existed. Kennedy had already seen some of the pages and reasoned that the rest were out there somewhere. The journalist was hoping that the full set of notes might contain a potential alibi. He had details of an interview in which one officer said the police surgeon had told him that Paula had possibly been dead six hours (and said that there was 'nothing suspicious'). That timing would have put the time of death at 2.30 p.m., when Gilfoyle was at work.

A week after *The Times* ran their story, the Crown Prosecution Service confirmed that the notes were indeed genuine. The Information Commissioner was later to clear Merseyside Police of deliberately withholding evidence.

Matt Foot recovered the tapes from Gilfoyle's police interviews. The two investigating officers interviewed Gilfoyle twenty-three times over five days in June and again in July.

The mood changes between the June and July interviews. The pair subjected Gilfoyle to a relentless attack in July in a blatant attempt to extract a confession from him. Foot, together with his colleague Sarah Flannigan, analysed the interviews and identified three different themes: suggestions that Gilfoyle was a 'fantasist'; references to him being a liar; and the suspect's own denials of guilt.

In the July interviews, the two officers called Gilfoyle a 'fantasist' no less than sixty-two times. Bizarrely, they repeatedly likened him to someone being snapped at by alligators. One officer says:

> The case is building up, and building up. Your story is disintegrating. You've reached the stage where the somersault goes full-turn and you're totally destroyed. I've told you you're in that

pit, them crocodiles, the alligators are biting lumps out of you and you're going to go down unless you do away with all the fantasies and start telling the truth.

And, again, the following day: 'These alligators are going to bite you away. Every one of them is an alligator biting at you, your story's just disappearing, you're going to lose, you can't keep it, you can't keep it going.'

They branded Gilfoyle a 'liar' twenty-two times in the July interviews.

I am calling you a liar because we have documentary fact [sic] which says you are a liar. You are known as a liar in the hospital, a nobody, you're a Walter Mitty character. You spin a yarn, you get found out and then it's: 'Oh, it's just Eddie Gilfoyle again.' They know you to be a liar.

This is immediately followed by his colleague: 'You get sussed out. You get sussed out as a liar, a pork-pie merchant and they don't want to know you after a while.'

In the face of this onslaught, Eddie Gilfoyle never yielded any ground. This was how the final interview closed. 'I have not had anything to do with the death of my wife,' Gilfoyle insists. 'I love my wife, there is no way that I would do these allegations that you are saying. You've got your own little ideas that, y'know, I've done it. I have not done it.'

Eddie Gilfoyle was interviewed for thirteen hours and twenty-seven minutes. He made a total of 122 denials of guilt. 'The police's attitude towards him is very, very aggressive,' says Matt Foot.

It shows a closed mindset. He answers every single question put to him, but they're not listening. Eddie himself is traumatised. He is actually being accused of murdering his wife and unborn child. It is clear that they are desperate to get his confession and they do not have enough evidence.

Not only that, but Foot points out that the police do not pursue any lines of inquiry raised by Gilfoyle.

• • •

The young Danny Major had no illusions about the realities of being a police officer. When he was young, his dad worked shifts on Christmas Day. Nor was Major oblivious to the dangers of a life in the force. 'Dad was almost killed during the miners' strike,' he told me.

Major's father was struck by a piece of flying masonry. The incident left him with a partially detached retina; he was nearly blinded in his left eye and had a brain injury. Ironically, his father had briefly been a miner before joining the force.

Why did he want to follow in his father's footsteps? 'I wanted to do my bit for the community,' replies Major, who has a degree in microbiology from Huddersfield University. 'I am very proud that my family has been in Yorkshire for centuries. I saw it as only right that I went out and got myself an education and give back to the community.'

Major, who is married with two children under the age of five, had until recently been working in a call centre. Shortly after the Operation Lamp report was published, he quit the job because of stress. He reckons that if he had stayed with the police without progressing he would be on £32,500 a year. 'I was earning just over £19,000,' he says. 'People always say: "You did your four months in prison – and it is done and dusted." But for me, I am still serving a sentence.'

Danny Major has always claimed that he was the victim of a cover-up. The experience devastated him and his family. 'It has been all-consuming. I still wake up in the night thinking about it. I am very determined to clear my name. I will never stop. In fact, everything that I worked so hard for is based upon me clearing my name.'

His parents never doubted him. They remortgaged their home to pay £30,000 in legal fees. 'I can take one corrupt police officer – you expect good and bad anywhere – but not a corrupt police force,' his mother, Bernadette, told me.

• • •

Both Danny Major and Paul Caddick feel that they were hounded out of the force. 'When you are a serving police officer, all your friends are police officers, all your wife's friends are policemen's wives,' Paul Caddick told me. 'Up to the trial, our closest police friends were there for us. Once the trial was over and done with, we were dropped like a stone.'

Paul Caddick was a 34-year-old police sergeant with a promising career ahead of him when he found Paula's body. Like Danny Major, he was committed to a career of public service.

'When I joined the police in 1976, I thought the system worked,' Caddick said. 'I thought that the police get it right nearly all the time. If they didn't, then it was one bad apple in the barrel who made the mistake and should be punished.'

The death of Paula Gilfoyle marked the end of a promising police career for her brother-in-law. That was the view of the assistant chief constable of Merseyside at the time, Alison Halford. She had been responsible for promoting Caddick to sergeant, before running into her own well-documented problems with Merseyside Police. Halford was the first woman in British police history to hold the rank of assistant chief constable. In a high-profile falling out with the force, she claimed to have faced sexual discrimination in her new post. Halford was suspended during the Gilfoyle trial and retired in 1993. 'I remember reading about the case in the local papers but at the time I was reeling from my own problems,' Halford told me.

She has called the Gilfoyle case 'a rank injustice'. Why?

> I have met the family and visited Eddie in prison. He's a nice, decent chap but perhaps he does not have the kind of intelligence to have concocted the sort of story he is alleged to have concocted. He isn't the sharpest knife in the drawer. But the police fouled up so badly. They didn't even take the body temperature, they weren't sure of the time of death, the rope went missing etc. At the start, they just thought it was suicide. I am amazed anyone found him guilty.

Halford felt that Paul Caddick was another 'victim' alongside Paula and, in her view, the wrongly convicted Eddie Gilfoyle.

Paul Caddick was the only witness to give evidence on Gilfoyle's behalf at the trial. He recalls taking the stand as a horrendous experience. The prosecution barrister, Rodney Klevan QC, asked him whether or not he expected to find Paula alive or dead when he was searching the house.

> I just thought: 'Well, if she is in the house then she's going be dead or else she would speak out'; so that's what I said. He turned my words around to infer: 'You knew all along she was killed.' It was horrible. I got upset. I had given evidence loads of times in court but this was awful. If anybody spoke in his favour, then it was me. I have known Eddie since he was little, since he was ten.

At the trial, Caddick, who as a police officer spent his working life investigating criminals, waited for 'this big piece of evidence' to appear so he could understand why the prosecution thought he was guilty. 'Obviously, we didn't know what the police had. It never materialised,' he said.

The worst moment was when the prosecution produced the 'practice noose'. 'They paraded it around the court like it was a trophy. At that point, I thought, this is really bad,' Caddick recalled. 'We were devastated after the trial – for a long time I just stayed on the sick.'

When Eddie Gilfoyle was sent to prison, the experience overwhelmed the entire family. 'It was such a deep trauma,' recalled Sue, Paul Caddick's wife. 'I could never have imagined you could be in that kind of state. We couldn't function. Yet I had four kids to look after. My youngest was four and the eldest was eleven.'

Life had to go on. 'The kids still had to go to sports day,' said

Paul. 'I still had to take our eldest, Ian, to rugby. And all the time people were looking at you, thinking: "There's the murderer's family." Even if they weren't thinking that, that's what we thought they were thinking.'

The family felt that they had to stay on the Wirral in the immediate aftermath of the trial for the sake of the campaign. 'I was like the Duke of Edinburgh,' Caddick said, 'walking three paces behind Sue so I could see who was in front of her, just to see if they might be about to upset her.'

The family felt completely isolated as old friends dropped away. As Paul Caddick readily admitted, they were not easy to get on with either. 'We were consumed by this. All we talked about was the case. It must have driven people mad.' Eventually, the family left the Wirral after their young daughter was bullied at school.

Shortly after the trial, a doctor from Merseyside Police turned up at Paul and Sue's house. Caddick was told that he was going to be retired on medical grounds.

> It was a massive shock. I understand why they got me out of the police – yes, I would have been a nuisance – I was furious at the time, but I came to understand that I could no longer wear the uniform. I accepted retirement for the sake of myself and my family. They ruined my career and the rest of my life.

Both Danny Major and Paul Caddick insist that, in spite of everything, they are not anti-police. 'Most do a great job,' Caddick says. Danny Major hopes to return to the force one day (although not West Yorkshire Police).

'The whole judicial system – the police, CPS and all the rest – swings on the impartiality of the officer who investigates,' Caddick said.

In this case, the impartiality of these officers was interfered with by the police hierarchy. They were compromised by their own bosses. You should never interfere with the impartiality of the police officer – it is the cornerstone of the entire system. That interference has always been what worried us. That is why we have pursued and pursued this case.

CHAPTER THREE

FROM ONE FIX TO THE NEXT

'My first guest witnessed the murder of a 26-year-old Korean student,' began presenter Jeremy Kyle as he introduced 'BB' (anonymised for legal reasons) on his eponymous weekday ITV chat show. 'After that traumatic event, she had to go into hiding for five years fearing for her life when she learned the gang had put a price on her head.'

Hers was, the chat show host told the live studio audience, an extraordinary account of self-sacrifice and personal courage. Even by Jeremy Kyle's high-octane standards, BB had one hell of a story to tell. She had been forced to leave friends and family, including her young daughter, in order to allow justice to be done and to ensure that a cold-blooded killer was put behind bars. 'Let's hear this story. Brave lady. Bev's on the show, ladies and gentleman.'

BB made her entrance.

The crime she was to describe was tragic beyond words. A young Korean woman – Jong-Ok Shin, known to friends as Oki – was stabbed to death on her way home from a Bournemouth night club in the early hours of the morning on 12 July 2002.

The attack was mindless and brutal. It took place just before

3 a.m. A number of people living nearby were woken by three piercing screams, then a moan followed by a dull sound as the dying girl slumped into a parked car. It took place just a few minutes' walk from her student flat.

Immediately before Oki lost consciousness, speaking in broken English, she told police and doctors at the hospital that her killer had been wearing a mask.

There were no signs that Oki had been robbed – neither her handbag nor her mobile phone had been taken – nor was there any hint of a sexual motive for the attack. It was brutal, though. The knife was plunged into her back three times with such force that it broke several ribs.

Dorset Police initially focused their energies on the young men in the student's circle of friends, including an ex-boyfriend. He was arrested, but later that year left the country.

Six weeks after Oki's death, the focus of the police investigation shifted to Bournemouth's large population of drug addicts. There is a surprisingly dark side to the town's tranquil and genteel image.

The police had picked up BB for shoplifting on 22 August 2002. BB was well known to the police as a drug addict and a street prostitute. She went on to tell the police, in an account that was to evolve over the course of a series of interviews, that three men had flagged her down when she was driving her car on the night Oki was stabbed, asking for a lift to a notorious crack house a few miles away.

• • •

'Let's just point out – because I don't want to concentrate on this – but you had a problem with drugs,' Jeremy Kyle said. That was a serious understatement, which BB herself corrected: 'I was a full-blown heroin addict with a large habit.'

The three men that BB claimed to have picked up were also drug addicts. This was how BB described to the TV audience a handbag snatch gone tragically wrong:

> I pulled over. One got out with the other one, followed after a couple of seconds or minutes by the third. Because I couldn't park straightaway, I pulled forward a little. And then I got out of the car to see what was going on, and as I looked around all I saw was shadows – not clearly, but I could see her. I saw Omar plunge a knife into her. She gave this scream. She just dropped down. I think he did it more than once. She dropped down, they got into the car, then they told me to 'drive, drive, turn the lights off'.

BB briefly mentioned that she had then been subjected to a horrific gang rape. She claimed still to be living with the appalling consequences of that attack. 'I had my womb rebuilt. They left me dead by the side of a river,' she said.

BB claimed to have paid a high price for her decision to (her words) 'take a stand': she was placed in the witness protection scheme and forced to live apart from her nine-year-old daughter. 'If this lady wanted to go outside for just a cigarette she had to put a bulletproof vest on,' Kyle claimed. The audience was told she wasn't even allowed to go to her father's funeral.

As Jeremy Kyle put it, it would take five years, three trials, including two hung juries, to 'nail this piece of scum'. Why, he asked, was she prepared to speak out? 'The girl [Oki] was bettering her life. I was killing myself anyway. I was a drug addict going off the rails. I was worthless anyway. I feel that it should have been me, not her, that was killed.'

The presenter interjected:

> You weren't worthless because, despite your drug addiction – and I would hope every single person watching this would agree with me – what you did was probably the most selfless and bravest thing that anybody can do. You put your own happiness to one side, and it took you five years but you nailed this scumbag. That's the truth.

But was it the truth? For the past seventeen years Omar Benguit has been in prison, convicted on the word of BB. Benguit's conviction was controversial from the start. Family and supporters, who had always believed in his innocence, watched the *Jeremy Kyle Show* with a familiar sensation. How on earth could anyone believe her?

BB had recounted the events of 12 July 2002 many times. Rarely had two accounts matched. The only consistent thing about her testimony was an uncanny knack for self-contradiction. Even in her brief TV appearance, BB managed to tie herself up in knots in relation to perhaps the most crucial aspect of her testimony.

The show came about as a result of a lengthy print interview in a now-defunct women's magazine published in November 2007. This was how BB described the moment when Oki was killed, in an article written up as a first-person narrative. 'I got out of the car to have a look, a gut-wrenching scream broke the silence. I spun around and there was Benguit plunging a knife into the woman's back.'

The problem was that BB had told three juries, and maintained throughout a series of interviews, that she had never actually seen the attack.

• • •

Omar Benguit was convicted on 27 January 2005, solely on the evidence of an addict who funded a hefty drug habit through prostitution and dealing.

The essential facts of BB's account were never independently corroborated. Instead, a woefully weak prosecution case was propped up by circumstantial evidence, provided by fellow drug addicts with lengthy criminal records and an obvious need to keep on the right side of the police. They attested to Omar Benguit's apparent agitation and guilty-looking behaviour immediately after Oki's death.

The police rounded up the addicts after BB had been picked up for shoplifting weeks after the murder. They all lived in the grip of their own demons in a desperate twilight world. Its epicentre was a notorious crack house and brothel: 47 St Clements Road, Boscombe.

By their own admission, most didn't know what day of the week it was, let alone what had happened six weeks before. There was no physical evidence linking Benguit or the two other men to the murder.

Nor was there any evidence to support BB's allegations of rape.

The Benguit case has an odd and convoluted history. Omar Benguit was sentenced to life with a minimum term of twenty years, but he was only convicted at his third trial. Of the three men BB identified as her passengers immediately prior to the killing, and who later were said to have gang-raped her, one did not even stand trial.

Delroy Woolry had been sent back to Jamaica. Bizarrely, he had been arrested after BB was picked up for shoplifting, but then deported from Heathrow Airport on 5 September 2002 courtesy of the Home Office.

In the first trial, the jury failed to reach a verdict on Benguit's one count of murder and one count of rape. The third suspect, Nick Gbadamosi, was acquitted on two counts of rape, and the jury failed to agree on one count of assisting an offender.

A retrial took place in 2004, and this time the jury acquitted Benguit of rape and Gbadamosi of assisting an offender. The jury failed to reach a verdict on Benguit's murder charge. Luckily for Nick Gbadamosi, he was caught on CCTV standing at a phone box by his car at 3:13 a.m., undermining BB's evidence.

Despite this inauspicious start, the DPP took the rare step of ordering a second retrial. The defence argued that it amounted to oppressive conduct on the part of the Crown.

• • •

'You may have despaired, members of the jury, on occasions during the trial at the sordid picture of the lifestyle that you have seen and heard emerge,' Mrs Justice Heather Hallett told the jury at the second retrial.

I do not know if you expected it to come from an area like Bournemouth. One witness seemed almost immune to her misery; you remember the girl that had no home and sold herself on the streets at night. A horrid, horrid tale. These witnesses just seemed to live from one fix to the next.

The jury of eight men and four women at Winchester Crown Court heard fourteen witnesses who claimed to have seen Benguit in the immediate aftermath of the murder. Of the key witnesses, all but one shared a common characteristic: drug addiction.*

June Sutton ran the notorious crack house at 47 St Clements Road. A Roman Catholic Liverpudlian, she cited the opening of the sectarian marching season as a reason for remembering the date of Oki's murder. Sutton recalled Benguit coming to the address in the early hours of the morning, looking for a change of clothes, shortly after Oki was stabbed. She claimed he was 'bouncing around' on account of the drugs he had taken. 'Although most of the time I was off my head, I had to keep my wits about me to a certain extent because I was dealing,' she told the court.

Life was cheap at No. 47. Sutton sold drugs to her own daughter who, in turn, prostituted herself to fund her habit. The daughter gave evidence but was described by the judge as 'useless' because she was 'so out of it'.

Shortly after the murder, June Sutton claimed to have kicked Benguit and Gbadamosi out of the flat. They then went

---

* The names of the drug addict witnesses have been changed.

downstairs to see another dealer, Steve McIntosh. He also recalled an agitated Benguit desperate to score. McIntosh's lifestyle was described by the judge as 'horrible and chaotic'. Rush hour for the Bournemouth addicts was 10 p.m. to 6 a.m. McIntosh told the court that typically he might sell drugs to between fifty and seventy people and on some days as many as 200. 'He must have spread a great deal of misery. Each day merged into the next,' noted Mrs Justice Hallett.

McIntosh and his girlfriend recalled Benguit coming in shortly after Oki's death and using a towel. They also remembered the date on account of the Orange Day parade, seemingly a big day in the calendar for those who lived at or used No. 47 as a place to crash out.

Other habitués of No. 47 who testified included Sarah Cooper, who recalled Benguit coming into her room sweating, looking flustered and wanting to change his top ('I wasn't totally obliterated,' she said). A lesbian couple, who had both had sex with Benguit in return for drugs, also gave evidence to support the claim that Benguit was sexually aroused after smoking crack despite there being no sexual motive.

Steve Roberts, who BB claimed to have ferried around as he robbed cars in order to pay for his crack habit on the night of the murder, recalled BB taking his car to give a lift to Benguit, who appeared 'panicky'. When Roberts was asked if he was 'out of it' at the time, he helpfully replied 'yes – and no'.

Helen Vine was a drug addict and prostitute who, on her own admission, would steal from her clients. She had only got out of prison a week before Oki's death and was living with Benguit after a row with a 'friend' who had sold all her possessions while she had been in prison. Vine claimed to have seen blood on Benguit's clothes and reported that he was 'not very stable'. She also recalled him boasting about having 'stabbed a student in Charminster'. Under cross-examination, she accepted that those precise words might in fact have been hers. Then there was Molly Andrews, an addict who claimed to have seen Benguit with a knife. 'You may remember she was emotionless, the one that described she had no permanent address. It just seemed the most dreadfully sad existence she was talking about,' Mrs Justice Hallet said.

There was only one witness to the events that night who was not (to use one of the addicts' own terminology) a 'smack head' or 'crack head': John Cutting, who lived in the same house as Benguit. He recalled seeing his housemate sharpening a knife. By his own admission, he had only caught a fleeting glimpse through the bay windows as he left the house.

And then there was BB. 'If ever there was an example of what drugs can do to you, you may think it was her,' Hallett told the jury.

Unlike all the other drug addicts paraded before the court, BB seemed blessed with uncanny recall and capable of producing a wealth of detail to add colour to her version of events – although the details themselves were often contradictory.

Her story was a tragic one. BB came from wealthy parents who stuck by their troubled daughter through years of addiction, paying for expensive but wasted periods in drug rehab. BB had trained as a nurse before falling under the spell of drugs. She had started smoking joints at the age of sixteen before graduating to class A drugs and eventually acquiring a £200-a-day habit. She funded her drug use through prostitution and some dealing.

BB was also a police informant.

Despite the heavy fug of addiction – and in contrast to the other No. 47 regulars – BB's recollection was always replete with detail. 'Omar got out. Nick got out. Darius got out. I got out and stood up. I couldn't see where they had gone. I got back in the car and started to make a cannabis joint,' she told the court about the moments before the killing. 'I didn't have time to finish it before they came back.'

The problem for the police was that nothing stacked up.

For example, BB claimed to have been in the Richmond Arms public house, popular with foreign students, a few days before the murder with Omar Benguit and Nick Gbadamosi. The pair was supposed to have made some unpleasant comments about Korean girls and their 'tight pussies'. There was no CCTV footage to support BB's claim that she or Gbadamosi had visited the pub in the run-up to the murder. Benguit was on camera – but it was only a brief visit.

On the night of the murder, BB recalled driving Steve Roberts around prior to giving the three men a lift. Roberts was a car thief and was supposed to have been on a robbery spree that night in order to fund his habit. According to BB, he would rob up to thirty cars a night.

That night was apparently more exciting than most. BB recounted that they had been involved in a chase with the police. 'I remember one police car had its blue lights flashing following us and it was then joined by two other cars with blue lights flashing. I had to put my foot down to lose them,' she recalled. Their car mounted the pavement. The police are required to document any such pursuits. No record was made.

Her account of the murder was strikingly different from the story the evidence told. With her dying words, Oki managed to tell doctors and police that her assailant wore a mask. BB never suggested that Benguit wore a mask. After the stabbing, Benguit had apparently got back in the car, wrapped the knife in his blood-sodden T-shirt and put it in a carrier bag. The evidence suggested that there would not have been much blood spilled from stab wounds incurred in a brief and vicious attack.

BB alleged that the three men had gang-raped her. Later, she claimed Gbadamosi raped her again. Luckily for him, there was the CCTV footage at 3.13 a.m. showing him at a phone box and close to his own car.

In the first instance, it was BB's boyfriend who made a statement to the police, detailing the attack in horrific and unsparing detail. On his account, she was told by Gbadamosi that she 'wanted this' as one of the other men held a knife to her stomach, cutting her. Delroy Woolry and Gbadamosi then raped her.

After that, all three men took tools from the boot of the car and used them to torture her.

> They initially used a socket-set, changing the size of the ratchets and inserting it into her rectum ... They used pliers, using the handle ends and also inserted the handle of a large screwdriver into her. During this time, all three males were goading each other on to more horrific things. Apparently above her cervix is a small plastic lump/ball and they inserted wire cutters into

her to try and cut it out. At this time, Nick also demands oral sex with [BB].

BB went on to claim that Gbadamosi raped her again on the Friday.

The potential for physical evidence from such an extreme attack was clearly vast. 'Extraordinary lengths' were taken by a forensic scientist to discover such evidence, noted Mrs Justice Hallett. Two cars were searched: a Renault and a Volvo (BB couldn't recall which car she had been in on the night). All the tools found inside them were tested.

The tests revealed no DNA evidence linking the men to the rape. Not only that, but there was nothing to suggest the men had been in either car. Benguit's jacket was also tested – but again no positive results came back. 'In my opinion, there is nothing in my examinations and my results to either support or refute BB's allegations of rape or assault,' the forensic scientist told the court.

BB was, in the words of Judge Hallett, an 'admitted liar'. The account that she offered the police when she was picked up for shoplifting on 22 August 2002 bore almost no resemblance to the account she provided on 12 September. This later version was the one that the jury heard.

The reason she gave for the discrepancies was her fear of reprisals. She said she wanted to disclose enough information to identify the killer but not enough to implicate herself. In her second statement, she said:

> I didn't tell the police everything straightaway as I was scared,

confused. I didn't know whether I wanted it to be brought up or if I could forget about it. I was very scared. I trusted the police, but not enough in the beginning. I needed to earn that trust before I said it all. I feel disgusted. I feel like I will feel like that for ever.

Both accounts offer considerable and very different detail as to the events of the fatal night even before she met up with Benguit, Gbadamosi and Woolry. For example, on 22 August she describes how Steve Roberts could not shift any of the stolen goods from that day's robbing spree. Roberts was 'a nightmare on the crack', BB told the officers.

Desperate for his next fix, Roberts attempted to blag money off BB's boyfriend. He threatened to use a stun gun on him. 'Andy had nicked it from a car when I was present. It looked like a torch. You could have it on as a torch or as the stun gun. The stun gun shoots out two pins on a thread that give you a big electric shock.'

BB's boyfriend would not lend Roberts money. He had ripped them off before. So the car thief offered a stolen car stereo as security for a loan. When BB returned with the money, Roberts immediately marched back into her boyfriend's flat and stole the stereo back.

In BB's later statement, on 12 September, that story is dropped in its entirety. Instead, she recounted the dramatic car chase with the police, which was not mentioned in her first account.

BB initially claimed that she met the three men after Oki had been killed. She said she had first heard two men, 'Mike Bigg' and 'Omar Hussain', talking at around 3.30 a.m.

They sounded agitated and spoke urgently. They came in and were visibly agitated and sweating on their faces and foreheads. Omar was carrying a cream plastic bag that was screwed up at the top. When he was in the room he never once put it down. They needed some crack. In my experience as a drug addict, crack users do not sweat when they need crack. They stated they had done a handbag snatch.

'Mike' was berating 'Omar'. 'You didn't have to go that far, you fucking idiot. You're a fucking wanker.' At this stage, there was no mention of a third man.

BB then gave them a lift in the Renault and saw Benguit zipping up his jacket. He was bare-chested beneath his jacket, and he reached inside for something in his breast pocket.

They went to Mike's flat. 'As we were all preparing to leave the house, both Mike and Omar are quickly going in and out of the rooms, searching for something. Mike was pulling open cupboards and doors, while Omar was just walking in and out.'

Mike asked BB to drop the bag off with a man called Darius and she refused. This was the first mention of Woolry.

In the second interview, 'Mike' became Gbadamosi, 'Omar Hussain' became Benguit and 'Darius' became Delroy Woolry. Mike, who was described as black in interview one, was now said to be light-skinned. In fact, he was given the moniker 'half-caste Nick'. The gang rape was described in horrific detail.

• • •

BB had a knack for leaving a trail of mayhem wherever she happened to be – not least, when she was in the witness protection scheme.

Dorset Police's star witness claimed that she had met with her handlers off duty. This would have been in direct breach of the rules. She also claimed that she received gifts from them, including CDs and a stereo.

The police were so concerned that BB's erratic behaviour might jeopardise the trial that Dorset Police's complaints and investigations team conducted its own investigation ahead of the second trial in April 2004.

BB told the investigation that she felt 'completely used, dumped and frightened' after the first trial ended. She alleged that her protection was reduced from twenty-four hours a day to 'virtually nothing'.

The officers denied BB's allegations. 'It is genuinely not known who is telling the truth, but if it is not resolved this will undermine [BB]'s credibility at the forthcoming murder trial at which she is the key prosecution witness,' the police report into the incident said.

Her time spent in witness protection was not a success. Far from kicking the habit, her dependency on hard drugs increased. She had to be moved from location to location as dealers learned of her whereabouts.

Her wildly sensationalised account of the murder, followed up with an appearance on the *Jeremy Kyle Show*, suggested at the very least a relaxed attitude to the threats that police were apparently protecting her from at the taxpayer's expense.

• • •

When the Criminal Cases Review Commission was set up in 1997, the likes of law reform and human rights organisation JUSTICE stopped investigating miscarriages of justice. The group said that they did not want to step on the toes of the new watchdog.

In reality, there was little enthusiasm from the human rights lawyers that ran the small charity to pursue such intractable cases. JUSTICE's interest in miscarriages of justice had historically been driven by the personal obsession of the group's first secretary, Thomas Sargant.

The CCRC had told prisoners claiming to be the innocent victims of miscarriages of justice that they did not need lawyers to apply. There has never been much financial incentive for lawyers taking on these difficult cases – certainly not under legal aid. While lawyers are caricatured as fat cats by the media, firms specialising in defence work have been going to the wall for years. Legal aid rates have been frozen for twenty years, and in 2014 fees were subjected to an 8.75 per cent cut.* Only one in four applications made to the CCRC is supported by a lawyer. There remains a small and committed group of solicitors willing to take these extremely difficult clients – but few defence lawyers are prepared to take something on unless a family is prepared to pay privately.

---

* When Lord Carter of Coles conducted a review of the defence profession for New Labour in 2006, the peer bluntly described the profession as 'if not dying, [then] time limited'. 'I was quite shocked, in certain parts, by the clear impoverishment of it,' he told me at the time.

• • •

It was into this vacuum that the university-based innocence movement came to the UK. In 2004, the University of Bristol launched its Innocence Project, where law students would investigate alleged miscarriages of justice.*

Shortly after an unsuccessful appeal in July 2005, Omar Benguit's sister Amie approached Barry Loveday, who was a reader in criminal justice studies at nearby Portsmouth University.

He quickly became convinced that a serious miscarriage of justice had taken place. 'I think the whole thing is bizarre,' he told the *Daily Echo* in 2007. 'The key witness in the case was a prostitute whose extraordinary version of events is just not believable.'

In a review of the case, Professor Loveday described BB's claim that she had been subjected to a gang rape as 'entirely fictional and a fabrication from beginning to end'. The academic found her story wholly implausible. The fact that the claims only surfaced when she herself was picked up for shoplifting only added to his suspicions.

Professor Loveday was also unconvinced by the apparent clarity of BB's recall. 'For an established drug addict, the ability to recall such detail one and a half months after the incident borders on the incredible,' he said.

• • •

---

* It has its origins in the New York Innocence Project, founded in 1992 by Barry Scheck and Peter Neufeld, and set up to exonerate wrongly convicted people through the use of DNA testing.

Soon after BB's dramatic appearance on the *Jeremy Kyle Show*, Omar Benguit's family made an application to the CCRC. It echoed many of the concerns raised by Professor Loveday in his review. Not only had the main prosecution witness contradicted herself on national television, but another far more obvious suspect – a convicted double murderer, no less – had emerged from the shadows.

Actually, Dorset Police had been made aware of this suspect well before they began to look at Omar Benguit. Three weeks after Oki's killing, Interpol in Rome faxed their colleagues in the UK a message headed: 'Query relating to murder of South Korean in Dorset'. The fax said that the man in question had moved to Bournemouth in May, and was 'strongly suspected' of another murder. 'It has to be underlined that he has a complex personality and is mentally unstable. His altered behaviour can result in violent reactions,' the Italian police warned.

When Danilo Restivo moved to Bournemouth, he was the main suspect in connection with the disappearance of a teenage girl called Elisa Claps. She had gone missing in 1993 in Potenza, Italy. Restivo was the last person to see her alive. He had arranged to meet her outside a local church. He was subsequently convicted and served a sentence for providing false information to the Italian murder inquiry.

Almost a decade later, in November 2002, Restivo bludgeoned to death a 48-year-old mother of two. Heather Barnett's body was found by her two children on their return home from school. He left strands of someone else's hair in her hands. Restivo was known to have cut hair from women as they travelled on buses in the Bournemouth area.

Restivo had come to live in Bournemouth in the spring of the year Heather Barnett died; Barnett lived opposite him. In June 2011, a jury at Winchester Crown Court found Danilo Restivo guilty of her murder. Later that year, a court in Potenza found Restivo guilty of the murder of Elisa Clapps and he was sentenced to thirty years in prison.

When the CCRC referred the Benguit case back to the Court of Appeal in April 2014, there were three grounds of appeal: BB's inconsistent post-trial accounts to the media; suspicions relating to Danilo Restivo; and previously unconsidered CCTV footage that appeared to undermine BB's rapidly shrinking credibility.

BB had claimed to be driving one of two cars – she couldn't recall whether it was a Volvo or a Renault Mégane – on the night of the murder. The CCRC considered the evidence of two CCTV experts who had studied the relevant footage from that evening between 2.30 a.m. and 3.05 a.m. The first had studied all of the cars driving down the road on that night and positively excluded each of them as BB's vehicle. The second was instructed to identify all the cars. He found that none matched BB's descriptions, although he was unable to identify four.

The Court of Appeal – comprising Lady Justice Rafferty, Mr Justice Cranston and Mr Justice Stewart – gave the case short shrift. They dismissed the CCTV footage brusquely: '...the issue is simply disposed of. Neither excludes the cars in which Benguit was on the evidence travelling, during a period in which he could have murdered Miss Shin.'

Noting that BB 'undoubtedly exaggerated' her account to the

police, Rafferty asserted that she did 'not exaggerate for monetary gain'.

On BB's own account, that was exactly what she had done. She had approached an online agency to sell her story. BB had been paid £500 for her account, and the agency sold her story to a magazine. 'I was getting a bit sick of actually having anything to do with it because it was only £500,' she later told Hampshire Police.

This was how BB recollected her response to reading the article: 'I remember when I saw it thinking it was a load of crap, but to be honest I wasn't really in a state to do anything about it.'

In the view of the appeal court, her credibility had been 'fully explored' before the jury. Nor did the court accept that Restivo might have been the murderer: he 'meticulously planned his attacks' on Elisa Claps and Heather Barnett, whereas the attack on Oki was 'opportune'. 'Striking similarities between the murders of Elisa Claps and Mrs Barnett did not feature in that of Miss Shin. Their bras were cut in the same place, their trousers partially lowered in the same manner and hair placed in their hands.'

The court acknowledged that 'searches and science did not link Benguit to the murder' (as it did in 2005 when it noted that the case for the prosecution was 'not supported by any forensic evidence'). However, it was reassured by 'significant circumstantial support' for Benguit's conviction. In other words, the testimony of a motley crew of heroin and crack addicts rounded up by the police.

The judges failed to mention the fact that their testimony formed part of a catastrophically bungled investigation in which the police did not so much as let one of three suspects slip through their fingers but, instead, provided for his one-way ticket to Jamaica.

Omar Benguit has always denied any involvement in Oki's death. In common with the other addicts interviewed by the police about their movements on the fatal night (with the notable exception of BB), Benguit did not have much of an idea what happened.

His older sister Amie will never forget the moment she learned that her brother had been arrested. The family owns a number of restaurants, including a fast food outlet. Her brother rang her up to tell her that Benguit had been arrested for murder.

'I was on the beach with my baby, dipping her toes into the sea in Sandbanks, Dorset,' she recalls.

> Omar was only allowed to make one phone call. He rang up his brother who was working. Unfortunately, he didn't want anything to do with Omar at that time. It was busy and there was a queue in the restaurant. My brother was so angry. Omar had to phone my other brother. He had just stolen from him, so he wasn't happy either. Omar was trying to work out where he had been that night. He was saying: 'Just tell me, was I there?'

The police taped the call, and later used the transcript as evidence of Benguit trying to drum up a false alibi.

Was Amie surprised that her brother had been arrested? 'No, he was always getting arrested for petty things,' she replies. 'Omar said it was his word against this other person – and that she was a crack addict prostitute. My first thought was that Omar was not capable of that kind of thing.'

Benguit was first interviewed on 22 August 2002. After confirming his name, date of birth and address, the verbatim transcript reads:

Interviewer: Right well, you've been arrested on suspicion of murdering Jong-Ok Shin, a Korean student, a 26-year-old who goes by the name of Oki – and that was in the early hours of Friday, July 12.

Respondent: Is it … I mean, is it a woman? It's a bloke.

Interviewer: It's a woman.

At the time of the arrest, Omar Benguit's life had gone into free fall. He was arrested as he left court. On that occasion, Benguit was the victim of a vicious beating at the hands of nightclub bouncers. They had hit him so hard that his eyeball was punctured. Benguit had a long list of 'previous', including two knife-related convictions. He had also threatened to stab someone with a syringe. These were nasty offences but consistent with the chaotic and scrappy life of a drug addict.

What had happened to Amie's brother? 'He had had a complicated relationship with his father from a very young age and he was dyslexic,' she said. As a result of his learning difficulties, Omar didn't go to the same school as the other Benguit kids in Lymington, a village in the heart of the New Forest. 'He was taken away from us and sent to a school for troubled children,' Amie recalls. 'He used to get into trouble. There was a bit of stealing, fighting and then he would go back home and get a hard time from Dad.'

Benguit also suffered from Crohn's, the inflammatory bowel disease which meant that he rarely drank. According to Amie, he started to take medication to deal with his condition. Then a doctor refused to prescribe the pills, and Benguit started taking the highly addictive painkiller dihydrocodeine.

He started hanging out with a bad crowd and, as Amie puts it, 'a bit of weed turned into a bit of cocaine'. 'He started going out with friends and he wouldn't sleep in the house, but he'd crash in the shed. I cannot blame myself but if I was there...'

Amie moved to London and then relocated to Italy for five years. In her absence, her brother's addiction spiralled.

> I knew he would end up back in prison because of the circle of friends he was hanging with. He was stealing from us. He would steal a box of chicken and try to sell it on down the road to a restaurant for £10 so he could get drugs. I would phone the police. I just wanted him to be arrested and be locked up for, say, six weeks and sort himself out.

It was a self-destructive pattern of behaviour that was as painful as it was frustrating for the family to witness. 'We almost disowned him. But, of course, we never did,' recalled Amie. 'We were just trying to teach him a lesson.'

When Omar Benguit was sent to prison for the murder of Jong-Ok Shin, the family was devastated. 'The case has ripped everyone apart,' Amie Benguit tells me. 'We try to be normal but there is a cloud over us. We are living it with him. It has completely destroyed our lives.'

• • •

It is a curious irony that, often, the only lawyers prepared to take a proper look at some of the most complex cases stuck in the justice system are students yet to start their careers. The first time I met Amie was at Portsmouth University's criminal justice clinic (formerly the university's Innocence Project). Omar Benguit officially became a client of the clinic in 2015. The case is now overseen by Marika Henneberg, who took over from Professor Barry Loveday as a senior lecturer at the university's Institute of Criminal Justice Studies.

In the conservative world of legal education, innocence work is a genuinely radical project. Not only does it offer a small number of prisoners a glimmer of hope where there is little room for any, but it has also provided a generation of lawyers with a crash course in the limitations of our justice system.

The innocence projects have become bogged down with problems. In the years since the pioneering University of Bristol Innocence Project launched in 2004, only one conviction has been overturned on the strength of a university application. This reveals as much about the shortcomings of the appeal system as it does about the limits of university innocence projects.

However, the movement has been in a state of disarray since, in 2014, the umbrella group Innocence Network UK disbanded. Its outspoken founder, Dr Michael Naughton, unilaterally pulled the plug on the scheme. The academic accused universities of jumping on the bandwagon, using projects as 'a recruiting tool' to attract students to their courses while merely paying lip service to the main mission of overturning convictions. Dr

Naughton has a point. University bosses quickly seized upon the marketing value of innocence work to spice up otherwise dull law courses.

It would appear that a genuinely radical project has become snagged on the jagged rocks of reality. At the end of 2012, there were twenty-seven projects investigating about 100 cases. At an Innocent Network symposium the following year, Dr Naughton argued that this was the perfect illustration of the CCRC's inaction and went on to argue that the organisation was not fit for purpose. It was a criticism that the CCRC turned on its head to shine a light on the work of its critics. The CCRC pointed out that they had only received seventeen applications from five universities, six of which came from a single university (Cardiff).

When I asked the CCRC chair Richard Foster, in 2016, to comment on the value of university projects, he was dismissive. 'If you think that you have a terminal illness, would you rather have your case considered by medical students in the bar on Friday night – or would you rather send it to a consultant oncologist?'

• • •

Amie Benguit reckons the family has spent (and largely wasted) a small fortune on lawyers' fees. As she said: 'When you are in my position and someone offers to help your brother, you're prepared to do anything.'

Her brother saw lawyer Giovanni Di Stefano – otherwise known as 'the Devil's Advocate' – while watching Sky TV.

Di Stefano was bragging about acting for high-profile clients including (so he claimed) Slobodan Milošević, Saddam Hussein, Ronnie Biggs and Ian Brady. Amie instructed Di Stefano ('Omar insisted...').

The 'lawyer' has no legal qualifications despite operating under the company name *Studio Legalese Internazionale* (The International Law Firm). In 2013, he was sentenced to fourteen years in prison for defrauding clients whom he had tricked into thinking he was a bona fide lawyer.

Sadly, Di Stefano is not the only legal adviser instructed by the family to end up behind bars. According to Amie Benguit, another legal adviser, who claimed to specialise in criminal appeals, is presently in prison for fraud. 'I have literally lost everything. I have just gone bankrupt,' Amie told me. 'I am very strong. I have to be strong. I am the pillar of the family.'

• • •

The Portsmouth criminology students hope to submit an application on behalf of Omar Benguit soon. 'The more you read the more you find yourself getting involved,' Izzy Linsell, an intern at the clinic who had just graduated in criminology, told me. 'We all feel Omar is innocent, but the way that the prosecution case has been constructed is unhelpful. The witness statements are incomplete and pages are missing. I started the process with an open mind.'

'No one who looks at the case thinks Omar did it,' said Marika Henneberg. 'It is hard to understand how anyone ever could have thought that he was guilty,' she added.

But then you have to see it in the context of a jury who did convict and who didn't see all the information we see. I think the way the case was presented to the court meant that a lot of the information was hidden. The jury got one side of the story. Put simply, there is no evidence.

I asked what the students made of the appeal process. 'If you fail in an appeal you can't use any of that evidence again. When someone has had previous appeals you have exhausted a lot of avenues already,' replied Linsell. 'Even if they have been badly presented and there is some substance to those lines of argument, we can't use them again. So we really do have to pull the case apart and investigate every single line possible.'

So – the big question – did the Portsmouth students have the requisite 'fresh evidence' to get the case back to the Court of Appeal? 'Oh, yes. We have found Omar's alibi,' replied Henneberg. In the summer of 2016, the academic travelled to Glasgow to interview Brian McGregor with Des Thomas, a former detective superintendent and former deputy head of Hampshire CID.

Thomas, a visiting lecturer at Cardiff University's law school, helps students review miscarriage of justice cases. He was present at the interview to ensure that it followed protocol and could be used at any future appeal.

McGregor claims to have known Benguit since 1996. The pair did time together in HMP Dorchester. McGregor is a recovering alcoholic who, for a time, lived rough in Bournemouth but, he insisted, that he was not part of the town's drug scene.

'I know for a fact Omar never did that murder,' McGregor told Henneberg and Thomas.

He never left my room that night. I locked my door all the time. I was living in bedsits. And I've got, by force of habit, into the practice of locking my door and then actually putting the keys in my pocket. I woke up in the morning and Omar was still there and none of my money had been touched or nothing.

McGregor claimed to have passed this information on to Benguit's solicitor when he heard his friend had been arrested. However, the lawyer apparently told him that he was not a 'credible witness' on account of his criminal record.

Des Thomas asked him why he never contacted the police. 'I don't get on with them,' McGregor replied. 'They've stitched me up in the past.'

When asked if there was a reason why he could remember the night of the Oki murder, he inevitably linked the evening to the sectarian marching season in Northern Ireland. 'There was a lot of bother at the time,' recalled the Glaswegian Catholic.

On his account, the pair only left the room once that evening – to walk to a nearby petrol station to get tobacco in the early hours of the morning. Other than that, Benguit was, MacGregor claimed, effectively locked in the room.

The Portsmouth students are presently wading through CCTV footage trying to find images of the pair buying tobacco from the garage.

• • •

Shortly after Amie Benguit arrived at the clinic, her mobile rang. It was her brother. At the time, he had been at HMP Wakefield in Yorkshire for seven years. All his family live on the south coast and she only visits once a year, but they speak every day.

Amie asked him how he was getting on with his latest book. Benguit had just finished Nelson Mandela's *Long Road to Freedom* and had moved on to Paulo Coelho's *The Alchemist*. The call ended prematurely.

Benguit was not in a good way. 'He's "down the block", in solitary. He is protesting because he wants to be closer to us,' Amie said. 'He was on hunger strike for eight days. It was really bad a couple of weeks ago. He went on a dirty protest. He is being assessed by a doctor every day to see what his mental state is like and whether he's suicidal.'

A couple of weeks later, I met with Amie in Bournemouth. We were there to retrace the route as described by BB on the night of the murder. We were joined by Nick Gbadamosi. Amie and Gbadamosi have become unlikely friends. Well over six feet tall and with the build of somebody who has spent a lot of time working out in the gym, he squeezed into the back of the car.

Gbadamosi claimed to have been clean for just over a year. He was well turned out, streetwise and whip-smart, but the years of addiction had taken a heavy toll.

He made little attempt to put a gloss on his criminal past. Talking admiringly about one of the trial barristers, he offered the following insight: 'Look, I am a criminal. I have been in and out of court a lot and I was highly impressed by this guy.'

Gbadamosi is a man who can take care of himself. When I asked how he dealt with prison, he replied: 'I was fucking furious. The case was high profile. It was on the telly. When I got to prison the governor asked did I want to go on "the numbers" [i.e. with vulnerable prisoners, such as sex offenders, isolated for their own protection]. I told him to fuck off. I am not going to live with paedophiles.'

He recalled walking onto the wing when all the prisoners were out 'on association'. 'I threw my bag down and screamed to get everyone's attention: "You all know who I fucking am. You know what those cunts have got me in for. I didn't fucking do it. If anyone has got anything to say you can fucking see me about it."' He was in prison for two years before the trial. 'Nobody said a word,' he said.

As we drove towards Malmesbury Park Road where Oki was killed, I asked Nick Gbadamosi what impact the rape allegations had had on his life. In an instant, his bravado evaporated. 'It ruined my life. It continues to ruin my life. It stops me from doing stuff that should come naturally. It inhibits relationships with women and my pursuit of employment. Companies check social media and see reams of shit about the case.'

Why did the police fight so hard to convict you and Benguit? 'They are just cunts. They wanted to convict somebody because they didn't want to look like the inept wankers that they are.'

Gbadamosi has a long criminal record, aside from the Oki case. He accepts that – but not the rape allegations. 'I had the two trials and I was cleared. It was such obvious bullshit,' he said. 'That was the wicked thing about it.' There was no evidence. 'You know, we've all been teenagers and had a shag in a back of a car. It gets hot and steamy. That would leave a wealth of DNA. She [BB] is saying three guys had done this to her in the car using tools from the boot.'

When BB gave her first interview, she identified two of the culprits as 'Nick' and 'Darius'. Gbadamosi reckoned she came up with these names as a result of two popular television shows, *Pop Idol* and *Big Brother*, which featured 'Darius' and 'Nasty Nick' respectively. 'Yeah, it really was that farcical.' Why would she do that? 'She just wanted to keep out of prison.'

There followed a dramatic grinding of emotional gears. 'It fucking kills me,' Gbadamosi said. We were both looking forward; Nick started shaking in his seat. When I looked over, he was in tears.

It is a ninety-second drive from Charminster Road, where BB supposedly picked up the three men, to the spot where Oki was brutally slain on Malmesbury Park Road at around 3 a.m.

Amie Benguit and I left Gbadamosi in the car to compose himself. It is a long and straight avenue of neat terraced houses. As we pulled up at the spot where Oki was brutally murdered, Amie asked me what was the first thing I had noticed.

The spot where Oki collapsed is opposite a long, narrow path between two houses and at the end is a blind corner to the right running behind the gardens. I was surprised. This was not a fact that I had gleaned from all my reading about the case. If this was a premeditated murder, and not the kind of spontaneous attack described by BB, then this would be the obvious point for it to happen.

We returned to the car and drove around the corner. In under two minutes, Amie pointed out Heather Barnett's house and, turning around, she motioned to Danilo Restivo's old flat.

• • •

In our digital age, almost every human encounter with officialdom is captured, documented and filed away. An audit trail is left whether we want it or not. One exception is our legal system, which frequently deals with situations where the stakes could not be higher – where the need for accountability and transparency could not be more obvious.

No area of civil society churns out more papers than our courts. It is ironic, therefore, that there is very little paper evidence of the judicial decision-making that led to Omar Benguit losing his liberty. What we have now is down to Amie Benguit and the hard work of Marika Henneberg and the Portsmouth students. In the case of Omar Benguit, there are no transcripts of his three trials apart from the forty pages of the judge's sentencing remarks in the 2005 trial.

To put this into perspective, in the Eddie Gilfoyle case, there is a full verbatim transcript of the four-week trial: over 1,800 pages contained in four fat lever-arch files.

What remains of Benguit's paperwork has been catalogued and scanned by the Portsmouth students. It is available on a single USB stick. They have not stopped looking for more material. Key documents such as prosecution witness statements and police interviews are incomplete. BB's key interview starts on p. 7. The Benguit case has passed through multiple sets of legal representatives, and at every stage of the process the paperwork has shrunk as files have been mislaid or else not returned.

Omar Benguit has protested his innocence from day one. He hopes one day to clear his name, but his ability to do that is significantly hindered by the absence of any court transcripts and other paperwork. This is the result of a policy on the part of our courts, as well as the fault of the legal representatives who have lost or refused to hand over files.

Every hearing in the Crown Court must be recorded in full, but audio tape recordings of those proceedings are destroyed after five years. This used to be justified on the basis of good housekeeping and conserving space occupied by tapes. Since 2011, proceedings have been recorded digitally. Those files are deleted after seven years under Ministry of Justice guidelines (known as the Crown Court Record Retention and Disposition Schedules). This policy applies to the judge's summing up, which is widely considered essential for any chance of an appeal.

The destruction regime is seemingly at odds with the thirty-year evidence retention policy of the National Police Chiefs' Council (formerly ACPO) in relation to murder cases. A Ministry of Justice spokesman told me that the 'practices, retention policies and records management procedures' of other organisations were 'not a factor taken into consideration' when deciding upon retention periods, nor are they considered when deciding whether records merit permanent preservation. 'And neither the Public Records Act 1958, nor the Data Protection Act 1998, nor any other piece of legislation requires that we do so,' the spokesman added.

Law firms do not preserve their clients' files for ever. Frequently they are disposed of after six years have elapsed. It used to be that the Solicitors Regulation Authority recommended a six-year minimum retention period under the 2007 code of conduct; but the watchdog says that this is not the case any more and it is up to individual firms to decide how long a file should be retained. 'This is an issue that we have been asked about time and again by solicitors,' a spokesman said. 'There's no set regulatory requirements for file retention. We expect solicitors to have appropriate arrangements for each client.'

• • •

Omar Benguit has been in prison since 2002 for a crime he claims he did not commit. Up until the end of 2017, Benguit had been in HMP Wakefield, hundreds of miles away from his family who live on the south coast.

The last time I spoke to Amie, her brother had been stabbed three times by a notorious child-killer, Stuart Hazell. She rang up to ask if I could recommend a decent prison lawyer. Amie believes that her brother has become a target for attacks because he maintains his innocence. 'He does not talk to paedophiles. They think he has an attitude problem,' Amie told me. Her brother has since been moved to HMP Long Lartin in Worcestershire.

Benguit continues to fight the authorities every step of the way. He has spent much of the past year in segregation. 'If he did not have us, I think probably he would have taken his life,' Amie said. 'Of course, if he had owned up to it and done a few courses, he would've been out by now.'*

---

* A number of criticisms have been made of the police's handling of the case: chiefly, that they pursued Benguit to the exclusion of other lines of inquiry (notably Restivo); they bungled the initial investigation (for example, by letting one of three suspects leave the country); as well as the unreliability of BB's evidence.

I put these to Dorset Police. Detective Chief Superintendent Mark Callaghan called the investigation 'thorough, detailed and very complex'. As he pointed out, there had been two appeals and the second specifically addressed the reliability of BB, and the possibility of Restivo being the killer. 'This case has been through a series of reviews and any issue surrounding concerns regarding this conviction is ultimately a matter for the CCRC,' he said. 'Dorset Police would follow the direction and instigate investigations, if directed by the courts and responsible authorities. As always, our thoughts are with Oki's family and friends who remain devastated by their loss.'

CHAPTER FOUR

DEFYING GRAVITY

On Tuesday 11 June 1996, Samuel Benefield, formerly known as 'Scotch Sammy', arrived at the Court of Appeal. The reformed gangster was taking no chances. He walked into the Royal Courts of Justice through the Carey Street entrance at the rear of the building, away from the press and well before court business started.

Benefield arrived with his minder from Scotland Yard's Criminal Justice Protection Unit. It had been over a quarter of a century since the armed robber had turned supergrass, putting his old gang mates behind bars for long stretches. He was fearful that they might decide to settle old scores. Benefield cut a bizarre figure, wearing a headscarf, a poorly applied fake moustache and beard with heavy sunglasses. 'He was dressed just like an Arab sheik,' recalled one lawyer.

Samuel Benefield was to be the star witness in an appeal by Tony Stock against a 1970 conviction for an armed robbery in Leeds. He had come to say three things: he and his old gang mates committed the robbery; Tony Stock was not part of the gang; and, finally, he had no idea who Tony Stock was.

• • •

Leeds, West Yorkshire, early one Saturday night in January 1970. The manager of the Tesco store at the Merrion Shopping Centre was carrying the day's takings across to the Lloyds Bank night safe. He was walking the short distance with the cashier's boyfriend.

It was dark and raining heavily. A Russian adaptation of *War and Peace* was playing at the Odeon. Locals and students queued for the early-evening showing.

The two men were rushed by a gang of men and attacked with coshes. The manager fell to the ground. Bleeding from a head wound, he refused to let go of the takings. He was carrying almost £4,200. It was a lot of money. The average family house cost £4,975 that year.

His attacker stamped on the manager's hand, breaking his fingers. The thieves grabbed the money and sped off in their getaway car. Only one witness was able to make an identification. The warehouse manager, Stewart Wilson, heard his colleagues' screams, ran to help and locked eyes for a moment with one of the robbers. Wilson was later shown police photographs of local criminals. The next day, Wilson assisted in the making of an identikit picture.

It looked a lot like Tony Stock.

It was to take a few days for police officers from Leeds to arrive at the home of the thirty-year-old father of four. He lived in Stockton-on-Tees, 72 miles north of the city. He denied having anything to do with the robbery and refused to take part in an identity parade.

With nothing else to go on, DS John Mather, a young detective who had come across Stock in connection with another investigation, decided to do something highly unorthodox. He and another officer drove their witness up the A1 to Stock's home. When Stock came to the door, the officers kept it open long enough for Wilson to snatch a look at him. There was a scuffle on the doorstep.

Wilson positively identified Stock and an arrest was made. Later, both officers wrote in their notebooks that, on seeing Wilson, Stock shouted: 'Get that man out of here, he knows me.'

Then the police did something else that would have been considered unusual even by the standards of 1970s policing. The two officers piled into their two-door Mini Cooper, with their witness and their suspect, for the 72-mile drive back to Millgarth Police Station.

The case against Stock consisted mainly of Wilson's identification and a series of apparently self-incriminating statements attributed to Stock, including an exchange with Mather in the cells when it is alleged that he said: 'The wife will get my share if the worst happens.'

Stock's defence was that the police were lying through their teeth. He claimed to have been at home on the night of the robbery with his family – his wife, Brenda, and their four children, all under the age of ten – celebrating his thirtieth birthday.

During a three-day trial in July 1970, Brenda and his nine-year-old daughter Charlene took to the witness stand to confirm that Stock had been at home that night. They were his only witnesses. Tony Stock was found guilty and sentenced to ten years in prison.

· · ·

Some twenty-six years later, reformed gangster Samuel Benefield turned up to the Court of Appeal to tell the judges what happened on that night. He came to deliver on a promise he had made to someone called Tom Sargant in 1979.

Tom Sargant was the first secretary of JUSTICE and a towering figure in the world of miscarriages of justice from the 1950s through to the 1980s. Every week prisoners would write to Sargant at the group's Chancery Lane office, claiming to have been wrongly convicted. Fiercely intelligent and driven by strong religious conviction, Tom Sargant took the then eccentric position of giving prisoners the benefit of the doubt. As a consequence, his name was well known on prison landings up and down the country.

When Tony Stock was sent to HMP Gartree, he did everything he could to protest his innocence. There were rooftop protests and a shattering 93-day hunger strike. Prison wardens force-fed Stock by wedging a wooden block at the back of his throat, with a circular hole through which a pipe is fed. Sometimes they used Vaseline to smooth the pipe's passage, sometimes not.

Stock wrecked his own health. He wrecked the health of his elderly mother, Mary, distraught at the strange fate that had befallen her son. While he was in prison, his wife, Brenda, divorced him. He lost contact with his four children.

Telling anyone who would listen, Stock would repeatedly assert his innocence and explain that he had been 'fitted up' by corrupt police officers. He wrote a furious letter to Tom Sargant, railing against the two police officers who 'invented the evidence' that put him away.

Sargant immediately wrote to Stock's lawyer, requesting all

the documentation relating to the case. The veteran defence lawyer who acted for Stock was only too happy to offload a difficult client. 'I feel that there really is nothing more which I can personally do,' he wrote to Sargant. 'I'm not at all happy about this case. I have considerable experience of criminal matters, but this is perhaps the first case in which I have been involved during many years of practice where I have felt that a man has been "framed".' The lawyer added that the lead officer on the Stock case, Mather, was well known in criminal circles as 'Mr Verbal'.*

Shortly after Stock had been sent to prison, John Mather's career came to an abrupt end. He was suspended and charged with corruption related to the taking of bribes. The judge at his trial at Leeds Crown Court in 1972 said that Mather and a fellow officer were 'either corrupt or stupid', and gave them the benefit of the doubt, dismissing the pair as 'complete idiots'.

Mather was put on traffic duty. Later, the officer was presented with ninety charges relating to disciplinary matters and resigned from the force. His file went to the Director of Public Prosecutions, but no charges in relation to those allegations were ever brought.

Tom Sargant read Stock's papers and wrote back to his lawyer, saying he was 'sure that Mr Stock is innocent'. Up until his retirement in 1985, Sargant fought to clear Stock's name. When Stock went on hunger strike, Sargant did everything he could to dissuade him from taking such a drastic course of

---

* 'Verballing' was the practice of falsely putting damaging remarks into the mouths of suspects during police interrogations. The Police and Criminal Evidence Act 1984 introduced the tape recorder into police interviews to stamp out the practice.

action. Stock's despairing mother could not cope. Not wanting to burden her son, she would write to Sargant, who did as much as he could to reassure her.

• • •

In November 1979, Tony Stock had been out of prison for three years and was putting his life back together. He was doing very well. He had moved to south Wales, started a new family and set up a business selling carpets in the Valleys.

Shortly after his release, Tony received a call from a reporter at the *Yorkshire Post* asking if he was he aware that someone had confessed to the Leeds robbery.

The Thursday Gang had become the Chainsaw Gang. It had apparently never occurred to the Leeds Police that the robbery in 1970 could have been the work of out-of-town thieves. This was a different era when, for example, armed robbers came equipped with coshes not guns. The M1 motorway only reached Leeds in 1968.

It was the building of a motorway network that inspired a new generation of armed robbers. The Chainsaw Gang, so-called because of their innovative approach to new-style Securicor vans, was pre-eminent. The police were desperate to bring to a close a crime wave that had lasted for almost a decade.

It ended with the arrest of Scotch Sammy. Samuel Benefield turned supergrass in 1979 and sang like the proverbial bird. He went on to testify in the cases of some ten defendants in connection with fifty robberies. Benefield was given a new identity and placed in the witness protection scheme. On the basis of his evidence, an entire East End crime gang was put behind bars. Benefield himself had a total of forty-one robberies taken into consideration, including the Leeds job.

• • •

'SQUEALER CLEARS IDENTIKIT VICTIM', screamed the headline in the *Daily Mail*. A *World in Action* special on the Tony Stock case on ITV told the dramatic story of his wrongful conviction at the end of 1979. The programme closed with Tony Stock's happy expectation of a pardon.

But then something very peculiar happened.

Home Secretary Willie Whitelaw decided not to pardon Stock. Instead, the minister cited an internal and top-secret report by West Yorkshire Police into the alleged perjury of the two officers who had investigated the case.

Tom Sargant was furious at the double standards. The government was only too happy to accept the Benefield admission when it served the purpose of putting away a vicious gang of armed robbers, but not to help an innocent man.

From that point on, JUSTICE used the Stock case to highlight the crisis faced by the criminal justice system. The group's 1980 annual report lambasted an indifferent Court of Appeal, which in its view had become 'unresponsive to clear indications of innocence' particularly in cases where the quashing of a conviction would involve an admission of 'police malpractice'.

This was a different time. Tom Sargant had direct access to government ministers. Researching the Stock case, I was given the JUSTICE file, which included a private exchange between Sargant and Home Secretary Willie Whitelaw.

At the end of a heated correspondence, Whitelaw noted that the outcome 'must be disappointing to Mr Stock – particularly if he had been led to believe that the uncorroborated statement made by Mr Benefield would be sufficient to secure the grant of a free pardon and compensation'.

Tom Sargant did not disguise his contempt for such a disingenuous line. Such a response was 'unsatisfactory and Machiavellian', he wrote back.

In 1981, Tom Sargant, described by the campaigning journalist Ludovic Kennedy as resembling 'a shabby eagle ... usually covered in cigarette ash', sat down with East End gangster Samuel Benefield. The interview was recorded with an eye towards an appeal and a transcript was written up.

Sargant asked Benefield if there was any reason why the police would not believe him about the Leeds job. 'There's no way they could believe that I didn't commit robbery, and there's no way in my opinion they could believe that Stock was involved,' Benefield replied.

'One of my troubles is that the Home Secretary says that he has not got absolute proof that Stock didn't do it, which the Home Secretary requires,' continued Sargant. 'Would you be ready to go back to court?'

Samuel Benefield, after a life of crime, was finally prepared to do the decent thing.

> I would be quite willing to go back to court. The man was innocent. I would like to put the record straight. I've already

admitted to about fifty robberies. This was one of them. I'm quite prepared to go to court to help in any way I can.

• • •

Samuel Benefield was as good as his word. More than a quarter of a century after the armed robbery, and eight years after Sargant died, the former East End gangster delivered on the promise. Tony Stock waited until his children from his second marriage were in their early teens and old enough to understand before renewing his fight to clear his name.

Unfortunately, something very odd happened – again.

Samuel Benefield gave his evidence to the court from behind a screen. 'I take it you can see me,' began Michael Mansfield QC. 'I wonder if you can help us by answering a plain and blunt question: is there anything in all of this for you?' Mansfield asked. 'Nothing. Nothing at all,' Benefield replied. 'I want to be here like I want a hole in my head at the moment.'

The Court of Appeal didn't believe Benefield. In fact, it was seriously unimpressed that Home Secretary Michael Howard had troubled them with the case in the first place.

Lord Justice Igor Judge did not accept that the subsequent revelations amounted to much.[*] 'In reality, there was very little additional material of any significance,' he said. 'We can only

---

[*] Lord Judge, who went on to become Lord Chief Justice, had considerable experience when it came to miscarriages of justice. As Igor Judge QC, he was prosecuting counsel on the Carl Bridgewater case in 1979 and appeared again for the Crown at the Birmingham Six's second unsuccessful appeal in 1987.

infer that the decision to refer the case simply represents a change of mind at the Home Office.'

Judge thought that the supergrass's description of his gang's return journey was 'outside any possible contemplation', so utterly illogical as to completely blow his credibility. The investigative journalist Paul Foot (father of Eddie Gilfoyle's lawyer Matt Foot) later wrote an article in *Private Eye* headlined 'Judge Dreadful'.

I met Tony Stock twelve years after his ill-fated appeal. He had with him a photocopy of the Paul Foot article. 'If anyone seriously believes that the Court of Appeal has reformed itself since the dark days of the Birmingham 6 and the Bridgewater 4, they should study the amazing and unreported case of Tony Stock,' it began.

If Samuel Benefield was not telling the truth, it followed, then he was lying. That was a proposition from which some obvious questions flowed, but it did not seem to bother the court.

As Foot explained:

> Someone, their Lordships guessed, had told Benefield all about the robbery so he could pretend he took part in it with others and thus exculpate Tony Stock. The judges surmised that Stock or some (unknown) agents of his had contacted (unknown) members of the Thursday Gang in some (unknown) prison and gave them details of the robbery so that they could pretend to the police that he was not there. For this fantastic hypothesis the judges produced not a single shred of evidence.

Samuel Benefield was a heavy-duty gangster. When he turned

supergrass, the media couldn't get enough of the Chainsaw Gang's alleged antics. 'The gang led by a man they called the General, planned an armed, commando-style raid at Southampton to steal £3.5 million in foreign currency as it was being loaded onto the QE2 before a world cruise,' ran one of many breathless reports.

One of the gang's members was Jimmy Moody. A psychopathic hitman, he was employed as an enforcer for the infamous 1960s south London criminal outfit run by Charlie and Eddie Richardson, as well as working for the rival London gang operated by the Kray twins. Moody's CV also included a stint as a freelance IRA hitman. The gangster was shot dead by an unknown assassin in a pub in Hackney in 1993.

And Tony Stock? At the time of the trial of Benefield and other Chainsaw Gang members, Stock was working as a sales representative, selling vending machines dispensing hot drinks in Stockton-on-Tees.

It made no sense for Samuel Benefield to admit to a crime that he did not commit – and for which a man had already done his time. Nor could a deal have been struck between the pair. Benefield was sentenced to five years because of his supergrass status. His former colleagues got over twenty years.

Supergrasses were separated from the rest of the prison population until trial. Any such deal would have to have been predicated on Benefield turning supergrass – not usually a turn of events criminals plan for.

If any of this occurred to the Court of Appeal, it didn't seem to trouble them. There was another question that followed from their suggestion that Benefield lied about the Leeds robbery:

where did it leave all those other convictions secured through his evidence?

'We should add, in fairness, that we have seen no reason to believe that his evidence in the trials at which a number of juries convicted his associates is now open to question,' said Lord Justice Judge.

Fairness had nothing to do with it. Judge made much of the apparent implausibility of Benefield's description of the gang's return, which, he said, comprised 'a series of assumptions which make scant sense'.

His Lordship continued: 'Setting our judgment of Benefield as a witness into the overall context of the remaining evidence on which we think it is proper to rely, we do not think this conviction was unsafe. Accordingly, this appeal is dismissed.'

This was all too much for Tony Stock. As Lord Justice Judge drew to a close, Stock shouted from his seat: 'Rubbish!' He stormed out of the courtroom, walking out of the Royal Courts of Justice and onto the Strand, leaving his wife and son James trailing behind him.

Tony Stock had succeeded in making a good life for himself after prison, but that, ironically, fell apart when Benefield made his confession. It was revealed that he was a convicted armed robber (albeit one identified as innocent in countless articles in the national and local media). His carpet stores, which relied on word of mouth in the Welsh Valleys, were dealt a fatal blow.[*] In 1979, Tony Stock had three carpet shops, but two years later he

---

[*] Ironically, this was largely as a result of ITV broadcasting its *World in Action* special on the Tony Stock case in July 1980. This was one of the first investigations into a miscarriage of justice case broadcast on TV. The BBC launched its pioneering *Rough Justice* series two years later.

emigrated with his young family to South Africa. He was as good as bankrupt and left the country with a trail of debts behind him.

• • •

James Stock had been sitting at his father's side in the Court of Appeal in 1996. He had only recently discovered that his father was a convicted armed robber and that he had half-brothers and half-sisters from his father's first marriage. 'My dad was pretty confident that he was going to be cleared,' James told me. 'He was just crushed, but he was down only for a few hours. It was amazing. That is something that I'm proud of my father for: his strength of character. Every time he was crushed he came back even more determined.'

Tony Stock crossed the Strand and walked into a pub. He had given up smoking, but bought himself a pack of cigarettes and lit up. 'It was the first time in my life I'd ever seen him down,' James recalled.

Before he finished his drink, Tony Stock decided to confront the other members of the Chainsaw Gang. He would persuade them to do the decent thing and tell the court that he had nothing to do with the Leeds robbery.

He downed his drink, jumped into a cab with his wife, Anne, and James and directed the driver to take them to the Blind Beggar on Whitechapel Road in the East End. The pub is where Ronnie Kray shot and murdered George Cornell and, ever since, has occupied a special place in East End gangster folklore. If you wanted to find an East End gangster, then that seemed an obvious place to start looking.

A couple of hours after leaving the Royal Courts of Justice, Tony Stock found himself in the flat of Clive Bobrow, a former member of the Chainsaw Gang. James and his mother were left in the taxi outside.

According to James, Bobrow was not in good health. Bobrow had told Tony that he might be prepared to leave a signed statement to be released after his death. 'That gave Dad enough of a glimmer of hope to carry on,' James said, before adding: 'That is when the case became an obsession.'

It was a bizarre end to a dismal day. What impression did it make on James, who was at this point studying for his A Levels? 'It made me very cynical about the British justice system. I still am,' he told me. 'I used to get very upset whenever I talked about it to anybody. It would always make me very angry, make me cry. I have let it go now.'

• • •

It was not the first time that Tony Stock had been crushed by the justice system – and sadly it would not be the last. James was right to say the case became an obsession for his father. It overwhelmed Tony Stock's life and cast a long shadow over the lives of his family and loved ones.

Following the Court of Appeal's 1996 rejection, Stock thought about taking his own life. The despair passed. However, the raising and crushing of his hopes would eventually prove devastating.

His case would go to the Court of Appeal four times. There was also a visit to the European Court of Human Rights. I first interviewed Stock in 2008, ahead of his final visit to the Royal Courts of Justice. He then told me: 'I would have been the first of the miscarriages of justice. Then there was a spate of cases: the Birmingham Six, the Bridgewater Four and the Cardiff Three. Each one was another nail in my coffin.'*

In the dispiriting litany of miscarriages of justice over the past forty years, there are many alleged crimes that are far more heinous than the 1970 Leeds robbery. No one died in Leeds.

But it was still a calamity, not just for Tony Stock, but also for his family. He lost contact for years with the four children of his first marriage and never managed to establish a proper relationship with them as a result. His heartbroken mother never recovered from the shock – and the case was to put a huge strain on his new family and, according to his brother, sent Stock to an early grave.

• • •

The year after Tony Stock stormed out of the Court of Appeal, the Criminal Cases Review Commission opened for business. The CCRC had unprecedented statutory powers, which allowed it to compel Yorkshire Police to release its report into the alleged perjury of Leeds detective John Mather and his police colleague. This was the top-secret report that Willie Whitelaw had cited when denying Stock a pardon.

West Yorkshire Police had accepted the truth of the supergrass, Samuel Benefield, the report revealed. Such was the detail

---

* Michael Mansfield acted in each of those cases, as well as for Tony Stock.

provided by Benefield that it 'inevitably casts doubt' on the safety of the conviction. Specifically, the report's authors had no problem with Benefield's description of his gang's return journey.

Unsurprisingly, Tony Stock's lawyers had wanted to get hold of the report ahead of the 1996 appeal. They went to considerable effort to do so but the Crown Prosecution Service blocked them, arguing that the report's release would damage the public interest. The lawyers challenged the CPS through the courts, only to be told by the Court of Appeal (before Lord Justice Taylor) that the report's contents were 'either not relevant or not worth fighting for'.

When the CCRC did open its doors in 1997, it was immediately overwhelmed. The Home Office deposited on the new body some 251 'old' cases. 'I don't know if we can cope,' its first chair, Sir Frederick Crawford, told journalists at its launch press conference. Amongst the first wave of new applications were the cases of Tony Stock and Eddie Gilfoyle.

In 2004, the CCRC sent the case of Tony Stock back to the Court of Appeal for the third time. Stock's lawyers and the CCRC believed that they had found new evidence that completely undermined what remained of the original case: the identification.

The newly disclosed 1979 report revealed that the sole witness, Wilson, had been shown five photographs, and that it was highly probable that those photographs included a picture of the one suspect, Stock.

It was never suggested that the police were looking for anyone other than Tony Stock. What possible reason could there be for the police to show Wilson photographs? The significance of the showing of such a photo was not so much that it breached Home Office guidance – it did – but the fact that it raised questions about the integrity of the investigation. It was a revelation that blew away the last slender shred of credibility that the original investigation had possessed.

It might have seemed a narrow basis upon which to build an appeal in a case that had so dramatically unravelled. After all, someone had confessed to the robbery, and there was now no reason to think that he was not telling the truth.

But the CCRC correctly anticipated that the Court of Appeal would not allow them to replay old arguments about Samuel Benefield – despite the fact that it was the court's own error that led to his testimony being rejected in the 1996 appeal.

The Court of Appeal did not hold back in its criticism of the upstarts at the CCRC for having the nerve to send a case back. It said: 'We question the value of this exercise thirty years or more after the original trial and appeal, when there was no new material.'

Lord Justice May accepted that Lord Justice Judge's court in 1996 failed to grasp Samuel Benefield's account of the exit route. 'There is little explanation of how the court in 1996 came to think as they did,' he said.

The Court of Appeal does not do apologies.

Tony Stock's guilt or innocence now hung on the narrow point about the five photographs. This became the focus of two appeals in 2004 and 2008.

In the first appeal, the court held that the photographs could feasibly have been shown prior to the police coming into possession of Stock's photograph.

This was a misunderstanding of the CCRC's submissions.

In 2008, the watchdog sent the case straight back. In its statement of reasons, the CCRC respectfully pointed out that the appeal judges had now twice failed to get to grips with the case in 1996 and 2004. They wrote that 'a number of matters were misunderstood' in 1996, and that in 2004 'the appellant's crucial submission was misunderstood'.

The CCRC confirmed that Detective Sergeant John Mather had indeed shown Wilson a selection of five photographs after they had shown him the Stock photo. This point was definitively clarified by the CCRC's head of investigation, Ralph Barrington, who interviewed Wilson himself on the point in 2005.

What could possibly go wrong?

• • •

Back to the Court of Appeal they went. In 2008, Lord Justice Latham, rejecting the appeal, suggested that, if there was a photograph of Tony Stock which the witness saw but did not recognise as his attacker, that 'seems to us to be capable of strengthening the reliability of his ultimate identification' – insofar as he was not prepared to identify him from a photograph ('which can often be an unrepresentative likeness') but was able to identify him in person.*

Another 'difficulty' for Stock, Latham suggested, was that

---

* 'Later this year, legal history will be made when a man convicted thirty-eight years ago of a robbery in Leeds gets a record fourth chance in the Court of Appeal to clear his name,' began another article by Paul Foot in *Private Eye*. 'But when the case of Tony Stock – first reported in the *Eye* twelve years ago – finally comes before m'learned friends, it will be the judges in the public spotlight. Can they finally admit their colleagues have previously got it wrong, not once but three times?'

he was making an argument 'dependent upon an evaluation twenty-eight years after the statements in 1979 and 1980 were made, statements which themselves were made nine and ten years after the events in question'.

That was hardly Tony Stock's fault.

This is how Lord Justice Latham closed the last judgment in the case of Tony Stock.

> We accordingly dismiss this appeal. We do so recognising the tenacity with which this applicant has fought to overturn his conviction. It may be suggested in some way that this of itself should cause us to doubt the safety of the conviction. He has certainly persuaded the CCRC to expend considerable time and resources in support of this case. Whether or not the truth may be that he has been angered by the evidence of Detective Sergeant Mather, we will probably never know.

• • •

Ralph Barrington was a former head of Essex CID who went on to advise the Criminal Cases Review Commission as their first head of investigations. When I first spoke to Barrington in 2011, he was about to step down from the CCRC at the age of sixty-seven after thirteen years' service.

He was furious at the Court of Appeal's treatment of Tony Stock. Barrington has since devoted a fair amount of his retirement to reinvestigating the case and continues to do so. He has described the Court of Appeal's logic in the 2008 judgment as 'defying gravity'.

Barrington joined Essex Police in 1964, became a detective constable in 1967 and rose to the position of head of Essex CID in 1987 after having been promoted to the role of detective chief superintendent. A former commissioner credited his part in many of the commission's early successes. He has called the Stock case 'the most outrageous miscarriage I saw in my time at CCRC'. The outrage he felt towards the role of the Court of Appeal was widely shared at the CCRC.*

In 2011, when I met Tony Stock, he was a 73-year-old pensioner. He told me how he was spending his state pension on private investigators, looking for fresh evidence in a case that had first gone to court more than four decades ago.

He was living alone in a flat in Llandrindod Wells, Powys, having separated from his second wife. Some eleven months after I met him, his brother Alan was unable to contact Stock, and so he rang up his old friend Keith who lived nearby. When Stock didn't come to the door, Keith rang the police. They broke down the door and discovered him fully clothed on his bed, dead.

His sister-in-law told me that when they cleared out his small flat they found two pictures on a wall. One was of the police officer who Stock believed had framed him. The other was a cartoon. Two mice fell into a bowl of cream. The first one gave up and drowned, the second one fought and swam so hard that it turned the cream into butter and then walked out. Stock had written underneath the second mouse: 'That's me'.

---

* I wrote a book about the case: *The First Miscarriage of Justice: The Unreported and Amazing Case of Tony Stock* (Hampshire: Waterside Press, 2014). It was written with the support of Ralph Barrington and Tony's lawyer, Glyn Maddocks, who has championed his case for more than twenty years.

• • •

The hopes of many – including the families of Tony Stock, Danny Major, Omar Benguit and Eddie Gilfoyle – reside in the Criminal Cases Review Commission (CCRC).

The CCRC celebrated its twentieth anniversary on 31 March 2017. Shortly after this date, a new application from Tony Stock's family was submitted to the watchdog. If the case is referred to the Court of Appeal, then it will be an unprecedented third referral. If not, it will inevitably raise questions about the point of a watchdog that refrains from referring a case back that is widely acknowledged to be (to quote its former head of investigations Ralph Barrington) 'a self-evident miscarriage of justice'.

At the time of writing, Danny Major's conviction has still not been overturned. The report by Greater Manchester Police (Operation Lamp) identifying the case as a likely miscarriage of justice came out at the end of the 2015. It was immediately referred to the CCRC.

The CCRC examined the Danny Major case but decided not to refer it back to the Court of Appeal. The commission has powers to instruct a body independent of the police force to examine the case. It declined to do so. It was the persistence of Danny Major and his parents, Eric and Bernadette, that persuaded West Yorkshire's police and crime commissioner to commission the review. Operation Lamp raises an obvious serious question about the competence of the CCRC's work.[*]

---

[*] In May 2014, BBC Radio 4's *File on 4* asked the CCRC's chair, Richard Foster, why the body had not commissioned a police force to investigate the case. 'I stand by that judgement and if that investigation turns up anything new and it's put to us, we would of course look at it,' Foster said.

As for Eddie Gilfoyle, it appears that the campaign to clear his name has hit another brick wall. In July 2016, the CCRC rejected the latest application, and the following year the High Court rejected the family's attempt to challenge the decision.

Omar Benguit's family expects an application to go back to the CCRC shortly.

• • •

The underfunded and understaffed organisation is the only route back to the courts for the victims of miscarriages of justice. In the bad old days before the Runciman Commission, a shadowy and discredited Home Office department known as C3 dealt with wrongful convictions – or, more accurately, failed to deal with them.

In 2016, the miscarriage of justice watchdog referred just twelve cases back to the Court of Appeal. The CCRC presently receives about 1,500 cases a year, mainly from prisoners claiming their innocence. That represents a referral rate of just 0.77 per cent, which marks a dramatic and unexplained fall from an already pretty meagre average of 3 per cent. In its last year, C3 received about 900 applications – it managed to refer nine cases to the Court of Appeal.

At the commission's twentieth-anniversary conference, its chair Richard Foster said that, so far, the group had referred 634 cases. 'Put another way, over the last twenty years we have referred on average two or three cases a month,' he said. 'About two-thirds of our referrals result in convictions being quashed or sentences changed. To date, 419 people have had their appeals allowed as a result of commission referrals."*

It was Tom Sargant who made the case for reform of the criminal justice system most forcefully. 'The present system for investigating possible miscarriages of justice is wholly inadequate,' JUSTICE said in 1989, the same year the Guildford Four were released.

Tom Sargant wanted a different model than the one proposed by the Runciman Commission. Sargant's commission would have been a 'determinative' body that would consider alleged miscarriages of justice independently of the courts. In other words, the cases would be taken out of the courts' hands.

Only cases with a 'real possibility' of being overturned can now be referred to the Court of Appeal. David Jessel, who presented the *Trial and Error* episode on Eddie Gilfoyle and went on to become a CCRC commissioner, called the 'real possibility' test the commission's 'baptismal curse'. The commission's critics argue that the watchdog was born into a subordinate relationship that forces it to 'second guess' appeal judges. In other words, the CCRC takes the pragmatic view that there is no point in referring cases back to the Court of Appeal if the court is just going to kick them into touch.

The CCRC will deny to the hilt that it has embodied the court's inbuilt conservatism but, when the number of referrals is only just into double figures, the statistics speak for themselves.

---

* The media was not invited to the CCRC's twentieth-anniversary conference, despite the fact that journalists played a significant part in making the case for its establishment. My own request was refused. The issue was raised by one of the few journalists present, David Rose, who was invited because he had previously chaired a CCRC conference.

Another revealing statistic is that, in its twenty years, the CRCC has only referred two cases back to the Court of Appeal for a second time. One of those two cases was Tony Stock's. So will it send 'a self-evident miscarriage of justice' (to use Ralph Barrington's phrase) back to the Court of Appeal for a third time? And what does it say about our justice system if it doesn't?

Tom Sargant's analysis of the Court of Appeal's failings was scathing. He began writing his autobiography but never finished it. Towards the end of the unfinished manuscript, he listed the court's 'self-imposed fetters' – for example, its 'unreasoning respect' for jury verdicts and its 'unwillingness to let down the police'. He acknowledged that some might think he had painted 'an unnecessarily black picture of the court's unwillingness to remedy miscarriages'. However, he concluded that the fetters were 'a necessary protective wall built by the judges against the flood that otherwise might overwhelm them; and, in part, inspired by the need to preserve public confidence in the jury system'.

The man himself gave a brilliant and uncompromising farewell interview to *The Observer* in 1982. 'I have had absolute cooperation from judges and lawyers. Many of whom are my friends,' he said. 'Although some of them hate my guts, and think I'm a damn nuisance. They don't believe juries make mistakes. I take a more jaundiced view. I take all the casualties.'

• • •

Over the past two decades the Criminal Cases Review Commission has often been criticised, sometimes fairly and sometimes not. But the problems anticipated by Tom Sargant's JUSTICE, as well as concerns about independence, chronic underfunding and its statutory straitjacket have dogged the CCRC since the day it opened its doors.

Some might take heart from the small number of cases going back to the Court of Appeal, and cite that as positive evidence of the justice system's effectiveness.

As reassuring as that might appear to be, it would be exactly the wrong conclusion to draw. Instead, it is a reflection of the sustained impoverishment of the criminal justice system. It is telling that the CCRC, the justice system's safety net, has suffered more under austerity than any other part of the system it is meant to safeguard.

In 2015, the MPs on the House of Commons justice committee launched an inquiry into the CCRC. The MPs offered a lukewarm verdict, concluding that the CCRC was performing its functions 'reasonably well'. That rather ambivalent endorsement did not reflect the concerns of practitioners and campaigners with first-hand experience of the body, who had appeared before the MPs to give evidence.

For years, critics have called upon the CCRC to abandon its adherence to a 70 per cent success rate (i.e. the proportion of referrals being overturned) to better reflect the 'real possibility' test – that call was echoed by the MPs. They urged the watchdog to be 'less cautious' and refer more cases back to the Court of Appeal. 'If a bolder approach leads to five more failed appeals but one additional miscarriage being corrected, then that is of clear benefit,' they said.

As it comes of age, the CCRC appears to be becoming increasingly timid.

The committee's inquiry revealed the extent of funding problems. The CCRC chair, Richard Foster, told MPs that for every £10 that the group had to spend on a case a decade ago, he now had only £4. This, Foster said, amounted to 'the biggest cut that has taken place anywhere in the criminal justice system'.

That funding crisis has been brewing for years. I interviewed Foster's predecessor, Professor Graham Zellick, who spoke of staff who were 'angry' and 'dispirited' as a result of the funding crisis. 'If you compare our £8 million budget with the amount of money spent on the other side by the police and Crown Prosecution Service, it is not even a crumb off the table,' he told me.*

While the justice committee's remit was the CCRC, many of those who gave evidence expressed their frustration at the Court of Appeal. A submission from Cardiff University, backed by eighteen academics at other universities, urged MPs to take a look at the Tony Stock case. It quoted Stock's solicitor, Glyn Maddocks, who claimed the case illustrated a problem at the heart of the justice system – 'that is the Court of Appeal's lack of willingness to engage with (or even recognise) the problem and its often intransigent, often arrogant and, dare I say, obdurate view that it knows best and is constrained by its own previous decisions, however wrong they may have been'.

That view was summed up by the veteran campaigner Paul May.† 'Much of the criticism levelled at the CCRC would in my view be better directed at the Court of Appeal, which remains

---

* 'Proving the Innocent Not Guilty: The CCRC is under fire', *The Times*, 21 January 2010.
† Paul May has run numerous campaigns on behalf of the victims of miscarriages of justice, from the Birmingham Six, Judith Ward and the Bridgewater Four through to Sam Hallam, Eddie Gilfoyle and Colin Norris.

capable on occasions of quite breathtaking obduracy towards appellants claiming wrongful conviction.'

Professor Michael Zander QC, emeritus professor at the LSE, was on the original royal commission that led to the CCRC's establishment. He explained to MPs that the problem dated back to the creation of the court. 'The Court of Appeal is the crucial issue,' Professor Zander said. 'It is hopeless, completely hopeless. They won't budge from their position which they have taken and held for more than one hundred years.'

The MPs seemed to take the point. Their final report called on the Law Commission to review the Court of Appeal's grounds for allowing appeals, as well as to look specifically at whether there needs to be a change in the law to 'allow and encourage' the court to quash a conviction where it has a serious doubt about the verdict even without fresh evidence.

However, the then Lord Chancellor Michael Gove rejected the proposal. The MPs took evidence from a dozen experts and received some forty-seven written submissions, but Gove rejected their work on the basis of an assurance from the organisation that was being criticised (and authored by Tony Stock's old adversary). 'We note the views expressed by the former Lord Chief Justice, Lord Judge, and we do not believe that there is sufficient evidence that the Court of Appeal's current approach has a deleterious effect on those who have suffered miscarriages of justice,' Gove wrote.

· · ·

At the end of 2017, the High Court killed off what might be Eddie Gilfoyle's last chance to clear his name. His lawyers had been challenging a decision by the CCRC in 2016 to reject the case through the courts. They had judicially reviewed the decision in a procedure that allows a court to review the lawfulness of a decision.

The High Court considered three arguments made by Gilfoyle's lawyers. At the heart of the prosecution case at the original trial was the notion that 'bubbly' Paula Gilfoyle had no history of depression. Merseyside Police has had Paula's diaries since at least 1994, and the CCRC since 1998. But they were not made available to the Gilfoyle family until 2010. Gilfoyle's lawyers argued that Paula had been subjected to 'appalling mental trauma' as a result of a formative relationship with the convicted murderer and rapist Mark Roberts. When the CCRC rejected the family's application in 2017, they dismissed the diaries as not revealing 'anything more than normal adolescent experiences'.

The second line of argument related to Eddie Gilfoyle's decision not to give evidence at his own trial. His lawyers argued that he was incapable of doing so because he was suffering from an anxiety disorder as a result of being denied medication during his trial. Gilfoyle's solicitor Matt Foot had obtained prison prescription charts indicating that Gilfoyle's medication had been withheld and, it was argued by Eddie's legal team, that withdrawal symptoms had compromised his ability to testify.

Finally, there were the arguments by Gilfoyle's legal team about the knot in the rope on the beam from which Paula was found hanging unaided. In the appeal in the Gilfoyle case in 2000, the court maintained that it would have been 'impossible for [Paula] to tie the knot where it was found'.

In the same way that the appeal judges had whittled away the

Tony Stock case to a single argument (the five photographs) on which the entire case rested, they reduced the Gilfoyle case to a single detail: the tying of the knot in the rope.

Gilfoyle's lawyers argued that the CCRC had failed to understand their contention that it would have been possible for Paula to have tied the knot in the rope on the beam from which she was found hanging unaided.

In an analysis of the Court of Appeal's treatment of the Tony Stock case, a former CCRC commissioner, Laurie Elks, complained of the court's 'atomistic' approach to these cases. The judges considered any fresh evidence only on the basis of whether it alone would provide sufficient justification to render the conviction unsafe.

'It has been Mr Stock's misfortune that the case against him has unravelled by degrees,' wrote Elks. Using the analogy of an onion, the former CCRC commissioner observed that at each sitting the court weighed up 'the onion peelings' (i.e., the new evidence) and in effect 'snorted: "That's not much compared with the towering weight of the verdict of the jury who were certain of Mr Stock's guilt."'

Elks argued that, instead, the court should have adopted 'a holistic approach'. The correct question would be: 'Are we in doubt, looking at the case in its entirety, whether Mr Stock was rightly convicted?' According to Laurie Elks, if they had asked that question, the court would have had to overturn the conviction.

In the Eddie Gilfoyle case, the Court of Appeal had reduced the entire case down to a question of whether his wife Paula could have tied the knot. In their latest application to the CCRC,

Gilfoyle's lawyers attacked that point. In October 2014, the CCRC commissioned *Trial and Error*'s knot expert to answer two questions: first, whether it would have been possible for Paula to have tied the knot under the beam; and second, whether, as a result of the force of a suspended body, the knot might have travelled upwards to the position in which police officers discovered it. The CCRC admitted that this was possible, but concluded it was unlikely.

Of course, the original rope, knot and all, had been thrown away at the post-mortem. How the knot was tied was based upon the recollection of the coroner's officer, who blithely assumed that Paula had taken her own life. Merseyside Police suggested that the same officer's judgement was questionable as a result of a migraine that meant he missed the post-mortem.

Matt Foot described the CCRC's approach to the rope as 'marbled through with incomprehension or illogical reasoning'.

• • •

Just before Christmas 2017, I visited Eddie Gilfoyle, his sister Sue Caddick and his brother-in-law Paul Caddick. The family's fury was aimed at the miscarriage of justice watchdog that had considered Eddie's application for six years before rejecting it. 'It's not independent,' said Gilfoyle. 'They are the same as the Court of Appeal. They have become the Court of Appeal. They are so scared of the Court of Appeal they might as well be the Court of Appeal.'

According to the family's lawyer, the CCRC is 'moribund, office-bound and file-based'. 'In Eddie's case, they haven't seen a single witness,' said Matt Foot. 'They haven't spoken to Eddie and they haven't been to the garage. They haven't been to the area. They aren't fit for purpose. They should be reformed or removed.'

The family believes that their progress has been blocked, not because of a lack of evidence, but because the CCRC simply won't stand up to the Court of Appeal. The group has become mired in its settled thinking that refuses to refer cases that have previously been refused by the Court of Appeal, argued Foot. 'We have to conclude there is no hope – no hope of establishing the truth for an innocent, wronged man and no hope of having a courageous, serious organisation capable of righting terrible historic wrongs.'

Unsurprisingly, the CCRC does not accept Foot's analysis ('not generally and not in relation to Mr Gilfoyle's case'). A spokesman pointed out that the watchdog visited No. 6 Grafton Drive and interviewed Gilfoyle for the first review, when the case was referred and, on its second, 'visited the area' and 'carried out a number of inquiries there'. He added that it was 'fatuous' to suggest that investigations always needed 'a boots on the ground approach' and that anything else was 'lazy or second best'.

'We have reviewed the case again in enormous detail,' the spokesman said. 'In order to refer it again for appeal we will need to find some compelling new grounds that have not been before the court in either of the earlier appeals. Thus far at least, we have just not seen that.'

As years pass, myths harden into facts – at least, that's how they are represented. For example, Paula Gilfoyle's death turned from a suicide into a murder investigation because three women went to the police with a bizarre story that Eddie Gilfoyle had got his wife to write fake suicide notes as part of a course at work.

How could three people (the three hearsay witnesses) tell the same bizarre story? It appears that those statements were never made independently of each other. Detective Superintendent Graham Gooch from Lancashire Police interviewed one of the three women, who admitted that her recollection had been prompted by her friend. That second woman, in her original police statement, denied any such collusion.

The Gooch investigation established that the third of the three 'hearsay' women had attended Paula's sister's house, Margaret Glover, at a gathering to (as Glover put it) 'clear Paula's name'. That was confirmed by an interview with another witness who attended. The name of the third of the three 'hearsay' women did not appear in Glover's statement.

In the wake of Paula's death, rumours were flying in every direction. All her friends, most of whom worked together and gossiped together on the assembly line at the Champion Spark Plugs factory, were devastated.

Into this febrile atmosphere, Eddie's father, Norman Gilfoyle, had told everyone that Paula had taken her own life because she was having an affair. The baby was not Eddie's, he said, and she had not been able to live with the guilt. That shocked and upset Paula's grieving friends. That is also the narrative as described in the police statements of the three hearsay witness. It is not the same story that the suicide notes tell.

Then there is the mystery of the keys. The prosecution argued that Eddie had removed Paula's garage key to prevent her from going into the garage and discovering the noose he had rigged up. That explained why Paul Caddick could not open the garage door, because the key had been removed from the bunch. That was also the reason why there were two identical Yale keys under the doormat.

Caddick insists that there never was a mystery. There was no missing key. He just couldn't open the garage door. He put in the correct key, the lock jammed and he asked Eddie for a spare. The two keys beneath the doormat were not identical. One was the spare garage door key and the other was a front door key. 'Of course, we can't prove it because the police never recorded it,' Caddick says.

There are also the three witnesses who put Eddie Gilfoyle back at No. 6 at about 5.30 p.m. It was never argued that Gilfoyle murdered Paula later in the day. It was suggested that this showed that Gilfoyle had lied and that he might have returned to the scene of his earlier crime. One of the three witnesses, the man, actively disliked Gilfoyle, rendering his evidence unreliable and his account was not checked out properly by the police. Another witness was a woman from Paula's courier company who came to deliver a parcel and claimed Eddie signed for it. Gilfoyle says that never happened and that she was mistaken. The paperwork did not prove it one way or another. The third witness was the neighbour who saw him leave noisily in his car. Gilfoyle argues that she is just wrong.

Finally, why would Merseyside Police go to such lengths to put the blame on Eddie Gilfoyle for the death of his wife? The family argues that its motivation comes from a desire to cover up a local practice on the Wirral, where the police control room were required to inform the coroner's officer about all deaths, including suicides. This, they say, was a disaster waiting to happen.

'What they couldn't afford to happen was for this case to go to the coroner's court,' Caddick told me. The purpose of an inquest is to find out how a person died. 'The first thing that they would ask is where is the police evidence, and, of course, all of that was destroyed,' he said. 'So they wanted to drive this case to trial. It was better for them to get a conviction. They wanted Eddie to be found guilty because that would exonerate them all. Nobody would care. Everybody would be fireproof.'

• • •

The devastation wrought upon the wrongly convicted is not just felt by that individual. The shockwaves spread wide. When Tony Stock was in HMP Gartree, he left his first wife, Brenda, and their four children to cope as best they could.

Ralph Barrington and I met with three of the children from Tony's first marriage for the first time ahead of an event in the House of Commons in October 2014. When Tony Stock was sent down, Anthony was just two weeks old, his brother Stephen was two years old, Antoinette (known as Twinnie) was six and Charlene was nine.

Stock's children from his first marriage didn't know much about their father and almost nothing about the strange fate that had befallen him. It was odd to be the one to tell them about it. 'We all knew Dad didn't do it but what happened to him broke up our family anyway. My mum was left singlehandedly to bring up the four of us,' Steve Stock told us.

'I didn't really know my dad,' he said. 'Life was hard for us growing up. Even now, just the other day, somebody came up to me and said: "You're the bank robber's son, I remember you."'

Twinnie had a vague recollection of her father's birthday party, which had taken place at the time he was supposed to have been committing an armed robbery in Leeds. When I asked how she felt about a book about her father's story, she told me she thought it was a great idea. She said that she really wanted to know that he didn't do it. 'But you know your dad didn't do it. You were there,' I pointed out.

When I recounted that exchange to her later, she was embarrassed. She wanted to clarify what she meant:

> Even though I have memories of the day – singing happy birthday and celebrating – I was only five years old. It is a blurred memory. People are cruel. Even though you tell them he didn't do it, you would hear the cynical remarks: 'They all say that.' It begins to chip away at you; it's years of people disbelieving you that wears you down. My father must have been a very strong character to continue his fight till he died.

When I last spoke to Tony's children it was two years after their father died. 'We feel we can't scatter his ashes till he has justice,' Anthony told me. 'My mum was left to look after us all,' Steve said, 'but life didn't move on for Dad. He never stopped trying to clear his name. Why should he? He was innocent.'

CHAPTER FIVE

SALEM COMES TO SALISBURY

Until eighteen police officers descended on his home in the grounds of the 16,000-acre Belvoir estate in Leicestershire in a dawn raid, Harvey Proctor had spent the best part of three decades living away from the public eye.

The former Conservative MP's political career had ended in disgrace. He was convicted of gross indecency for crimes relating to encounters with male prostitutes aged between seventeen and twenty-one, a few weeks ahead of Margaret Thatcher's third consecutive election victory in June 1987.

Proctor had been, to use a contemporary phrase, 'monstered' by the media. Hounded by reporters, his face was splashed over newspaper front pages for weeks on end, leaving his reputation irretrievably trashed.

A comeback from the political wilderness for Harvey Proctor – MP from 1979 to 1987 for the Essex constituencies of Basildon and then Billericay – was never on the cards. Nor did he desire it. 'I didn't want to be in the public arena,' Proctor told me when we met in early 2016. 'I wanted to be private. I had always wanted to be private after what happened in 1987.'

Proctor recalled the humiliation he felt at the time of his fall.

'I became public enemy number one. With the exception of Princess Diana, I was the only person on the front page of the newspapers six weeks running,' he said. 'I couldn't walk down the street without people spitting at me.'

But 'what happened in 1987', as he repeatedly put it, was nothing compared to the sheer horror of the allegations directed at Proctor by a single witness known only as 'Nick'. Proctor stood accused of child sexual abuse and three murders.

• • •

In December 2014, Detective Superintendent Kenny McDonald made an extraordinary appeal for witnesses to step forward. He was launching a new investigation, codenamed Operation Midland, into alleged sexual abuse and murder committed by a Westminster paedophile ring. The Metropolitan Police was seeking help from witnesses to the activities at Dolphin Square in Pimlico, an exclusive residential development near the Houses of Parliament that was home to politicians and peers, as well as senior members of MI5 and MI6.

'Today, I want to appeal directly to those other young boys – now men – who were also subject to abuse at the hands of these men,' he told the TV cameras. 'I believe that there were other boys who were abused or who were present when that abuse took place. I would ask you to trust me. I will support you and do everything in my power to find those responsible and bring them to justice.'

Lurid tales of a 'VIP paedophile ring' had been doing the rounds for years in the wilder parts of the press where libel laws hold no fear. For example, a 1994 article in the now defunct *Scallywag* magazine linked the scandal about child sex abuse in children's homes in north Wales to Westminster. It quoted 'a source in Dolphin Square': 'We often have underaged boys wandering around the corridors, totally lost, looking for the room of a particular MP,' the source said. The arrival of the internet provided fertile territory for such stories to ferment and grow.

In October 2012, the approach of our criminal justice agencies to historical allegations changed overnight. The ITV documentary *Exposure: The Other Side of Jimmy Savile* revealed that the former national treasure, whose recent funeral in Leeds had been attended by 4,000 mourners, was a shell-suited sexual predator. The programme was the result of nearly a year's investigation and featured women claiming that Savile had abused them. It was, as the Metropolitan Police Commissioner, Sir Bernard Hogan-Howe, said at the time, a watershed moment in abuse investigations. 'A dam had burst,' he later wrote.

The sorry saga showed how trusted institutions – the police, politicians and the BBC – had failed and, at worst, conspired to cover up abuse of the powerless and vulnerable.

Three weeks after the documentary aired, the Labour MP and now deputy leader Tom Watson, lit the touch paper. Buoyed by a successful campaign against phone hacking, the MP said a file collected by the police to convict paedophile Peter Righton in 1992 contained 'clear intelligence' of a widespread paedophile ring. 'One of its members boasts of his links to a senior aide of a former Prime Minister, who says he could smuggle indecent images of children from abroad,' he told the Commons. 'The leads were not followed up, but if the files still exist, I want to ensure that the Metropolitan Police secure the evidence, re-examine it and investigate clear intelligence suggesting a powerful paedophile network linked to Parliament and No 10.'

A former child protection officer who supplied information to the MP spotted a tweet from a possible victim. It read: 'I was abused by the gang.' The author of that tweet was reported to have been 'Nick'. Nick and Watson later met. It was 'a very traumatic and difficult conversation', Watson later told *The Guardian*. 'He only told me about one murder. He spoke very slowly, very intermittently and I didn't need to hear any more.'

The first time Nick went to the police, he was accompanied by a journalist from Exaro, a news agency since closed. It was set up by seasoned journalists and headed up by Mark Watts, with the noble aim to 'hold power to account'.

A month before Detective Superintendent Kenny McDonald's appeal, Nick, now in his forties, told *BBC News at Ten* how he had first been abused. As he put it, physical abuse at the hands of his own father gave way to sexual abuse, before he was 'handed over' as a young boy to 'the group'.

Nick was a black silhouette, his face and body hidden and his words spoken by an actor. 'It was a group of men, very powerful people and they controlled my life for the next nine years,' Nick explained. 'They created fear that penetrated every part of me, day in day out. You didn't question what they wanted, you did as they asked without question and the punishments were very severe.'

The men were from the 'military, law enforcement and the political establishment'.

When Detective Superintendent Kenny McDonald made his

2014 appeal, he was understandably keen to persuade victims that, this time, their claims would be taken seriously.

But he went one step further. 'Nick has been spoken to by experienced officers from the child abuse team and from the murder investigation team and they, and I, believe what Nick is saying is credible and true, hence why we are investigating the allegations that he has made.'

• • •

The Office for National Statistics has a name for the massive surge in reported sexual offences in the wake of the October 2012 revelations. They call it the 'Savile effect'. The police are currently deluged with allegations. The number of child abuse reports had increased by 80 per cent over the three previous years ending in 2017. It had reached the point where the police were receiving an average of 112 complaints a day. More than 70,000 complaints of child abuse came in each year, and forces were preparing an estimated 40,000 reports of abuse for the Independent Inquiry into Child Sexual Abuse, launched in 2014. Similarly, the children's charity, the NSPCC, reported an 81 per cent increase in calls to its helpline in the year after Operation Yewtree commenced in response to the scandal.

• • •

When the Operation Midland team arrived at Harvey Proctor's home near Grantham, the former Tory MP was living in quiet and happy obscurity, working as private secretary to the Duke and Duchess of Rutland. He lived with his partner and their two dogs in a house in the grounds of the 16,000-acre Belvoir estate.

In a coordinated sweep, the homes of Lord (Leon) Brittan and Britain's most decorated soldier, D-Day veteran Lord Bramall, were also raided. The Met sent twenty officers to Lord Bramall's house, a man in his nineties who lived with his dying wife.

The officers spent fifteen hours searching Harvey Proctor's house as well as his office at the castle. They seized photographs, papers and archives related to his 1987 case, and confiscated telephones, iPads and laptops. They even bagged up his sleeping tablets for later inspection. 'Just before they left, I said to the officers: "Is this likely to be in the newspapers?" They said no,' Proctor told me. 'I was thinking back to 1987. I have said as little to the press as I possibly could. It was the press who were the motivating force against me.'

• • •

Some thirty years ago, Robert Maxwell's *Sunday People* newspaper went to town on Harvey Proctor. In June 1986, it ran a lurid three-page story featuring an interview with a male prostitute about the MP's 'spanking sessions'. The following Sunday, the paper accused Proctor of using the services of a rent boy network. A gay massage parlour boss told the newspaper that he used to take part in sex games at the MP's flat, 'while he watched by-election results on television'. 'Given the direction of subsequent Tory fortunes at by-elections, it is surprising the practice did not become more generalised,' quipped the former Tory MP Matthew Parris in his 1998 book *Great Parliamentary Scandals*.

The journalist summed up the Proctor scandal thus: 'Harvey Proctor never did anything more shocking than spank people – and willing victims at that, for he paid them for their pains.'

Harvey Proctor had previously successfully sued the *Sunday People* in the libel courts for having wrongly alleged that Margaret Thatcher had refused to call the MP 'my honourable friend' in Parliament. But this time the MP kept his silence. He told friends that his sexuality was his own business and, anyway, he couldn't afford another battle in the courts.

The *People* ran the story of the 'bottom-spanking Billericay MP' on its front page for six weeks. Proctor's phone line was tapped, and the paper paid off an eighteen-year-old rent boy who visited the MP with a concealed tape recorder. Proctor maintained that those he had slept with were over twenty-one years old. The wired-up rent boy had told the MP that he was over twenty-one (their exchange was recorded). Proctor later admitted to four counts of gross indecency with two underaged rent boys who were seventeen and nineteen years old. At that time, the age of consent for homosexuals was twenty-one. Proctor was convicted and fined £1,450 plus £250 costs.

• • •

Operation Midland kicked off in front of the nation's media with Detective Superintendent Kenny McDonald's 'credible and true' appeal and was conducted in its full glare. While the Operation Midland team was still searching Harvey Proctor's home, a journalist from the news agency Exaro put in a call to his office asking Proctor to confirm details of the raid.

The following morning, Harvey Proctor was back in the public eye again, insisting that he was not part of a rent boy ring. But this time the MP felt compelled to break his silence and rang up BBC Radio 4's *Today* programme. Presenter James Naughtie asked Proctor what he knew about 'the rumours and allegations that are flying around in great quantity' about paedophilia in the 1970s and 1980s. The former MP told him that if he had known anything at the time he would have contacted the police himself. 'The number of victims grows by the day, the number of alleged perpetrators through death, diminishes. That's a problem. It is certainly a problem for me,' he said. 'I suppose my problem is I am still very much alive.'

Three weeks later, Harvey Proctor had lost his home, his job and future security. 'I may not look destitute, but I am,' he told me. 'I have no money. I have no assets.'

If it wasn't for the support of friends, he would have been homeless. 'I have a roof over my head for my partner and my dogs,' he said. He called his new home 'a glorified shed'. 'It is an outbuilding on a farmhouse away from the house. There is no running water.'

• • •

This time around, journalists were not so quick to jump on the bandwagon. In fact, Harvey Proctor turned the tables on his tormentors by calling his own press conference in August 2015.

It was a brave move by a former politician who, if he was still remembered, was associated with a rent boy scandal and an unpalatable brand of 1970s right-wing politics. Now he was about to appeal to the media's better nature in a press conference unlike any other.

The extreme stress of taking such a risk was written all over Proctor's face. 'Anyone of a delicate or a nervous disposition should leave the room now,' he began. The text of his speech had been emailed widely to the press ahead of the conference. Proctor quoted directly from a police disclosure document that was arranged under three headings: Circumstances, Homicides and Sexual Abuse. It had been sent to Proctor two days before he had been interviewed. The allegations were graphic, horrific and bizarre.

Under 'Circumstances', the Met explained that 'Nick' claimed he was the victim of 'systematic and serious sexual abuse by a group of adult males over a period between 1975 and 1984'. Allegedly, that group included Proctor.

Nick went on to name Proctor as the man who had abused him, and also claimed that he had witnessed the murder of three young boys. The former MP was 'directly responsible for two of the allegations and implicated in the third', Nick said.

Under 'Homicides', the document read:

- 1980: at a residential house in central London. Nick was driven by car to an address in the Pimlico/Belgravia area where a second boy (the victim) was also collected in the same vehicle. Both boys, aged approximately 12 years old, were driven to another similar central London address. MR PROCTOR was present with another male. Both boys were led to the back of the house. MR PROCTOR then stripped the victim, and tied him to a table. He then produced a large kitchen knife and stabbed the child through the arm and other parts of the body over a period of 40 minutes. A short time later MR PROCTOR untied the victim and anally raped him on the table. The other male stripped Nick and anally raped him over the table. MR PROCTOR then strangled the victim with his hands until the boy's body went limp. Both males then left the room. Later, MR PROCTOR returned and led Nick out of the house and into a waiting car.

- 1981–82: at a residential address in central London. Nick was collected from Kingston train station and taken to a 'party' at a residential address. The witness was among four young boys. Several men were present including MR PROCTOR. One of the men told the boys one of them would die that night and they had to choose who. When the boys wouldn't decide, the men selected one of the boys (the victim). Each of the four boys, including Nick, were taken to separate rooms for 'private time'. When they all returned to the same room, Nick was anally raped by MR PROCTOR and another male as 'punishment'. The other males also anally raped the remaining boys. MR PROCTOR and two other males then began beating the chosen victim by punching and kicking. The attack continued until the boy collapsed on the floor and stopped moving. All of the men left the room. The remaining boys attempted to revive the victim but he was not breathing. They were left for some time before being taken out of the house and returned to their homes.

- Between May and July 1979: in a street in Coombe Hill, Kingston. Nick was walking in this area with another boy (the victim) when he heard the sound of a car engine revving.

A dark-coloured car drove into the victim knocking him down. Nick could see the boy covered in blood and his leg bent backwards. A car pulled up and Nick was grabbed and placed in the car. He felt a sharp pain in his arm and next remembered being dropped off at home. He was warned not to have friends in future. Nick never saw the other boy again. Nick does not identify MR PROCTOR as being directly involved in this allegation. However, he states MR PROCTOR was part of the group responsible for the systematic sexual abuse he suffered. Furthermore, he believes the group were responsible for the homicide.'

Under 'Sexual abuse', the disclosure reads:

- 1978–1984: Dolphin Square, Pimlico. Nick was at the venue and with at least one other young boy. MR PROCTOR was present with other males. MR PROCTOR told Nick to pick up a wooden baton and hit the other boy. When Nick refused he was punished by MR PROCTOR and the other males. He was held down and felt pain in his feet. He fell unconscious. When he awoke he was raped by several males including MR PROCTOR.
- 1978–1981: Carlton Club, central London. Nick was driven to the Carlton Club and dropped off outside. MR PROCTOR opened the door. Inside the premises were several other males. Nick was sexually assaulted by another male (not by MR PROCTOR on this occasion).
- 1978–1981: swimming pool in central London. Nick was taken to numerous 'pool parties' where he and other boys

were made to undress, and perform sexual acts on one another. He and other boys were then anally raped and sexually abused by several men including MR PROCTOR.
- 1981–1982: large town house in London. Nick was taken to the venue on numerous occasions where MR PROCTOR and one other male were present. He was forced to perform oral sex on MR PROCTOR who also put his hands around Nick's throat to prevent him breathing. On another occasion at the same location, MR PROCTOR sexually assaulted Nick before producing a pen-knife and threatening to cut Nick's genitals. MR PROCTOR was prevented from doing so by the other male present.
- 1979–1984: residential address in central London. Nick was taken to the venue. MR PROCTOR was present with one other male. MR PROCTOR forced Nick to perform oral sex on him before beating him with punches.
- 1978–1984: numerous locations including Carlton Club, Dolphin Square and a central London townhouse. Nick described attending several 'Christmas parties' where other boys were present together with numerous males including MR PROCTOR. Nick was given whisky to drink before being forced to perform oral sex on several men including MR PROCTOR.

• • •

'I am a homosexual. I am not a murderer,' Proctor told the assembled journalists. 'I am not a paedophile or pederast.' Referring to the 1987 convictions, he pointed out that those offences were no longer offences at all.

The other members of the 'gang' as identified by Nick were the late Lord (Leon) Brittan, the late Sir Edward Heath, Lord Janner, a former Labour MP, former chief of the General Staff Lord Bramall, and the former heads of MI5 and MI6.

Former Prime Minister Ted Heath had sacked Proctor from the Conservative Party's parliamentary candidates' list in 1974. Thatcher came to the MP's rescue eighteen months later. There was little love lost between Proctor and Heath. 'Edward Heath despised me and he disliked my views, particularly on limiting immigration from the New Commonwealth and Pakistan, and my opposition to our entry into and continued membership of what is now known as the EU,' Proctor said. 'I opposed his corporate statist views on the economy. I despised him too ... He had sacked the late Enoch Powell, my political hero, from the Shadow Cabinet when I was chairman of the University of York Conservative Association. I regarded Enoch as an intellectual giant in comparison with Heath.'

Now Proctor stood accused of trying to castrate a boy with a penknife – which, it was alleged, he would have done but for the intervention of his political nemesis. This attack was said to have happened in the former Prime Minister's London house: 'A house to which I was never invited and to which Heath would never have invited me, and to which I would have declined his invitation.' It was so far-fetched as to be unbelievable, Proctor told the assembled media. 'It is unbelievable because it is not true. My situation has transformed from Kafkaesque bewilderment to black farce incredulity.'

These were the allegations that Detective Superintendent Kenny McDonald had described as 'credible and true'. How had he come to that conclusion?

• • •

In November 2016, the former High Court judge, Sir Richard Henriques, in a damning review of eight investigations into historical abuse allegations, found forty-three failings by the Metropolitan Police in relation to its conduct of Operation Midland alone. The Henriques report was brave enough to name the madness at the heart of the investigation and other police failures. 'The policy of "believing victims" strikes at the very core of the criminal justice process,' Sir Richard wrote. 'It has and will generate miscarriages of justice on a considerable scale.'

The College of Policing policy book, as of March 2016, reads: 'At the point when someone makes an allegation of a crime, the police should believe the account given and a crime report should be completed.' This provision is also contained in a 2014 statement of Her Majesty's Inspector of Constabulary, which expresses the opinion that 'the presumption that a victim should always be believed should be institutionalised'.

The presumption of innocence, which relies on the police investigating cases 'without fear or favour', was suspended as a response to criticism of the years of inaction that the Savile revelations highlighted. Collective remorse on the part of the police was hardwired into policy. What resulted was the Operation Midland debacle.

Chief Constable Simon Bailey heads up Operation Hydrant, which was established as a way to share good practice between forces investigating historical abuse cases. He attempted to justify the rationale to Sir Richard. 'If we don't acknowledge a victim as such, it reinforces a system based on distrust and disbelief,' he said.

The officer went on to describe the police as 'the conduit that links the victim to the rest of the criminal justice system', and argued that there was 'a need to develop a relationship and rapport' with a victim 'in order to achieve the best evidence possible'.

Sir Richard, who spent over forty years in the criminal courts as a barrister and a judge, was scathing. The High Court judge took the chief constable to task for 'inaccurate terminology', and said that he preferred to regard the police service as 'a critical part of the criminal justice system' (as opposed to a 'conduit') under an absolute duty to use 'accurate language'. 'Since a complainant may or may not be telling the truth, the present policy causes those not telling the truth to be artificially believed and, thus, liars and fantasists and those genuinely mistaken are given a free run both unquestioned and unchallenged,' Sir Richard said.

His report also highlighted the inappropriate proximity between the police and the media. Nick first made his allegations on the now defunct Exaro website, and one of its reporters attended his first police interview.

Exaro collapsed in 2016, claiming that its demise was due to a failure to capitalise on commercial opportunities rather than the controversy over the VIP abuse claims. It stands accused of sensationalism over its reporting, as well as exploitation of the victims of abuse.

The Henriques report focused on the mutual dependency between police and the media. When the Operation Midlands dawn raids were launched, press releases were issued and journalists were tipped off. The Met's officers denied the tip-offs and claimed that there was not enough information in their press releases to reveal the suspects' identities.

Henriques was not convinced. For example, one press release said: 'a man in his nineties from Farnham was today interviewed under caution'. Journalists from the BBC, Press Association and Exaro all managed to figure out that the suspect was Lord Bramall. Exaro identified 'a man in his sixties from Grantham' as Harvey Proctor. When Bramall was interviewed by police for a second time, his wife had just died. 'Out of respect', the Met issued no press release. There was no coverage.

Not only did South Yorkshire Police tip off the BBC over the 2014 raid on Cliff Richard's house in connection with historical sexual allegations, they also sent them an aerial photograph of his home the night before. The BBC duly sent a helicopter to film the event.

Harvey Proctor has called for anonymity for suspects until they are charged. At his press conference, the former MP said: 'Anonymity is given to anyone prepared to make untruthful accusations of child sexual abuse while the alleged accused are routinely fingered publicly without any credible evidence first being found.'

Metropolitan Police Commissioner Sir Bernard Hogan-Howe begrudgingly acknowledged that Proctor, Brittan and Bramall were entirely innocent. It came after months of insisting that the Met had nothing to apologise for.* Hogan-Howe confirmed

---

* '[If] we were to apologise whenever we investigated allegations that did not lead to a charge, we believe this would have a harmful impact on the judgements made by officers and on the confidence of the public,' said the Met's assistant commissioner Patricia Gallan in January 2016. 'Investigators may be less likely to pursue allegations they knew would be hard to prove, whereas they should be focused on establishing the existence, or otherwise, of relevant evidence.'

that an investigation, which had cost £2.5 million and tied up officers for sixteen months without making a single arrest, had found 'no credible evidence'.

• • •

When I interviewed Proctor, I asked him why he had called a press conference, given his own history with the media. 'The police were using the media. I had my hands tied behind my back. I could not defend myself,' he told me. 'I was nervous because I was doing everything I didn't want to do…'

At this point, his words trailed off. There followed one of three extended pauses during our conversation, in which Proctor struggled to compose himself.

Harvey Proctor's reputation precedes him. The rent boys aside, his right-wing politics speak for themselves. As an interviewee, though, he is a surprise: straightforward, even self-effacing – every question receives a very precise and thoughtful answer.

But discussing the trauma of his experience was off the table. At one point he explained that he could get 'very emotional', which he suggested was a weakness. 'I apologise about that. I would prefer not to say anything about the emotional side of things.'

Except for these alarming surges – eyes welling up, his cheeks reddening as he gulped to keep a lid on extreme emotions – he remained composed throughout our conversation.

• • •

A few months before I met Proctor, I spoke to Paul Gambaccini at his South Bank apartment close to London's Royal Festival Hall. The veteran broadcaster and DJ had also been subjected to the dawn raid treatment – this time, under Operation Yewtree, the investigation set up in the wake of the Savile inquiry.

Gambaccini had been awoken at 4.38 a.m. on 29 October 2013 by a ring on the doorbell. He was arrested in connection with allegations of historical sex abuse against two teenagers, his possessions taken away by the sackload as he was carted off to Charing Cross Police Station.

It had been over fourteen months since the Crown Prosecution Service dropped the case when we met, but Gambaccini's fury over his treatment at the hands of the police had not diminished. 'The state as expressed through its agencies – the police and Crown Prosecution Service – warred against me for a year,' he began. The DJ had been on bail for a year, or 'twelve months of trauma', as he put it.

Gambaccini told me that he did not want to be a 'rent a quote' – he had only done one interview since his book about his experiences, *Love, Paul Gambaccini*, came out in 2015. In fact, he wanted to do another interview about his wretched year like 'a hole in the head'.

But there was no stopping him once we started. He spoke with an articulate rage, and his contempt for what he saw as the wilful stupidity of his pursuers was withering. 'Bernard Hogan-Howe's Metropolitan Police tried to destroy my life and end my career for their own public relations purposes,' the broadcaster told me. 'That is a stark sentence. But that's the entire episode distilled to a kernel.'

The allegations against him amounted to nothing more than 'a science fiction case' dreamed up by a fantasist, he said. Since the charges were dropped, Gambaccini discovered that the original police investigation had been closed because of 'insufficient evidence' a month before he was arrested. The later investigation only began when the first complainant – Gambaccini called him 'Primary' – alleged that a second witness ('Secondary') was able to corroborate claims of sexual activity between 1978 and 1984 when the pair were teenagers.

The police are compelled to act when someone is accused by two different people – a point explained to Gambaccini by his friend Lord Brian Paddick, a former Metropolitan Police deputy assistant commissioner. But Gambaccini protested that Primary and Secondary were not two different people 'in the way that someone from Hull and someone from Taunton would be'. Instead, he claimed they were lifelong friends who had had three dozen years to concoct their story.

Unsurprisingly, a conversation with Gambaccini (aka the Professor of Pop) is littered with music references. When he was arrested, he penned the following memorable denial:

> On Monday night, I attended an excellent production of the Kander and Ebb musical *The Scottsboro Boys* at the Young Vic Theatre. It concerned a group of black men in Alabama in the 1930s who were falsely accused of sexual offences. Within hours, I was arrested by Operation Yewtree. Nothing has changed, except this time there was no music.

The DJ drew a parallel between the American lynch mob and

what he repeatedly called the 'witch-hunt'. 'I lived through this, just as I lived through McCarthyism. This is why I recognise this not as a unique event but as a recurring event in history, like the witch trials in Salem.'

Gambaccini attacked what he called the 'fundamental misconception', shared by the police and CPS, that if an accuser came forward they must be telling truth, simply because it took courage to come forward. 'Problem: it takes equal courage for fantasists and distressed individuals to come forward as it does for a genuine victim,' he said. Gambaccini reckoned that Secondary might never have been interviewed by the police.

The DJ described himself as one of a generation of gay men 'traumatised' by Scotland Yard's 'pretty police' campaign, where good-looking officers acted as agents provocateurs to entrap gay men in public toilets. That said, he stressed his belief that 90 per cent of police 'joined the force undoubtedly to do good and not to take on the Orwellian zealotry of their leaders'.

According to Gambaccini, the Met was paying for its officers to jet around the world to interview witnesses who might assist their case against him, while failing to chase up easy leads that might have proved his innocence. Unbeknownst to his accuser, Gambaccini was a virgin when the abuse was supposed to have happened. The DJ told the police the identity of the man to whom he lost his virginity. The police never contacted the man. 'It would've taken ten seconds to have tracked him down. The guy is an RAF veteran,' Gambaccini said. 'They spent eighteen months on the fraud and they wouldn't bother to spend ten seconds on the real guy.'

Gambaccini's book breaks new ground for the typically

self-aggrandising celebrity bio genre. It is an unflinching account of a successful man – popular and venerated by his peers – who overnight finds himself ostracised and cut off from society.

'My name is Kafka, Franz Kafka,' is how his book begins. He wrote about how much it meant for him to receive an invitation into someone's house in those dark days: 'It is a personal commitment in the face of the opposition of the state.'

Towards the end of our interview, Gambaccini recalled a police officer using his toilet who, pointing at a photograph, later asked: 'Who are these boys?' They were his godsons. 'Throughout this witch-hunt there has been this ludicrous tendency to conflate homosexuality with paedophilia – a point made by Harvey Proctor,' Gambaccini told me. 'They are interested in results, not justice, and public relations rather than truth. If it helps their PR to paint elderly gay people as paedophiles, they will – even if it is intellectually preposterous and morally repugnant.'

• • •

Attitudes towards homosexuality have changed beyond all recognition since Harvey Proctor's political career came to an abrupt end. The offences to which he pleaded guilty three decades ago would not even be illegal today. The legal age of consent for gay men at the time was twenty-one but, as of 2000, it is sixteen.

The former Tory MP and self-declared disciple of Enoch Powell was said by *Private Eye* to be so far right 'as to be somewhere in the North Sea'; but his politics are perhaps more nuanced than the caricature. He insisted he was never hypocritical about his sexuality. He always voted in support of gay rights (as well as, he points out, in favour of penal reform).

'It is extraordinary that as the so-called liberalisation of the laws on homosexuality have developed, there has also been this offensive behaviour towards homosexuals,' Proctor told me.

Harvey Proctor MP was not 'out', but, as he explained: 'No one at the time would come out and say that they were a homosexual as a Conservative because they would not be an MP. It never occurred to me when I was a MP that it mattered a damn to my constituents.'

• • •

In October 2017 we learned that, in Wiltshire Police's view, if Harvey Proctor's political nemesis Sir Edward Heath was alive today then the police might call him in for questioning over allegations that he raped and indecently assaulted boys as young as ten.

As utterly shocking as such a statement is, they also assured us that 'no inference of guilt' should be attached to their conclusion. This was the main finding contained in Wiltshire Police's 'closure report', which sought to bring to an end a two-year investigation known as Operation Conifer, reckoned to have cost taxpayers £1.5 million.

Supporters of the late Conservative Prime Minister immediately called for a Henriques-style inquiry into the handling of the allegations. 'Sir Edward's reputation has been unfairly tarnished,' former Cabinet minister (and long-term supporter of Eddie Gilfoyle) Lord Hunt of Wirral said. 'No living person would be subject to a process which involves a trawl for accusations, followed by the publication of those accusations with no independent assessment of the 'evidence', or any details of the supposed place, time and circumstances of the alleged assaults.'

Operation Conifer had been set up – if not to fail – then certainly to disappoint, frustrate and anger all sides. Those who believe in the existence of an establishment cover-up to protect the late PM will no doubt see the report as further evidence; and those who dismissed the allegations as outrageous smears against a respected former PM will take the view that such a report offers anything but 'closure'.

It is not the job of the police in a criminal investigation to reach a conclusion as to likely guilt or innocence of a suspect, as the Conifer report reminded readers. It also explained that, given that the subject of the investigation was dead, Wiltshire Police did not have the option to send the file over to the Crown Prosecution Service to consider a decision to charge.

Conifer's task was to establish if the hypothetical threshold of whether to interview a dead man under caution had been met. But that is not much of a threshold. As former Director of Public Prosecutions Ken MacDonald put it, the bar is 'as low as the police want it to be – and in the case of a dead man, virtually non-existent. They are covering their backs at the expense of a dead man. Shame on them.'

Wiltshire Police Chief Constable Mike Veale has defended the investigation, saying it was 'the right moral, ethical and professional thing to do'. According to Veale, it would have been 'an indefensible dereliction of my public duty as a chief constable' not to have investigated such serious allegations against a former Prime Minister – even a dead one.

The Operation Conifer report is a curious read. Much space is set aside to justifying why it went to such extraordinary lengths to deliver an inevitably ambiguous outcome. Savile's ghost – and the need for action, no matter how futile – looms large.

As well as moral, ethical and professional considerations, Wiltshire Police claimed they were operating under a 'legal requirement' to investigate the dead. In support of their argument, they invoked Article 3 of the European Convention on Human Rights ('No one should be subjected to torture or to inhuman or degrading treatment or punishment'). According to Operation Hydrant, 'the closer the alleged suspect is to the state and the more serious the allegation', the greater the duty on the police to investigate.

Veale complained publicly about the risks of taking on the establishment. He told the *Mail on Sunday*, 'It can be quite sinister. I was told early on in Conifer, "You'll lose your job; the establishment will get you." I'm not a conspiracy theorist. I don't believe in Martians. I used to think, "What are these people on about?"'

Apparently, the title of chief constable no longer guarantees membership of the establishment. 'He is a chief constable, for goodness sake,' exploded Daniel Finkelstein in *The Times*. 'Where does he get off suggesting that he is the victim of the power of others?'

The investigation known as Operation Conifer began with another public appeal in August 2015. Detective Superintendent

Sean Memory was filmed standing outside Sir Edward Heath's former home, Arundells, in Salisbury. 'This is an appeal for victims. In particular, if you have been the victim of any crime from Sir Ted Heath or any historical sexual offence, or you are a witness or you have any information about this, then please come forward,' Memory said.

Two weeks later, 118 people contacted the force with information. Prior to that, four people had made allegations. In total, forty people made allegations dating from 1956 to 1992; 1,580 lines of inquiry were generated; 284 statements taken; and three people unconnected to Heath were arrested.

Wiltshire Police concluded that in respect of seven allegations, including one of raping a young boy and a series of indecent assaults, Heath would have been interviewed under caution. In relation to twenty allegations, the threshold to interview was not met because of (as the report puts it) 'undermining information', including two cases where the allegations were 'false'. The report reveals nothing about the credibility of any of the other allegations. Ten were made by third parties on behalf of complainants – including two who had died and three that were made anonymously without the complainant even being interviewed.

Throughout the report, the individuals making as yet unproven allegations are inaccurately labelled 'victims' (as opposed to 'complainants') despite the recommendations not to do so in the Henriques report.

Immediately after the Conifer 'closure report' came out, the *Daily Telegraph* ran an interview with the sister of the man who made the single most serious allegation: rape. According to the report, the man is a convicted paedophile and, in the view of his own sister, a 'born liar'. She claimed that the police failed to interview her or her brother. 'My brother should have been hung, drawn and quartered,' she said.

• • •

We have been here before. In 2005, the late author Richard Webster compared the child abuse scandals of the 1980s and 1990s to medieval witch-hunts in his book *The Secret of Bryn Estyn*. 'There is a view of history which suggests that, as we progress towards civilised rationality, we are less and less likely to fall prey to unreason, or to be gripped by those episodes of collective insanity which have scarred European history,' he wrote. He referred to the 'demonological anti-Semitism' of the middle ages or European witch-hunts of the sixteenth and seventeenth centuries. The writer argued that the comforting notion of history as enlightened progress was 'not only mistaken but dangerous'.

Webster reckoned that in relation to the north Wales children's home scandal, which related to allegations of abuse made between 1974 and 1990, the police made unsolicited approaches to 650 witnesses who went on to accuse 365 people. Only six people were prosecuted. There were two convictions for sexual abuse. Webster recognised that some abuse had clearly taken place, but was deeply alarmed at how many innocent people at the end of long careers of public service had had their lives destroyed as a result of totally baseless allegations.

The notion that abuse was somehow endemic to our

residential care homes quickly gained traction amongst commentators without evidence or challenge. The author quoted an example from June 1996, when a presenter on BBC Radio 4's *World at One* casually asserted that 'we might have to face up to the possibility that abuse in children's homes was the norm rather than the exception'. A few days later, speaking in the House of Commons, Labour's Welsh affairs spokesman Rhodri Morgan said that although children's homes were meant to provide care, they had dished out 'a diet of sadism by day and sodomy by night'. The following year, writing for *The Guardian*, the journalist Linda Grant referred to the 'bureaucracy of paedophiles' who ran children's homes.

• • •

A 2002 House of Commons select committee on home affairs into allegations of child abuse in children's homes makes for a disturbing read post-Savile. The MPs preface their report by acknowledging that there was 'much justified concern' about child sexual abuse. Their focus, however, was directed at a bizarre and disturbing proliferation of false allegations.

The MPs concluded that 'a new generation of miscarriages of justice' had arisen from 'the over-enthusiastic pursuit of allegations'. The investigation heard from twenty-seven witnesses in seven evidence sessions and received more than 200 submissions.

When the MPs began their inquiry, thirty-four of the forty-three police forces in England and Wales were actively investigating abuse. The journalist David Rose, then special investigations reporter for *The Observer*, reckoned that fifty or more of the 120 former care workers found guilty of sexual abuse could have been wrongly convicted. Chris Saltrese, a defence lawyer specialising in abuse cases, estimated that the number might rise as high as 100.

Richard Webster told MPs that 'in excess of 80 per cent or 90 per cent of the 581 suspects' identified by the police in north Wales alone were 'completely innocent'. The Labour MP Claire Curtis-Thomas, chair of the all-party group on abuse allegations, said that she knew of twenty cases where there was 'an overt indication' that there had been significant abuses of the criminal justice system. The MPs took evidence from four people accused of abuse: two were acquitted; the charge against the third was dropped at the eleventh hour; and the fourth had his conviction quashed on appeal.

The report quoted the despairing words of one judge, Mr Justice Crabtree, as he dismissed charges against one defendant:

> Anyone who is in charge of protecting children is vulnerable to allegations of assault from some dissatisfied or angry child, and if no complaint is made for months or years, how can any teacher, social worker, nurse defend themselves? How is he or she going to be able to prove his or her innocence when so much time has passed?

The committee highlighted the danger of police 'trawling' operations, the practice of making unsolicited approaches to former residents of care homes. The MPs explained that in any police investigation, the police (obviously) contact the person named by the complainant. 'Trawling refers to the process when the police go one step further and contact potential witnesses who have not been named or even mentioned,' the report said.

In a trawl, the police might contact 'all or a large proportion' of former residents – a practice the police, conscious of criticism, had misleadingly relabelled 'dip sampling'. David Rose told MPs that the whole process was 'almost tailor-made to generate false allegations'.

Perhaps the most shocking finding contained in the 2002 report was that the CPS rejected a 'staggering' 79 per cent of institutional abuse cases referred by the police. This compared to a general discontinuance rate of just 13 per cent.

In 2002, MPs made a series of sensible recommendations. For example, they called for clear justification of police trawls; more rigorous analysis of witness evidence; reform of similar fact evidence; fuller disclosure, including of 'evidence inconvenient to the prosecution'; and, finally, for the CCRC to lower their threshold for referral to the Court of Appeal.

Not only did the Labour government reject the conclusions, but it also rejected the well-evidenced premise of the investigation, refusing to believe that such allegations led to a large number of miscarriages of justice.

• • •

It is a sad fact that half of all children in custody came through the care system. Inevitably, therefore, a fair number of the former residents of care homes in the 1970s and 1980s ended up in prison.

Ben Gunn pleaded guilty to killing a friend when he was fourteen years old. In the late 1970s, he spent around three years in care in north Wales. As a prisoner, he made a false allegation of historical abuse against an innocent man who spent twelve years in prison. Gunn knew he was innocent all along. He candidly explained how it happened at a Falsely Accused Carers and Teachers conference in 2013.

Why did he make the allegation? Gunn was fifteen years into his sentence and he was, in his words, 'in a hole, psychologically'. 'My parole recommendation was way overdue and I couldn't see any light whatsoever,' he said. Then the police turned up to interview him in prison. He added: 'I'll go anywhere for a free cup of tea. So I went along.'

He was questioned in relation to a trawl of north Wales care homes. The police came back. Gunn claimed that he was then told that they were certain they had their man; that their suspect was going down; and that, if there was a conviction, then the local authority wouldn't contest any compensation claims. It was at this point when Gunn admitted that his ears pricked up.

Gunn made his false allegation, which, he claimed, was 'mild' and never used in the man's later conviction. It was only later that, by talking to other prisoners on the wing from that part of Wales, he found out that they had also made allegations. Their allegations had not begun the trawl, but Gunn recollected they had all taken the view that it was 'just a compensation scam'. The police led them to believe that there was overwhelming evidence. 'What is it to you if you put the boot in, and claim a few quid of easy money?'

• • •

The police do not need to trawl when they have lawyers willing to do it for them. The home affairs select committee investigation in 2002 heard evidence from leading child abuse lawyer Peter Garsden, who was then handling twenty group actions and 800 individual claims. His firm employed twenty-one lawyers wholly reliant on abuse work. The MPs noted 'in passing' that there might be 'an element of self-interest' amongst lawyers to generate business by encouraging complainants to launch civil compensation claims, as opposed to directing them to the Criminal Injuries Compensation Authority.

The journalist David Rose interviewed Garsden as part of a BBC *Panorama* investigation into the issue ('In the Name of the Children'), which led to the home affairs committee investigation. The lawyer made the startling claim that he believed himself to, quite literally, be doing the Lord's work. 'I believe that really, we're messing with the Devil, because you know, child abuse is evil, and the people that get involved in it are powerful, manipulative people. They will do their level best to stop us succeeding and stop us getting justice for the victims.'

Rose asked him: 'Is this the Devil at work?' Garsden replied in the affirmative – 'and that was something that never occurred to me before I became involved with a Christian pressure group'. He also claimed that false allegations did not exist.

In a section of the interview that did not make the final cut, Garsden was candid about the lawyers' closeness with the police. 'It very quickly became apparent that it was important for us and the police to have a symbiotic relationship with each other. They depended on us, and we depended on them.'

Modern personal injury law firms are volume businesses these days.* Sexual abuse lawyers place advertisements in the prisoners' newspaper *Inside Time*, aiming to reach out to prospective clients. It could not be easier to begin a claim. 'Find out how much sexual abuse compensation you could be entitled to,' reads one typical ad.

This calculator has been designed to provide prospective applicants with a rough guide to the likely sexual abuse compensation that they may be entitled to under the Criminal Injuries Compensation Authority scheme. To use the calculator please choose a sexual abuse type and then click next and follow the instructions. Call us now or complete our contact form.

• • •

When Paul Gambaccini appeared before the House of Commons' justice committee in 2015, he told MPs that he had been a victim of what he called a 'flypaper' investigation. This is where a high-profile suspect's name is hung up in public. That person is then endlessly re-bailed to keep the investigation live, in the

---

* In 2000, Labour scrapped legal aid for accident claims. It created the regulatory environment to allow market forces to flourish, enabling accident victims without legal aid to have access to justice through revamped 'no win, no fee' deals. The reforms unleashed a compensation culture to fill the vacuum left by legal aid. Law firms and claims companies now aggressively market their services targeting volume business.

hope that the original accusation draws further complainants out of the woodwork.

The broadcaster reckoned that his serial re-bailings were deliberately timed to coincide with developments in the cases of other celebrities. The justice committee agreed. 'Police use of the "flypaper" practice of arresting someone, leaking the details, then endlessly re-bailing them in the vague hope that other people come forward is unacceptable and must come to an immediate end,' said the group's chairman, Keith Vaz.

Operation Midland was wound up in March 2017. It took seven months for Metropolitan Police Commissioner Sir Bernard Hogan-Howe to meet Harvey Proctor and offer an apology in person.

Nick, on the other hand, has received continuous support – a point made by Sir Richard Henriques. 'The allegations have had a profoundly damaging effect upon the characters and reputations of those living and those deceased,' he said. 'In differing ways those reputations have been hard won over several decades, and yet in Operation Midland they were shattered by the word of a single, uncorroborated complaint.'

CHAPTER SIX

STARING INTO THE ABYSS

When Hannah Stubbs took her own life in August 2015, Elgan Varney felt she might as well have taken his life, too. The pair met as mature students on a physiotherapy course at Keele University at the start of the 2014 academic year. They began a brief relationship that would end in tragedy on both sides.

Varney ended the relationship, but Stubbs went on to accuse him of sexually assaulting her before spending several weeks in a mental health unit at St George's Hospital in Stafford. She hanged herself at her parents' home on 29 August 2015.

Despite her death, Varney stood accused of rape. Just three days before the trial was due to start in March 2017, he was cleared of all charges after the Crown Prosecution Service decided it could offer no evidence against him. 'When my solicitor told me there was to be no trial, she was happy for me,' the 33-year-old told me.

> I was incredibly frustrated. I was anxious about the trial and fearful of yet more press coverage but I thought at least I'd be fully exonerated. Finally, I thought all the facts would come out

in a court and then I could see what was left of my life. I wasn't even allowed that opportunity.

The allegations contained in Stubbs's statement to the police made on 12 March 2015 bore no relationship to the allegations she had originally made to university friends. The pair had been part of a tight-knit group of students at Keele University. They studied together, hung out at the KPA bar for mature students on campus and shared a passion for climbing. The others were shocked when one of their number made such serious allegations against another close friend.

• • •

The police and Crown Prosecution Service has come a long way in dealing with cases of violence against women. Stung by criticism of years of inaction, they have finally begun to take the issue seriously.

In 2007, prosecutions relating to violence against women and girls accounted for just 7 per cent of the CPS's total caseload; in 2016 it was up to 19 per cent.* In 2013, the then Director of Public Prosecutions, Keir Starmer, blamed a 'misplaced belief' that false accusations of rape were commonplace on a failure on the part of the police and prosecutors to investigate offences properly. The DPP was launching a CPS study conducted over a seventeen-month period in 2011–12. This was 'a trailblazing report', Starmer said. It was the first time that the CPS had 'clear

---

* According to the CPS's annual 'Violence against Women and Girls report' 2015/2016.

evidence' on this important issue. 'This report shows that false allegations of rape and domestic violence are very rare, but that they are very serious where they do exist,' Starmer said.

According to the report, there had been 5,651 prosecutions for rape but just thirty-five prosecutions for false accusations. 'Victims of rape and domestic violence must not be deterred from reporting the abuse they have suffered,' Starmer wrote in the foreword to the report. 'We have worked hard to dispel the damaging myths and stereotypes which are associated with these cases. One such misplaced belief is that false allegations of rape and domestic violence are rife.' The DPP urged the police not to adopt 'an overcautious approach' because of the 'understandable concern' that some allegations were false.

Rape Crisis reckon that, of the 60,000 women and girls who get in touch with them every year, only 15 per cent then contact the police. One of the main reasons the group attributes to this statistic is the fear of not being believed. 'The widespread myth that false reporting is common and that women routinely lie about being raped, perpetuated by disproportionate and distorted media coverage, fuels this fear,' the group argues.

• • •

When Hannah Stubbs and Elgan Varney were not with each other during their brief friendship, they were glued to their phones, messaging and texting each other, often into the early hours. They exchanged over 10,000 messages during the course of their five-month relationship. An estimated 6,696 messages were sent via WhatsApp, with an additional 4,848 through Facebook. Varney's legal team transcribed all of them. An additional batch of Varney's texts was forensically downloaded from his mobile phone.

It was later alleged that over the course of their relationship, Varney had raped Stubbs on two separate, unspecified occasions. The first allegation related to an incident that was said to have taken place sometime between 1 October and 31 December 2014, with a second taking place at some point in February 2015. Then there was an allegation of an assault on a single day (27 February 2015).

But the huge pile of correspondence between the pair undermined the account that Hannah Stubbs had given to the police. Not one message supported the prosecution case or Stubbs's account. 'It reveals nothing at all untoward about Elgan's conduct,' Varney's solicitor, Mark Newby, said. 'It is striking that all their exchanges are entirely good-natured on both sides.'

According to Newby, the overall impression was of a young man trying to extricate himself from a relatively casual relationship but, he added, 'doing that with sensitivity and trying to remain friends. Hannah wanted the couple to be going steady.'

The great shame is that the police never bothered to read them, despite Varney offering them his phone.

In a statement read outside Stoke Crown Court, Elgan Varney said: 'Time and time again I read about people in similar positions. The pendulum has swung too far and fairness and balance needs to be restored so that the presumption of innocence is not completely eroded. That is the only way for true justice to be done.'

Elgan Varney never wanted to talk to the press. He found the prospect terrifying. He just wanted to try to get on with his life. The first time I spoke to Varney, he described himself as 'a *Guardian*-reading feminist'. Varney was wary of being misrepresented after seeing the way the press had reported the original allegations. He was also frank about his own history of anxiety prior to meeting Hannah Stubbs.

Varney would not have agreed to an interview had it not been for another article which ran immediately after the CPS dropped charges. A journalist had approached Varney for an interview after the CPS offered no evidence, but Varney had declined. The journalist then spoke to the parents of Hannah Stubbs.

After reading the interview, he realised he had to set the record straight. Not only were there factual inaccuracies in the article but, more importantly, it heavily implied that Varney had raped Stubbs, notwithstanding the dropped charges. Varney was devastated.*

* * *

'When I started at Keele I wasn't looking for a relationship,' Elgan Varney told me. Back in September 2014, he had just turned thirty years old and he dreamed that one day he would become a physio for Nottingham Forest Football Club.

Varney used to work in the club shop and played for its

---

* The newspaper's readers' editor eventually agreed to take the article off its site. It took the best part of a year to achieve this outcome. According to the readers' editor, a decision to take down an article is only taken in 'exceptional circumstances'. Elgan Varney has only given one interview.

Junior Reds team. He didn't want to spend all his time hanging out with eighteen-year-olds. He told me he was at a different stage of his life. He wanted to focus on his studies and meet people who were interested in doing more than drinking at the student bar.

Hannah Stubbs appeared to fit that category. Both were mature students. Varney recalled his first impressions of the 22-year-old physio student when they briefly spoke at an introductory lecture: 'bubbly, talkative and a bit cheeky'. 'After all that happened, people might think that Hannah was withdrawn and vulnerable,' he said. 'She was outgoing and could be pretty forthright.' It is a view of Stubbs echoed by her other friends.

The pair chatted properly for the first time online in a Facebook group for students on the course. Their exchange began at 11.31 p.m. and ended at 1.27 a.m. 'Hey, are you a mature student as well, Hannah?' Varney began.

They messaged each other about their excitement for the new course. Conversation flowed as they discussed their travels and their romances. They traded pictures of each other's pets. Stubbs had two dogs and twelve chickens; Varney had recently lost his childhood dog, Dingo. They swapped numbers.

The two students struck up an easy rapport. Varney was renting a room in a house a five-minute drive from campus and Stubbs was living with her parents, a thirty-minute drive away. Varney didn't have a car. Stubbs would drop by to chill out and give him a lift into college. Varney insisted on paying her petrol money.

One thing the two students had in common was a history of anxiety and depression. Both had dropped out of earlier university courses. Varney, a straight-A student from a Nottingham comprehensive, left a degree in history and politics at Nottingham University in 2005. He had originally started studying at Keele in 2012 but had taken a leave of absence due to glandular fever and anxiety.

Stubbs had previously studied medicine at Birmingham University, but had also dropped out. When she started at Keele, she was taking antidepressants.

Varney, a keen sportsman, threw himself into university life at Keele. He played tennis for the university, ran with their running club and captained the 'Neil Baldwin' football team, its unofficial side. Baldwin, a man with learning difficulties who has become a mascot for the university as well as a kit man for Stoke City, was the subject of the BAFTA-winning BBC 2 film *Marvellous*.

The couple shared around fifteen hours of lectures each week, socialised together and spent a lot of time at their favourite hangout, the university's 22-metre climbing wall. Most days they met with two other friends, fellow mature physio students Steven and Hazel, whose names have been changed to protect their privacy.

'It was very evident they both cared about one another,' Hazel told me. 'They always seemed happy together. I would describe their relationship as caring, playful and happy.'

Steven agreed: 'Elgan and Hannah got on very well throughout the time I knew them both. He was caring towards her, and they always seemed to have a good time together. Hannah enjoyed being in Elgan's company and wanted to see him as much as she could.'

Hazel's first impressions of Stubbs was that of someone who was 'friendly, compassionate – but anxious'. 'I recall Elgan as being energetic, outgoing and friendly. He could be outspoken, but in a likeable way. He saw both sides of things. He would often go out of his way to help both myself and fellow classmates.' Steven described Varney as 'a kind, caring and genuine person'. 'If anyone needs help, he's the first one there. I've seen that for myself on a number of occasions,' he said.

The couple never made their relationship 'official' (it fell apart because Varney didn't want anything serious). The relationship was sexual, 'but it was never just about sex. I genuinely cared for Hannah,' Varney said.

Their constant messaging revealed that while both were enjoying their time at Keele, Stubbs was struggling with anxiety; something she had been dealing with since before they had met.

She looked to the older Varney for advice and he was more than happy to help. In November, Stubbs started seeing a university counsellor at Varney's suggestion. 'I think you're going to be a little proud of me,' messaged Stubbs when she reported back on her first appointment.

The two were so close that at the end of the first term Stubbs repeatedly messaged Varney to ask him to spend Christmas with her family. He was reluctant, and although they spent Christmas evening and Boxing Day together, they exchanged more than 750 messages in the few days either side.

'We have to [wrap] presents in a second. Currently hiding in the toilet,' Stubbs messaged at 8.43 p.m. on Christmas Eve. 'Is it bad that I'd rather be at yours watching a film? Dislike all the faff of Christmas at times.'

If exchanges were intimate, then they were affectionate. 'Not got my grizzly bear to cuddle up to though unfortunately,' Stubbs messaged the day after Boxing Day. 'I like falling asleep with you,' she wrote in the early hours. 'I like waking up with you too though ;),' she added a minute later.

At the start of January, when Varney's landlady unexpectedly gave him notice to quit his flat because her boyfriend was going to move in, Stubbs's first response was to ask Varney to move in with her family. The boyfriend never moved in, Varney continued to live at the flat and his landlady volunteered to speak in court on his behalf. Later that month, when Stubbs realised that her period was late, Varney was concerned. As ever, he was ready with support, suggesting that she take a pregnancy test. When it turned out to be a false alarm, she messaged: 'There's no need to worry about baby Elgans ☺☺☺.'

· · ·

As well as the two counts of rape, Varney was also charged with a sexual assault that Stubbs alleged took place on 27 February 2015 – the day after Varney told Stubbs he didn't want to be in a relationship. Her messages show that she wanted to see him: 'Could watch a film maybe ☺?' Varney wasn't keen. He replied: 'Up to you… but if it's gonna make you feel bad…'

Stubbs later told the university that Varney had persuaded her to go to his flat 'against her better judgement'. The following evening, the pair continued to exchange friendly messages, with Stubbs imploring Varney to go over to her house. Stubbs told Varney that her family was asking after him, keen for him to visit and curious as to whether she was still 'seeing' him.

It was clear that Stubbs was struggling to come to terms with Varney's decision to call it a day. He was polite and the exchange ended on good terms. 'Have a good match tomorrow ☺,' she said.

They signed off.

• • •

Stubbs made her first allegation in early March after a strange episode at the university climbing wall, when she claimed to have injured her back while play wrestling on gym mats with fellow students (not Varney).

Varney recalled students, especially the trainee medics, crowding around and 'making a fuss over Hannah'. Varney thought that this was an overreaction and that Stubbs was attention-seeking. Nevertheless, when Stubbs asked if he would accompany her to the hospital, he agreed and got into the ambulance with her. Although Varney was sceptical about the hospital visit, he still took pictures at Stubbs's request of her smiling on a spinal board. She later posted them on Facebook along with a thank you for going with her.

Other students joined them at the hospital and one, James, drove everyone home after Stubbs was given the all-clear after 3 a.m. That evening, Stubbs told James that Varney had inappropriately touched her.

James was shocked by this allegation. He then messaged his friend Michelle; she seemed like the right person to turn to. Michelle, whose name has also been changed to protect her privacy, had blogged for the university's mental health awareness week the previous year about her own long history of self-harm after she said she had been raped.

A few days later, Michelle spoke to Stubbs.

The following day, Varney received a Facebook message from Stubbs. It would be the last:

> Elgan, due to what happened last week when I came over to yours I have decided that I don't want any contact with you. I don't feel like you respected me or how I feel. I had been clear with you on the phone that I didn't want things to happen again, and yet you still went ahead. I think I made it clear by sitting on the floor and not wanting to join you on the sofa that I meant what I had said on the phone.

The day prior to this, the two students had exchanged friendly messages.

• • •

Hannah Stubbs was not alone when she sent Varney the message. One of those who was present was the former couple's close friend Steven. He later said in a witness statement: 'I fully believe that [Stubbs] was not raped or sexually abused by Elgan.'

He said that the message had been 'formulated by Michelle'. 'It seemed that Hannah had little input into this,' he said. He also mentioned that Michelle was 'the first person to mention the word "rape" to me'. 'I was shocked by this. I recall that Michelle soon became heavily involved with Hannah and seemed to have a lot of influence over her.'

Steven, who later went to Hannah Stubbs's funeral, also said that Stubbs had previously made allegations against James, claiming that he had touched her inappropriately. Hazel was also prepared to go to court to speak on Varney's behalf. 'Prior to the wrestling incident, Hannah and Elgan were very comfortable with one another,' she said.

She also claimed that Stubbs had made allegations to her against another student. She is convinced that the allegations were unfounded. 'I do not think she understood the consequences of the allegations. I am not sure it was entirely a malicious act. I don't think it was a thought-out process.'

It was Michelle who first rang the police about the allegations. Several weeks after the allegations were made, Michelle self-harmed again. This time it was on a camping trip in front of a group of freshers. Steven helped run the climbing club and was present when it happened. The club decided to ban Michelle, who unsuccessfully appealed the decision, arguing that she had not been in control of her actions on account of her mental illness.

Over thirty people signed witness statements attesting to Varney's good character, including ten Keele students, and more were prepared to go to court. Hazel described Varney as 'a very sensitive individual, if not too sensitive'. 'He tries to help people and goes to extremes to help them.' It was a perceptive comment.

• • •

Three weeks later, Elgan Varney was asked by the police to attend a voluntary interview. 'The interviewing officer seemed friendly and polite, but I had no idea what to do. I had never been in this position before,' he recalled. 'I thought I didn't need a lawyer because I had nothing to hide, but was told by a friend in the police I needed one.'

Varney spent much of the interview trying to persuade the officer to read the messages. 'I was surprised she didn't just take my phone then but she told me the tech team would be in touch,' he said. 'I thought the whole thing was completely crazy and that the truth would be clear from the messages.'

Two weeks before speaking to Varney, the same officer had interviewed Hannah Stubbs. The transcript and video interview was later made available to Varney's legal team. Stubbs was reluctant to make any concrete allegations and repeatedly referred to her lack of faith in her own memory. In Stubbs's description of her first sexual encounter with Varney, she said she couldn't 'really remember if I wanted him to or not, but I think I must've done'.

She mentioned Michelle's role. 'People have said to me, like my friend Michelle … if you've said to them you don't want them to then they shouldn't.'

Six months after making the allegations against Elgan Varney, Hannah Stubbs took her own life. 'Hannah's death has left a sense of loss that is impossible to put into words,' said her family in a message posted on Facebook.

Friends and family remember her fondly – but there is no doubt she was deeply troubled. The full history of her mental health never emerged; instead, it was widely reported in the press, as a result of interviews with her family, that the trauma of being raped had led her to take her own life. Yet her suicide note did not mention Varney or being raped.

The inquest into her death recorded that she had been suffering from post-traumatic stress at the time of her death – but this was not a result of her being raped. According to notes provided by the university to the inquest, Stubbs disclosed to her personal tutor that she had a history of mental health issues and was 'burnt out' by her experience at Birmingham. That experience resulted in 'a long period of mental illness during which she had suicidal thoughts'. She also spoke of a previous suicide attempt that took place before she started studying at Keele.

Also disclosed was her internet search history in the run-up to her suicide. This included multiple searches in August 2015 on false allegations, searches on how to withdraw prosecutions, as well as research into the kinds of personality disorders that drive such allegations. Two weeks before her death, Stubbs downloaded CPS guidance on perverting the course of justice and making false allegations – twice.

Dr Peter Naish, a senior lecturer in psychology at the Open University, was instructed by the defence team to act as an expert witness in the case. He had access to a wide range of confidential documents, including Hannah Stubbs's medical notes. He was so concerned he volunteered to go public after it was announced that the case would not proceed.

From time to time, Dr Naish is called upon to act as expert witness. He regards it as 'interesting work and a service to society', but that doesn't mean that he fails to see problems in the system.

He believes the Varney case provides a stark illustration. I asked him for his thoughts on the case and he wrote me a note. 'It is a human characteristic that, when we incline towards a particular belief, we seek evidence to confirm it,' it began. 'Evolution gave us that habit as a rough and ready solution for a brain of limited processing power. This is not the scientific way.'

'If we are developing a theory that seems to fit the facts we have so far, then rather than trying to find yet more facts that fit, we should test the theory by seeking out any facts that do not,' Dr Naish reflected. 'Many miscarriages of justice would be avoided if the police adopted this approach. In this distressing case, a miscarriage was avoided, but the last minute rescue was no real escape.'

Dr Naish argues that there were two victims of this case.

No one would dispute that Hannah was a victim, because, whatever the cause of the unfortunate young woman's suicide, something has gone disastrously wrong when a person of her age feels that death is the only course remaining. It is less obvious that Elgan, too, has been a victim; after all, he has 'got off' without even having to go to court.

But what if he had gone? It's said there's nothing to fear if you are innocent, but what about those miscarriages of justice? Elgan was staring into that abyss. Had he been found guilty, not simply of the horrible crime of rape, but also, in effect, of the victim's death, then he would have been facing a long custodial sentence. Those convicted of sex crimes are not treated kindly in prison.

For month after month, Elgan lived in this dread, his life on hold, his mental health besieged. As an expert, I was privy to a wide range of information, not just the mental health issues of the key players, but communications between them, family matters, actions of friends and so on. If the case had come to court, I would have presented what I knew in Elgan's defence and everyone would have heard it. With no trial my lips must remain sealed. This is very unfortunate. If people care to wonder why the Crown Prosecution Service decided not to pursue the case, they might assume that it was because the CPS had insufficient evidence to prove Elgan guilty, not because there was so much that proved him innocent. The hope of humane treatment for the accused has been thwarted by publicity where there should have been privacy, and silence where there might have been explanation.

The frailties of the finite human brain are inescapable; errors are inevitable. That is why safeguards are required. Protective measures have been likened to slices of Swiss cheese – they inevitably have holes. In safety-critical situations, such as an aircraft cockpit or a nuclear power station, multiple levels of protection are employed: lots of 'cheese slices', in the hope that the holes will not line up. Air or nuclear accidents destroy lives, but so do errors in the administration of justice. Elgan, and those like him, deserve and demand effective safeguards.

• • •

Hannah Stubbs's death was traumatic and confusing for Varney. 'The news of her death made me physically sick. I cared about her. It was shocking and difficult to process. I was confused, sad and angry all at the same time.'

After her death, Varney didn't hear from the police for over six months. He was eventually charged on 11 March 2016. 'After I'd considered the evidence it was very clear that Elgan was innocent and should never have been charged,' Anna O'Mara, his solicitor until she took maternity leave, told me. 'It was remarkable that the CPS and police held so much evidence which undermined their case and strongly pointed to Elgan's innocence, but that they failed to act on this until a few days before the trial.'

She repeatedly asked the CPS to review the case. The judge at a preliminary hearing also urged the CPS to rethink dropping the case. O'Mara was particularly shocked by the police interview. 'Hannah initially was reluctant to commit herself to making an allegation against Elgan,' she pointed out. 'This eventually led to the officer explaining the legislation to Hannah, pointing out to her what the police would need to prove a case. It was only after Hannah had received prompts from the officer that she hesitantly developed a disjointed allegation against Elgan.'

At one point the officer encouraged the young woman to close her eyes and try to recall the events. An approach that perhaps might only be considered appropriate when dealing with a historical allegation. Stubbs's interview occurred only days after she alleged that the last assault had happened.

The lawyer points out that the defence continually sought disclosure of further material that they claimed to know existed, but that the police were not forthcoming. 'The police knew that the complainant had made previous similar complaints, but took no steps to investigate this whatsoever until they were continually pressed by the defence,' she said. Hannah Stubbs was eventually questioned by the police about previous allegations of rape she had made against another man, but that only happened because Varney's legal team raised the issue in court that previous complaints would need to be considered.

'It is awful that the CPS took so long to act, and the traumatic impact it has had on Elgan's life can't be underestimated,' O'Mara said. 'Something in the system needs to urgently change to prevent innocent lives being torn apart.'

His barrister, Matt Stanbury, has described the failed prosecution as 'perhaps an unrivalled case study in how a false allegation can come about'.

> It is often assumed that a false complaint must be the result of a vendetta. This case shows that it can be very much more complicated. It seems there were numerous factors at play. There can be little doubt that Miss Stubbs was influenced by her more mature friends, and ultimately the police, to believe that she had been a victim. Her reluctance to complain was mistaken for a misplaced loyalty; her vulnerability mistaken for victimhood.

Hazel and Steven both believe that Stubbs would not have gone to the police had it not been for the intervention of Michelle. 'Similar allegations had been made in the past with previous partners and they had not escalated to the point of getting the police involved,' Hazel told me.

When Stubbs took her own life, neither friend thought that it was because she had been raped – they didn't believe she had been.

• • •

Elgan Varney's case was not a one-off. Liam Allan, a 22-year-old criminology student at Greenwich University, spent two years on bail after being charged with twelve counts of rape and sexual assault. He told police that he had had sex with the alleged victim but that it had been consensual.

The two students' cases are different in significant ways and alarmingly similar in others. Both came very close to being sent to prison on the word of their accusers, despite a wealth of digital evidence.

In Varney's case, the police didn't bother to go through his messages with Stubbs. In Allan's case, the police downloaded 40,000 text and WhatsApp messages from the complainant's phone but refused to pass this evidence on to the defence, despite repeated requests from Allan's lawyers for the messages to be disclosed before the trial. They were told there was nothing to disclose. The case against Liam Allan collapsed three days into his trial at Croydon Crown Court.

The messages revealed that his accuser had pursued Allan for what she called 'casual sex'. She had told friends how much she had enjoyed sex with him and discussed fantasies of being raped.

It was the prosecution counsel, Jerry Hayes, who demanded that the messages be passed over to the defence. This move averted near-disaster. The barrister had only taken on the case the weekend before the trial started.

Hayes, who describes his approach to law as 'old-school', took the view that if the defence wanted to see evidence then they should have access to it, unless the case was 'a fishing expedition'. All 2,400 pages of messages were handed over. 'It blew the prosecution case out of the water,' he said. 'Clearly the officer hadn't reviewed it in any detail. He had failed in his duty of disclosure.'

The barrister told the judge that this was the most appalling failure of disclosure that he had ever encountered. According to Hayes, the forced disclosure took place in 'the fifty-ninth minute of the eleventh hour'. By then, the complainant had given her evidence and Hayes had started giving his evidence to the jury. Hayes had been told by the officer in charge of disclosure that he had seen it but that it was 'clearly not disclosable as it just contained very personal material and nothing capable of undermining the prosecution case or assisting the defence'.

'The system nearly failed,' Hayes said. 'This is a criminal justice system which is not just creaking, it's about to croak.'

The public was rightly appalled by the Allan case. As a broadsheet leader put it, there were 'competing narratives' over the reasons for the debacle. The prevailing view was that this was a consequence of the fact that the pendulum of criminal justice had swung too far towards protecting victims and away from defending the rights of suspects. The Criminal Bar Association accused the police and CPS of 'unconscious bias', which prevented them from properly investigating complaints in sexual offence cases.

Secondly, the case was cited as further evidence that our criminal justice system was becoming increasingly overstretched. Noting that the rules around disclosure had been introduced in response to cases like the Birmingham Six, *The Observer* argued that over twenty years the amount of data involved in criminal cases had 'ballooned' as a result of computers, tablets and mobile phones. It was argued that this made the investigation and prosecution of criminal offences 'far more complex and time-consuming than ever before' and the massive volume of data confronting the police in all sorts of cases made 'meeting their obligations on disclosure increasingly difficult'.

Following Liam Allan's case, it was revealed that the number of prosecutions in England and Wales that collapsed because of a failure by police or prosecutors to disclose evidence had increased by 70 per cent in the past two years. But the idea that this is all about deficits in resources seems fanciful. After all, how long does it take for an officer to turn on a mobile phone and scroll through messages? It took around six hours to read over Varney and Stubbs's conversations.

Liam Allan has accused the police and CPS of chasing rape convictions 'like sales targets'. As it currently stands, only 11 per cent of rape allegations end in a conviction, and the Met are under increasing pressure to improve this figure. The Met have revealed that there has been a dramatic rise in the recording of rape allegations, which has gone up by 60 per cent in the past four years.

• • •

In August 2017, Jemma Beale was jailed for ten years after having made a series of false rape claims. She alleged that she had been seriously sexually assaulted by six men and raped by nine, all strangers, in four different incidents over three years. The judge, Nicholas Loraine-Smith, described her life as a 'construct of bogus victimhood'. 'These false allegations of rape, false allegations which will inevitably be widely publicised, are likely to have the perverse impact of increasing the likelihood of guilty men going free,' he said. 'Cases such as this bring a real risk that a woman who has been raped or sexually assaulted may not complain to the police for fear of not being believed.'

Writing about the case, *Guardian* journalist Zoe Williams said it was 'a well-documented nightmare to bring a charge of rape', before asserting that to do so falsely was 'vanishingly rare' for that reason. She quoted the 2013 CPS study which found that there had been 5,651 prosecutions for rape but just thirty-five prosecutions for a false accusation – in other words, 0.6 per cent of all prosecutions involving rape were for false allegations.

Obviously, that figure did not include allegations of rape that failed to reach court. Many false allegations, if they come to light at all, are not deliberately false, and as such they do not constitute a chargeable offence.

The 2013 report found that a significant number of false allegation cases involved young and often vulnerable people. Around half of the cases involved people who were twenty-one or younger and a significant number suffered from problems with their mental health. It was the notion of a false allegation of rape or domestic violence made purely out of malice that was 'extremely rare'.

A 2005 Home Office study suggested that only 4 per cent of cases of sexual violence reported to the police were found or suspected to be false. A 2010 Ministry of Justice Evidence and Practice Review estimated that as many as 11 per cent of rape allegations could be false. The ministry noted that the overestimation by police and prosecutors, poor communication with complainants and limited understanding of the law all contributed to misconceptions about the number of false allegations. 'This means the view that false allegations of rape are common and/or are made by vengeful or desperate women cannot robustly be supported or denied,' it added.

Against that uncertain and unsatisfactory backdrop, some police officers have taken the view that false allegations are so scarce as to be negligible. Chief Constable Simon Bailey, who is in charge of the national initiative set up to share good practice between forces investigating historical abuse cases (Operation Hydrant), has said that 0.1 per cent of all complaints might be false. That was the figure he gave to Sir Richard Henriques, the judge appointed to the Operation Midland review.

Sir Richard said that the claim 'bore no relation' to his own judicial experience or to his experience during the review. 'I remain most concerned that the Hydrant team fail to appreciate the danger of false complaints and that a cardinal principle of the criminal justice system is that the complaint may be false.'

Why do people make false allegations? Perhaps, unsurprisingly, the reasons are varied and complex. Felicity Goodyear-Smith, a professor at the University of Auckland, has created a 'typology'.*

She has identified a number of individual 'motives and drivers'. Categories include 'self-serving false narratives of abuse' (e.g. seeking revenge against a former partner, as well as the desire for sympathy and attention); 'sincerely believed false allegations', where people persuade themselves that an

---

* In an essay for Dr Ros Burnett (ed.), *Wrongful Allegations of Sexual and Child Abuse* (Oxford: Oxford University Press, 2016).

incident they have imagined, heard, read about or seen on film actually happened to them; and 'partly true allegations', where details are embellished or else there are inaccuracies that are honest mistakes.

According to Professor Goodyear-Smith, it is wrong to attribute blame or responsibility solely to those who make false allegations. Allegations can be 'jointly constructed' with psychologists, victim support workers and the police who are 'on the lookout for signs of abuse, who recognise symptoms and jump to conclusions'. In this context, she highlights the dangers of suggestive interviewing techniques, particularly in relation to developing memories in children and young people.

• • •

Elgan Varney remains furious at the police and the CPS for their lack of impartiality in investigating the case. 'It collapsed because there was no evidence. I should never have been in court in the first place. Two years of my life have been ruined, my career prospects have been ruined, family and friends have suffered, and public money wasted,' he told me.

'I want to be clear how tragic Hannah's death was. As someone who only ever cared about her, I would like to send my sincere condolences to her family. I always treated Hannah in a respectful way,' he said. 'I know that I was not responsible for her death. I am completely innocent and should never have been in court in the first place.'

Steven was a friend of both young people and went to Stubbs's funeral. He wanted to make the following point: 'It is clear to me that Hannah was ill, and I have absolutely no doubts about Elgan's innocence. It's crazy that he was charged and put through hell, only for the CPS to admit their mistake at the eleventh hour. The whole thing is just so tragic for all concerned.'

Elgan Varney wants to get on with his life, as he should be allowed to. But, as he put it: 'You can't move forward when the fact that you have been accused is one click away on Google. Being cleared is not enough. Except in the most exceptional circumstances, there needs to be anonymity for anyone accused of rape while due process takes place.'

CHAPTER SEVEN

COLLATERAL DAMAGE

For months, Louise Long would sift through the mountain of documents on her living room floor. 'I would do the school run, come home and get the paperwork out,' she recalled. She was looking for new evidence to clear her husband's name. He had been accused of a series of sexual assaults, which were said to have taken place almost four decades ago. 'For weeks on end the kids weren't allowed to open the windows in the lounge because the papers were all over the carpet,' she said. 'They weren't allowed to touch anything.'

Geoffrey Long, a 67-year-old building and decorating contractor living on the south coast with his second wife Louise, was convicted of five sexual assaults in October 2010. He spent twenty months in prison as a result of allegations made by his daughter from his first marriage. In June 2012, the Court of Appeal quashed his conviction. But he did not walk out a free man. A fresh trial was ordered.

In January 2015, a second trial at Lewes Crown Court collapsed after his daughter's erratic testimony cast serious doubt on the reliability of her previous account. This was the second attempt at a retrial – the first collapsed in February 2014, after it was revealed that the main prosecution witnesses had been recording the trial.

This all happened despite the fact that Long's son from his first marriage, previously a prosecution witness, had gone to the police in 2012 to report his sister's admission that she had made the claims up.

I first met the couple shortly after the collapse of the trial. Just before, Geoff Long had been accused of being 'a paedophile' and asked to leave the house of a prospective new client in Brighton. The two men knew each other. They had played together in a golfing tournament years ago. 'I'll never be totally free of it. The stigma follows you,' Long told me. 'When you get to the age of sixty-seven, you haven't enough years ahead of you to feel normal again.'

• • •

It was obvious that the allegations made against him were false back in 2012, solicitor Mark Newby told me. 'That the Crown stuck doggedly to a case – there was not one but two attempts at a retrial – is not only a scandalous waste of money but, even more alarming, reveals a credulous approach to self-evidently flawed evidence. It always was a nothing case. What was the prosecution thinking?'

A loving couple, both have resolved to put a deeply traumatic experience behind them as best they can. However, they disagreed on the wisdom of talking to the press. Geoff Long did not want to add more misery to an already wretched situation. His wife felt that they had no reason to be ashamed, and were also under a duty to help people who had been through similar experiences.

'As a society, we accept there are miscarriages of justice and that there has to be collateral damage,' Long told me as soon we sat down. 'For every eight people who get sent to prison in relation to these types of allegations, two might be innocent. They're the collateral damage.'

Fortunately for him, Louise Long had not been prepared to let her husband be written off. 'There are people out there who are in the same boat as us. It's important that they know that they can fight back – and win,' she said. Her husband cut in: 'Look, what you did was fantastic and resulted in me being a free man.' In his view, in the majority of cases, the convicted partner would be abandoned by their other half. 'So what's the point?' he asked. 'If everyone thought the way you did,' he chided his wife.

After the initial meeting, I didn't hear from the couple for several weeks. I assumed that that was it. The couple only agreed to speak on the record after Long was accused by his would-be client of being a paedophile.

• • •

Most sexual abuse happens in secret. There are no witnesses and, in the case of historical allegations, no physical evidence. As a consequence, all too often abusers are never brought to justice and victims are forced to live with the burden of their trauma for the rest of their lives.

But a false historical abuse allegation can also ruin lives. The absence of corroborating witnesses and evidence may seem like an insurmountable hurdle for crimes that are supposed to be proved 'beyond reasonable doubt', yet what Geoff Long experienced suggests otherwise.

In October 2010, Geoff Long was sent to jail for five years. He was convicted on five charges of sexual assault but acquitted of rape. 'I was just numb,' Long recalled. 'In the lead-up to the trial, the barristers told me the case was a total farce and would immediately be seen as such by the jury. When I left my son in the morning, I told him I would see him later.'

As it turned out, Long did not see his four-year-old son James for a year. Louise watched her husband and the father of their child as he was led down from the dock to the cell beneath the court. 'All I could hear was her family behind me cheering,' she said. 'I just sat there staring at where he was standing. It was horrible. I waited for everyone to leave the courtroom and then went home.'

Before leaving for prison, his barrister told him there was no chance of an appeal: 'If you're found guilty by a jury, that's it.' His first night behind bars at HMP Lewes was horrific. Following a recent heart attack, Long had had a stent fitted in his upper thigh to regulate the flow of blood to his heart. 'I thought about taking the plug out – lying there, quietly bleeding to death,' he said. 'If I could have ended it, I would have. I did try, but obviously not hard enough.'

The following day he was visited in his cell by a prison listener, a fellow inmate assigned to help vulnerable prisoners. Long broke down and burst into 'unstoppable' floods of tears. He told the prisoner that he had been convicted of abusing his own daughter. He did not get sympathy. Instead, Long was offered practical and realistic advice: 'Whatever you do, don't tell anyone what you're in for – or you're dead.'

• • •

Our jails are filling up with men of pensionable age convicted of offences allegedly committed decades earlier. The over-sixties are the fastest growing section of the prison population. There has been a 125 per cent increase in the decade up to 2015 according to the Prisons and Probation Ombudsman, Nigel Newcomen. Of the 234 over-eighties held in prison in 2017, 204 had been convicted of sex offences.

Prison is bad enough for genuine criminals. For those who are innocent, prison is a place of extreme torment. Those who are convicted sex offenders or 'nonces' are prime targets for violent attacks. Those wrongly accused of sexual offences might well share the revulsion felt for sex offenders – the difference is that every day they are reminded that the justice system considers them to be someone capable of such abuse.

Geoff Long was brought up on a housing estate in Moulsecoomb, Brighton. He describes himself as streetwise. 'I was the eldest of ten children brought up on a very tough estate,' he said. 'But it was a strict upbringing and there was discipline. I was brought up to respect the police.'

He described his time in prison as 'horrendous'. After two months in Lewes, he was moved to HMP Maidstone for the remainder of his sentence, but he still insists that he got the better deal. 'Louise was out there in the world taking all the flak because of me. When she came for her first prison visit I told her there was no way out for me and the best thing she could do was sell the house, downsize and apply for a divorce.'

A year after Long was convicted and sent to prison, his

daughter sold her story to *Chat* magazine, which ran the headline: 'PAEDO DAD CREPT INTO MY BED' on its cover.

Louise Long recalls other parents spitting on her as she dropped James off at school. On one occasion, she was physically attacked. She was sitting in her car with her seatbelt on when another mother came over, punched her in the face and keyed her car. James, who was only seven years old, was sitting behind her in the backseat. Apparently the mother had flown into a rage when her daughter told her that James had asked if she wanted to play with him. 'To be honest, I understand her response but I had to press charges,' she said. Her attacker received a two-year suspended sentence.

• • •

'You are free to go. I am very sorry.' With these words, Lord Justice Leveson quashed the conviction of David Bryant in the Court of Appeal in July 2016. A former fireman of seemingly impeccable character, he had been accused of abusing a boy four decades earlier. The boy's name was Danny Day.

Danny Day went to the police in 2012 shortly after ITV's Savile exposé. As a fourteen-year-old, Day had worked at the British Legion in Christchurch, Dorchester, where the firemen used to drink. He claimed that Bryant and a colleague, Dennis Goodman (who has since passed away), invited him back to the fire station to play darts. Day went back with the men and nothing untoward happened. But he explained that the second time he was at the station they were more 'hands-on'. On the third occasion, Day alleged that he was subjected to a horrific rape. He stated that he had been 'held down over a table by the pair, who then took it in turns to rape him while having sex with each other'. Day was left screaming with pain. Goodman then apparently chucked some money at Day and asked if he would like to come back.

Danny Day did not report the attack at the time but claimed that he had confided in an old school friend called Chris White. Day only went to the police with his story after returning to the area in 2012 and discovering that Bryant had become a respected member of the community. He pushed a note through Bryant's letterbox:

> Dave, its Danny Day. 35 yrs [sic] ago I used to collect the glasses in the Legion and I am the same one that you ... played darts with in the fire station (remember!) At 6 o'clock tonight, I am going to the police station to report what went on and at 7 to the national papers. I think it is time you and me had a chat. One way or another you will pay for what you done [sic].

The retired firefighter told the court Danny Day had not crossed his mind since the mid-1970s. The court had received more than thirty letters from friends, family and former colleagues of the ex-fireman attesting to his good character. At the trial, a witness explained that Danny Day's description of the fire station, while consistent with the modern station, was different from how the building looked at the time of the alleged attack. Nor, it was argued, would it have been possible for other firefighters to have ignored an attack that involved twenty minutes of screaming.

Danny Day waived his right to anonymity to talk to the

press. 'I don't think justice has yet been fully served in this case,' he told the *Bournemouth Daily Echo* after Bryant was sentenced to six years. Bryant's upstanding position in the community had been a cunning cover for his crimes, Day argued. 'It is as though because he has led an unblemished life since then that somehow makes up for it,' he said. 'But I do still want to encourage anybody who has experienced this sort of thing to come forward. It can't be left alone.'

Bryant's application for an appeal was dismissed by a single judge. Day offered his thoughts to the *Echo*, noting with apparent pleasure that his abuser 'didn't even get past the first hurdle'. 'The first judge looked at it and dismissed it,' he said. 'I don't know how he got that far to be honest, he's in the place he should be in.' As a result of an appeal by Day, the sentence was increased from six to eight and a half years.

Danny Day was awarded £12,000 from the Criminal Injuries Compensation Scheme. He then launched a £200,000 damages claim against Bryant and Dorset County Council.

That civil claim ended up on barrister Rupert Butler's desk. A clerk at his chambers, 3 Hare Court, asked Butler to draft a defence to the claim as a favour to keep sweet a firm of solicitors that was new to chambers. Butler, a commercial barrister, reluctantly agreed to take a look.

'I took the papers thinking: "Crikey, there really is not a defence as it has been through a jury trial to the criminal standard of proof,"' he recollected. Then the barrister began to read the medical reports attached to the particulars of the claim, including a report by a psychiatrist that Danny Day's solicitors had instructed. He could not believe what he read.

Giving judgment, Mr Justice Singh summarised the evidence: '[Over] a period dating from 2000 to 2010, Day had to seek medical attention from his GP in relation to what can only be described as his being a chronic liar.' On 17 August 2010, Danny Day was referred by his GP to mental health services with a letter noting that he had 'a history of lying and cheating and that it was suspected he has an underlying personality disorder'. According to the medical records, Day said that his psychological problems came from several sources, one being his poor relationship with his parents. He never mentioned being raped.

Danny Day claimed he had to forsake his place on the British boxing team at the 1984 Los Angeles Olympics because of the trauma the assault caused him. In the unused material from the original trial, there were two statements: one was from Nick Gregory, said to be a former England boxing coach, who wrote about Day's boxing career and his selection for the Olympic Games in 1984; another came from Day's partner and described his boxing achievements – Day had apparently won fifty-seven out of sixty-one bouts, a better record than the legendary Muhammad Ali (who also fought sixty-one bouts but only managed to win fifty-six).

While in prison, David Bryant happened to be on the same wing as Chris White, the old school friend that Danny Day claimed to have confided in. White told Bryant that he had not been friends with Day, nor had he been told of any abuse.

• • •

Barrister Rupert Butler had not done personal injury work for years until this case. He now represents the estate of the late

Labour peer Lord Janner, whose life was dogged by allegations of child sexual abuse.

As soon as he read Danny Day's claim form, the barrister was suspicious. 'Instinctively, I thought, "How on earth could a jury buy this story?" It just sounded like a load of cobblers,' he told me. The medical report convinced Butler that Day was a compulsive liar. 'I did not understand the dynamics of the way these things work. I understand them better now. After a while, compulsive liars become very good at lying.'

The fact that an accuser is a compulsive liar does not necessarily mark them out as easy to discredit. In fact, Butler reckons that compulsive liars can make pretty formidable opponents in court. 'As a defendant, you have very little ammunition to challenge that person because your case is: "I scarcely knew this person. It wasn't me. I wasn't there."' The narrative goes almost entirely unchallenged unless there are internal inconsistencies. 'But then the compulsive liar can shrug their shoulders and blame it on the passage of time,' Butler continued. 'Furthermore, they become plausible in their mistakes because they believe the narrative themselves. By the time they stand up and tell the courts, it is in their own minds a fact.'

Butler has met Danny Day. He has, if not sympathy, then pity for the man who has wreaked such damage.

> I have said to David Bryant and his supporters, you might have a strong negative view about Danny Day, but give him credit for the fact that he is the only person I have ever heard of who went to a doctor and said: 'I am a liar.' Imagine how different the world would be if politicians did that. People don't tend to admit

dishonesty as a medical failing; Day recognised that he had a personality disorder and wanted help. He threw himself on the mercy of doctors who did not or could not help him.

Butler believes that Day's accusation was not motivated by a hatred of Bryant and Greenway, but was instead an attempt to win over a psychiatric nurse with whom Day was besotted. According to Butler, Day is a man 'who has not been loved in his life' and who 'goes to extreme measures in order to get attention'. Butler does not believe that Day had any malicious intent against Bryant, nor was he driven by the possibility of compensation.

'Our system of justice is incompetent at dealing with these cases,' Butler told me. 'It is unfair to ask a jury to unravel the complexities of Danny Day's psychological make-up. We have got to get better at dealing with these cases and one way to do that is for the police not to believe complainants when they walk through the door.'

> I have discussed this with Danny Day. We both agree that he was as much let down by the police as David Bryant was. Danny should never have been allowed to go into the witness box. Dorset Police let him down horribly, the CPS has let him down horribly and the criminal justice system has let him down horribly, and now the civil justice system was doing the same. If somebody had got hold of the case in a sensible way at the start, no charges would have been brought.

• • •

It might seem impossible to imagine that a daughter could accuse a father of such terrible abuse unless there was some truth in those allegations.

For years there had been a growing rift between Geoff Long and his first wife and their children, following a bitter divorce. According to Long, his business success angered his first wife, who felt their children were losing out on his new-found prosperity. By the time Long and Louise married, the only contact he had with his first wife and daughter were abusive, late-night calls. In 2009, Long and Louise were about to set up a children's nursery. According to the couple, this was when – and, indeed, why – the allegations of abuse first surfaced. Long refused an application to admit his own eldest grandchild into the nursery. The couple reckon the first allegation was a vindictive attempt to close down the business.

His daughter went to Brighton Police's historical sexual abuse inquiry team to say that thirty years earlier, when she was just eight, she had been abused by her father.

As an act of malice, it was immediately effective. 'I had to sell the nursery,' Louise Long said. 'The childminding business which I had run for six years closed the day after the police came to arrest Geoff.' Then the allegations snowballed; rape was mentioned.

When Geoff Long visited the police station, his was accompanied by a local solicitor who specialised in conveyancing. His legal representative had no experience of criminal law. 'He just let me go on and on,' Long recalled. He readily conceded that he was not the perfect husband. He married too young and started a family before he was ready for the responsibility. He had a number of affairs. 'I'm the first to admit it, I was no angel,' he said. 'I didn't behave as well as I should.'

It just so happened that Long, a keen football fan, had a pretty good memory of his weekend activities in 1979, when it was claimed he was abusing his daughter. 'That was the year that Brighton got promoted to the old first division for the first time in their history,' he said.

He had followed his team across the country and his girlfriend at the time had been with him. Long was an open book with the two interviewing officers, pouring his life out, even including details about his affairs. 'If you are an innocent person, you think that you have nothing to be scared of,' he said.

The prosecution re-enacted that interview at his subsequent trial.

> One played my part, the other played the police officer and they went through the statement in front of the jury in which I said I had had two affairs. One resulted in me being divorced and having a child outside my marriage. It made me look like a devious person. The prosecution turned to the jury and said: 'How can you believe this man who is an obvious liar?'

• • •

Despite having no income and a husband in prison, Louise Long was not entitled to legal aid because she had equity in their property. Fewer than one in three people are now eligible for legal aid. She approached one of the very few solicitors who specialised in representing those accused of sexual abuse.

Mark Newby and his team at QualitySolicitors Jordans have been inundated with requests for help relating to historic sexual allegations. 'Some weeks requests come in every day. If we have a big win in the courts then we get swamped,' said Newby. The Savile revelations have caused 'a deluge', he told me, and there was 'little sign of common sense returning'.

Newby sent Louise Long a pamphlet explaining how to research for an appeal on her own. The solicitor, together with barrister Mark Barlow, from Garden Court North chambers, went on to represent Geoffrey Long at the Court of Appeal on a pro bono basis. Rupert Butler, together with his colleagues Peter Knox QC and Rachael Earle from 3 Hare Court, did the same for David Bryant.

The two wives, Louise Long and Lynn Bryant, did the digging themselves. Under a Freedom of Information Act request, which cost around £800, Louise Long managed to recover 3,600 pages of previously undisclosed evidence, including copies of the investigating officer's notebooks. She also spent £3,000 on getting hold of the original trial transcript. Both men's wives were convinced that the accusations levelled against their husbands were demonstrably untrue.

Long's daughter had always alleged that her father would wash himself and her in a sink in the bedroom after the attacks. According to Louise Long, there was no sink in the bedroom where she claimed the attacks had occurred. And another inconsistency soon emerged: the bingo hall where Long's first wife claimed to have been when he was supposedly abusing their daughter had closed decades before the alleged assaults.

Similarly, Lynn Bryant found that the police had been

working off old plans of the fire station; however, the actual layout at the time of the alleged incident did not match Day's evidence.

Ahead of the 2013 trial at which David Bryant was convicted, his wife discovered that the pool table upon which Day claimed he was pinned down and raped was actually purchased years after the alleged attacks in 1992.

In October 2012, Geoffrey Long's son told the police that his sister had drunkenly confided in him that she had fabricated all the allegations. Instead of investigating the claim, the police prosecuted the son for attempting to pervert the course of justice. In January 2015, the Crown Prosecution Service dropped charges against the son.

When the second retrial collapsed, the CPS issued a statement. They explained that the evidence in the retrial was 'inconsistent with that in the original trial, and the prosecution case was therefore fatally undermined'. 'This could not have been foreseen and as soon as this became apparent, the CPS offered no evidence,' it said.

A spokesman for Sussex Police confirmed that there had been 'no request or suggestion' that there should be any re-investigation and that there were 'no grounds for carrying one out'.

'I do not want to see anyone else going to prison now,' Geoffrey Long told me. 'I worked my feelings of revenge out when I was in prison. Obviously, I felt very angry then. You have to work through the anger. It happened, you cannot change it. We aren't over this by any means, but we are still together and getting on with our lives.'

Only six months after David Bryant's conviction was overturned, his wife tragically passed away. Her immune system had not been able to fight off an infection and sepsis had set in. Bryant was convinced that the traumatic experience had killed her. 'You couldn't prove it, but it stands to reason,' he said.

Alex and Simon Stanley have known David and Lynn Bryant since the 1980s. Simon worked alongside David as a firefighter and was best man at Lynn and David's wedding. 'Nobody believed the allegations. We just couldn't make the police see that. They just didn't investigate it – they didn't bother. They didn't want to know. That was what got to Lynn the most,' Alex told me.

The couple supported Lynn throughout her campaign and visited David in prison. On what happened to be Alex and Simon's twenty-fifth wedding anniversary, the four of them were at the Court of Appeal, where David's conviction was finally overturned.

The anger, Alex said, 'ate away' at Lynn. 'I lost my mum in 2010. That feeling of hopelessness is what it was like,' Alex told me. 'You can't turn to anyone for help. Nobody wants to help. He had been found guilty and you can't do a thing about it. Normally, you can pick up a phone, write a letter, find a way out – but this was like losing somebody.'

She described the phone call from barrister Rupert Butler offering pro bono help as being like 'a tidal wave'. 'We thought: "Oh my God, at last, somebody believes in us." But how could he see it for what it was so easily, and yet the police couldn't? I don't get it.'

She describes Lynn Bryant as force of nature. 'She would always be on at Rupert. She wouldn't let anything drop and if someone wasn't doing what they should, she would tell them. She said, "I am not stopping until he's out of prison and his name is cleared." That's what we have done.'

Geoffrey Long's formidable wife, Louise, is determined to look on the bright side of their ordeal. 'I am just glad I found the strength to carry on and find the evidence to prove Geoff's innocence,' she said. 'Life really can get better – no matter how bad it seems at the time, or what people throw at you.'

CHAPTER EIGHT

A MEDICAL DIAGNOSIS OF MURDER

Carla Andrews and Craig Stillwell, like many first-time parents, spent the initial weeks of their new baby's life veering between feelings of joy and terror. The first time they felt something might not be right with Effie was when she was four weeks old. 'We would give her a bottle and the whole thing would come straight back up,' recalled 24-year-old Andrews. 'She would sleep all day, every day.'

Their doctor explained that Effie's sensitive stomach was most likely caused by acid reflux. He suggested the couple stock up on Gaviscon, which would help to settle her stomach, but the vomiting continued. Andrews and Stillwell were so anxious that they would regularly ring the GP's out-of-hours line. They were told that it was most likely a case of overfeeding, and were advised to try feeding Effie less. Despite their best efforts, Effie's condition did not improve, and they found themselves making regular visits to Stoke Mandeville Hospital in Aylesbury, Buckinghamshire.

In the early hours of 15 August 2016, when she was just three months old, Effie suffered her first seizure. Andrews and

Stillwell were housesitting for his father; the couple were asleep on the floor, with their daughter resting in a wicker Moses basket beside them. When they checked on Effie, they found that her face was drained of colour and her body floppy; Effie's eyes weren't moving and she was gasping for air. It was a terrifying experience for the young couple.

The parents rushed their daughter to a nearby hospital. They arrived there at 3.50 a.m. and Effie was taken straight to the resuscitation ward. Shortly afterwards, a scan picked up on a brain bleed. 'We didn't really know what that meant,' Andrews said.

With doctors unable to identify a natural cause for the seizure, the couple were informed that social workers had been called. But Andrews and Stillwell were both so alarmed by Effie's vulnerable state that they didn't think too much about the implications of this news. After a few hours, Effie was moved to the children's ward. 'Doctors kept walking past and looking at us. They just held us there,' recalled Stillwell, also twenty-four years old.

The young couple were busy soothing Effie, when a man and a woman walked into the room. They thought that the pair were from social services, but they were actually officers from Thames Valley Police. The couple were told their daughter had suffered a 'non-accidental injury'. 'As soon as we understood that they thought Effie had been vigorously shaken, we completely broke down,' recounted Stillwell. The police officers explained to the young parents that they could proceed in one of two ways: either they went to the police station voluntarily, or they could refuse and be arrested. 'I just wanted to be by Effie's bedside,' her father recalled. 'I told them I wasn't going anywhere. As I moved towards my daughter, the officer jumped me.'

Stillwell was pinned to the floor by the policeman, as two of the officer's colleagues ran into the room. His left hand was handcuffed. When he refused to surrender his other hand, one of the police officers forced a baton under his armpit. The 24-year-old, who had never previously been in trouble with the police, volunteered to leave peacefully, without handcuffs, but the police did not give him this choice. 'I have never been arrested before,' he said. 'I was scared and upset because of what happened to my daughter, and also because I was being accused of hurting her.'

• • •

Mainstream medical orthodoxy holds that a combination of symptoms known as 'the triad'– swelling of the brain, bleeding between the skull and brain, and bleeding in the retina – indicates trauma through shaking. This is better known as Shaken Baby Syndrome.

In a 2009 paper for the *Washington University Law Review*, Professor Deborah Tuerkheimer said that the symptoms in their classic formulation were as close to 'a medical diagnosis of murder' as it was possible to imagine. 'Prosecutors use it to prove the mechanism of death, the intent to harm and the identity of the killer,' she wrote.

It is not known how often Shaken Baby Syndrome is cited in our courts, but according to an investigation by the BBC's *Panorama* team, who aired an episode of the show titled 'Shaken

Babies: What's the Truth?', there were more than 100 cases in 2016. Dr Waney Squier, one of the few experts prepared to question the existence of Shaken Baby Syndrome in court, reckons that there might be as many as 250 such cases each year. The triad is invoked in courts in Sweden, France, Australia, New Zealand, as well as in the US and UK. Critics of Shaken Baby Syndrome argue that there is no science to support the notion that it is conclusive of abuse.

In 2017, SBU, a Swedish agency tasked by the government to make independent health technology assessments, published a review of over 3,700 research papers into the triad, and found only two of them were of 'moderate quality'. The 'methodological flaws which characterise this field of research' troubled the study's authors, who noted that features of the scientific literature included 'circular reasoning and inadequate presentation of data collection'.

Niels Lynöe, who led the review and who is a senior professor at Stockholm's Karolinska Institute, said in the *New Scientist*: 'You can't use these studies to say that, whenever you see these changes in the infant brain, the infant has been shaken – it's not possible according to current knowledge.'

In her 2009 paper, Professor Tuerkheimer, formerly a prosecutor in the Manhattan District Attorney's office, argued that scientific thinking now accepted that the symptoms of abuse might well have natural causes. But, she argued, the courts had not caught up with the science and the result was 'a criminal justice crisis'. Tuerkheimer has since said that there could be more than 1,000 innocent people imprisoned in the US after being convicted of wilfully harming their babies.

In 2006, the UK's Attorney General, Lord Peter Goldsmith, conducted a seven-month review of eighty-eight cases relating to Shaken Baby Syndrome. In his view, just three of those convictions needed to be looked at again by the courts. In her 2009 paper, Professor Tuerkheimer was sceptical about the UK review, noting that admissions by defendants were treated as corroborative of the diagnosis. The UK's Crown Prosecution Service, in its 2011 guidance, dropped the Shaken Baby Syndrome tag because of the emotive connotations, and noted that it did not adequately describe the range of causes of head injuries. According to the 2011 guidance, the mere presence of the triad would no longer be considered enough to show that a dead infant had suffered Shaken Baby Syndrome.

Dr Geoff Debelle, a consultant paediatrician at Birmingham Children's Hospital, reckons the most recent study points to about twenty-four such cases per 100,000 live births. 'So not many, thankfully,' he told me. 'That said, there are three cases in the paediatric intensive care unit in my hospital now. We get about one a month.'

The doctor argues that a major preventative public health programme is needed for new parents. 'There does seem to be a reaction to infants persistently crying: where you pick up a child, they still cry and then you lose it. It is tragic.'

Dr Debelle, who is the Royal College of Paediatricians and Child Health's child protection officer, was unimpressed by the Swedish report ('very poor methodology'). The college is working on its own peer-reviewed response. Dr Debelle takes exception to those medical expert witnesses who go to court and argue that doctors make a simplistic judgement: 'a collapsed infant with haemorrhages equals shaken baby'. 'We say trauma has to be close to the top [of probable causes],' he says. 'These things don't happen of themselves. Infants don't suddenly develop these conditions. There must be some cause or reason.'

'So-called experts use highly selective evidence,' Dr Debelle continued, adding that he was not specifically talking about Dr Waney Squier. 'She is a pathologist of repute, there is no doubt about that, but I don't think she has ever seen a live child and how they present at hospital.'

• • •

The couple had arrived at Stoke Mandeville Hospital at 3.50 a.m. on 15 August 2016, with a desperately ill child. Twelve hours later, they were in a police station accused of abusing that child. As they were being interviewed, their daughter was unresponsive and struggling to breathe.

They were held in the police station for nine hours and interviewed separately for about three hours each. 'The officers kept repeating questions, but wording them in a slightly different way. Sometimes when I answered, they would make a little smirk as if I was lying,' Carla Andrews said.

According to Craig Stillwell, it was 'a case of guilty until proven innocent'.

They asked Carla if she thought I would do it and they asked me the same question: 'Do you think Carla would do it?' They tried to suggest Carla did it because she had suffered from depression. Because of my outburst, as they put it, they asked me about my aggression. I'm not aggressive. They took my child away from me.

The couple left Aylesbury Police Station at 11.50 p.m. Stillwell was released on bail on the condition that he could only see his daughter under supervision. The following day, social workers paid a visit to his mother's house. They wanted the couple to sign an emergency protection order, giving the local authority parental responsibility for Effie. One of the social workers kept calling their daughter 'Ellie'. Eventually, Stillwell's mother threw the social worker out.

Two days later, Andrews and Stillwell were in court. Meanwhile, their daughter fought to stay alive. Effie's health deteriorated and she suffered two more seizures on 17 August.

After the emergency protection order had been signed, the judge allowed Carla Andrews to see her daughter – but Stillwell had to be subjected to a risk assessment. That took a week. Andrews remembers the judge being 'quite nice'. Lawyers for Buckinghamshire County Council had argued that Stillwell had acted aggressively in the hospital, but the judge said any parent would have behaved that way given the circumstances.

The couple were then allowed supervised contact, three days a week, for an hour and a half each day. They were summoned to Stoke Mandeville Hospital for a meeting when Effie was being discharged into care, and watched as the foster carers visited their daughter. But they were not allowed to visit Effie themselves. 'We had to walk past the room where she was. We weren't even allowed to look in the window to see if she was OK,' Stillwell said.

In Effie's case, tests for the rare genetic condition Ehlers-Danlos syndrome (EDS) revealed that she suffered from Type IV, which can cause easy bruising and spontaneous bleeds on the brain.

The court recorded that Effie was assessed and 'a definite pathological mutation' was found. She had a collagen deficit, which impacted on the formation of all tissue, particularly the arteries and veins. 'It is characterised by thin and translucent skin, easy bruising, vascular and arterial rupture which may occur spontaneously,' the court noted. It was the first time a case of EDS Type IV had featured in court. After the condition was identified, the local authority withdrew their application. Proceedings at Milton Keynes Family Court ended on 26 April 2017.

It took nine months from Effie's seizure for the application to be withdrawn. In the meantime, Judge Karen Venables acknowledged that the couple had been forced to endure 'unimaginable horror'. The judge noted that Craig Stillwell and Carla Andrews had 'always conducted themselves with extraordinary dignity' at each hearing.

The court had access to the couple's texts and WhatsApp messages. There was, Judge Venables recorded, nothing of concern in their private exchanges. Instead, the correspondence showed Effie to be 'a much-loved and much-wanted baby', and that the parents were 'delighted with the birth ... bonded well with Effie [and] there have been many happy times'.

Unbeknownst to the couple, the judge had also seen a photo album prepared by Carla Andrews. On its back page was written the message:

It's December 24th 10:15pm Xmas eve. I'm ready for bed, but

as I write this I am dreading Christmas tomorrow, because our baby won't be here. I am missing you Effie ... we all are. Me + daddy promise to have you home soon. We love you, always have. Always will xxx

• • •

When hospital staff suspect abuse, they understandably act quickly. In the wake of social care disasters like Baby P – the seventeen-month-old boy who died in London in 2007 after suffering more than fifty injuries over an eight-month period – doctors and social workers feel duty-bound to be vigilant. In 2005, the House of Lords ruled that child protection professionals owe a duty of care to the child – not the parents. In other words, parents who have been wrongly accused of harming their children cannot sue doctors (or social workers) for any negligence in carrying out investigations into child abuse.

As Effie lay in hospital, neither parent was allowed onto the ward for a week. According to William Bache, the veteran lawyer who represented Carla Andrews, a nurse will quickly take the view that they are dealing with child abusers. 'They're judge and jury, and executioner, all in one. They immediately start to treat the parents like lepers.'

Bache has been a solicitor in Salisbury for most of his fifty-year legal career. He was deputy corner for Swindon and Wilshire for twenty years and represented Angela Cannings, who in 2002 was wrongfully convicted of smothering her two baby sons.

Controversial paediatrician Sir Roy Meadow gave evidence

against Cannings, but it was later ruled that her babies had probably died as a result of a genetic disorder. The former head of the Royal College of Paediatrics was later struck off by the General Medical Council, in 2005, after giving misleading evidence at the 'cot death' trial of solicitor Sally Clark. Clark was jailed in 1999 after the deaths of her two infant children, but she was freed in 2003. Sir Roy had claimed the chance of two children dying naturally in such circumstances was 73 million to one – a claim the Royal Statistical Society disproved. Sally Clark never recovered from her ordeal and died at the age of forty-three, three years after being released.

William Bache has acted in a large number of sudden infant death cases, including approximately twenty-five Shaken Baby Syndrome cases. He has been 'around the legal block' very many times, as he put it when I spoke to him. 'You get a sense, when you are talking to people, whether they are telling you the truth or not,' he told me.

The lawyer believes that sudden infant death cases are in a category of their own. As he put it to me, when talking about accused parents: 'Their innocence seems to me to be absolutely obvious. It just shines through. I am quite convinced that they have not done the things that they are accused of doing.'

In one respect, Effie's parents were lucky. She had a particular form of Ehlers-Danlos Syndrome that was, according to Bache, 'clearly established' from a genetic screening. However, in most cases things will not be so clear-cut. Dr Geoff Debelle said it was 'a good judgement – but whether it was the right judgement is a moot point'. The condition is extremely rare and mostly present in adults, he added.

William Bache sees a close consonance between the symptoms described by different people from different walks of life in different situations. 'If one accepts what these people are saying is true, then there has been a death or a serious injury to a child, but the answer is not that it is as the result of abuse. The answer lies somewhere in a naturally occurring phenomenon which has caused it,' he said. 'I have regarded this as my duty to go and look for it.'

In terms of the science, Bache believes:

> We are in the same situation as Galileo when he said that the earth moved around the sun. And we all know what happened to him. It is precisely the same thinking. If you dare to come up with something that does not fit with the so-called mainstream medical thinking, then all sorts of very nasty things happen to you.

Bache divides schools of thought in the medical profession into two camps: the mainstreamers ('many of whom have vested interest in maintaining the status quo'); and the sceptics ('people I have a much greater respect for').

• • •

The highest-profile sceptic is probably the world-renowned neuropathologist Dr Waney Squier, formerly a consultant at John Radcliffe Hospital in Oxford. She is reckoned to have written reports and/or testified in more than 160 cases in Canada, Germany, Hong Kong, Iceland, Ireland, Israel, the Netherlands, New Zealand, Sweden, Switzerland, the UK and the US.

When Dr Squier first began giving expert evidence, she appeared for the prosecution and cited the triad as conclusive of abuse. 'I was just an ordinary day-to-day working neuropathologist who happened to be fascinated by the development of a child's brain,' Dr Squier told me. 'For thirty-four years, I studied the brains of babies who died either shortly after birth, or in childhood, or at the termination of pregnancy or miscarriage. I was totally enthralled by what was going on.'

Until about 2000, Dr Squier went along with what she had been told at medical school and read in textbooks. 'I don't know how many cases I have written reports on, saying this baby's brain is swollen, but because there are retinal haemorrhages and subdural haemorrhages, it was Shaken Baby Syndrome,' she said.

What changed her mind was a paper written by Dr Jennian Geddes, a neuropathologist colleague from London, who showed that the brain damage in babies alleged to have been shaken was not due to tearing of the nerve fibres of the brain, but to a lack of oxygen. This was a finding that was common in babies dying from many natural illnesses, and in babies who collapsed and died after being nursed on a ventilator. As a result of the Geddes research, Dr Squier went on to read everything she could about Shaken Baby Syndrome. She was startled to discover that there was, in her opinion, no scientific support for the Shaken Baby Syndrome hypothesis.

According to Dr Squier, some years later brain scans showed that almost half of normal babies had subdural haemorrhages and retinal haemorrhages. These features were also seen in young babies who were dying from a whole range of natural illnesses, including minor accidents and low falls.

So Dr Squier switched sides and began to give evidence for the defence. In the case of Lorraine Harris, Dr Squier originally provided a report arguing that Harris's baby had suffered injuries consistent with shaking – but then subsequently backed Harris's appeal.

On 4 December 1998, Lorraine Harris took her four-month-old baby, Patrick, for his third immunisation. Early in the hours of the following morning, she rang her GP because she was concerned about his breathing. The GP noted that Patrick's temperature was up, but his chest was clear, and, although snuffly, he appeared fine. The GP left the house at 1.30 a.m.

An hour later, Lorraine Harris rang 999 and said she could not wake up Patrick. An ambulance crew arrived at her home and tried to resuscitate Patrick, but the crew could not find any pulse. He was rushed to Derby children's hospital and placed on a life-support machine, but he died on 6 December. A post-mortem found swelling of the brain, small amounts of subdural haemorrhaging and extensive retinal haemorrhaging. Lorraine Harris was interviewed and charged with manslaughter.

On 7 September 2000, Lorraine Harris was convicted and sentenced to three years' imprisonment. After being advised by her original lawyers that they saw no grounds for an appeal, Harris's family approached solicitor Campbell Malone, who had acted for Stefan Kiszko and Eddie Gilfoyle. Her new legal team was able to cite the Geddes research and, as a result, her conviction and those of three other people was overturned in 2005.

It was a landmark ruling.

But it was too late for Lorraine Harris; her life had been ruined. Baby Patrick had died and been buried without his mother even being told. While on bail awaiting trial, she became pregnant and gave birth to another child in prison after her conviction. Meanwhile, Harris's relationship with Patrick's father collapsed. That child was taken from her and placed for adoption, and even after the appeal she was not allowed any contact. According to Dr Squier, the story of Lorraine Harris was no 'dystopian nightmare'. 'It is a story repeated day in, day out, all around the world,' she said.

• • •

In 2008, Suzanne Holdsworth was acquitted by the Court of Appeal of murder. She had been jailed for life three years earlier, after being found guilty of murdering two-year-old Kyle Fisher, who died from severe brain damage while in her care.

The prosecution alleged that Holdsworth had smashed Kyle's head against the banister at her home, with as much force as that caused by a 60 mph car crash. There was no forensic evidence, no blood or hair on the bannister. 'They didn't do a DNA test on the alleged murder weapon,' Holdsworth's partner, Lee Spencer, later told *Newsnight*'s John Sweeney. 'I'm no Sherlock Holmes – I drive a cement mixer – but what kind of investigation was that?'

Defence experts, including Dr Waney Squier, identified that Kyle had five separate brain disorders. 'That child obviously had multiple injuries. He had been to casualty so many times,' Dr Squier told me. 'Nobody took it seriously. We don't get these things right. We focus on this idea of shaking to such an extent that we miss all these obvious signs along the way. His mother demonstrated that she was not fit to look after him.'

Just one look at Kyle Fisher would have revealed that something was profoundly wrong. The baby had an obviously enlarged head and a drooping eye. Kyle allegedly fell from his pram onto a fire prong, which punctured one of his eye sockets and stabbed into his brain. This happened when he was in his mother's care.

Suzanne Holdsworth spent three years in Low Newton Prison, just outside Durham. I interviewed her, and her partner Lee Spencer, at their home in Leeds shortly after she was released. She was so traumatised by the prison experience that she could barely talk about it without breaking down. Lee, a bear of a man and devoted to her, told me she rarely left the house or even got dressed. It was a hot summer's day and we sat in their garden, which had what looked like an enormous paddling pool. 'When I got to prison, I didn't know what I was doing there,' she told me. 'Prison officers would come to me later saying: "Do you remember me? I saw you when you came in." They told me I was just oblivious to everything. All I was doing was sitting in a corner, crying.'

The depth of her trauma was shocking. The grim mood of the interview was only broken when Lee suddenly exclaimed: 'For God's sake…' and, gathering her up in one enormous scoop, threw her into the pool. It was the only time that Suzanne Holdsworth smiled.

A few weeks later, Holdsworth spoke at a meeting at the House of Commons. Sitting between Lee and her lawyer, Campbell Malone, she only managed to speak a few words. Barely audible between sobs, she talked of wanting to get into the car 'and just run it off a cliff'. 'I got sent away to jail for something I never did. I was taken away from my kids. I missed everything. No one has ever said sorry to me for that. That's all I want. It would make me feel better.'

• • •

On 13 September 2010, Detective Inspector Colin Welsh, then lead investigator with Scotland Yard's child abuse investigation team, addressed a conference in Atlanta, Georgia. His session was called 'A National Co-ordinated Approach to Cases of Non-Accidental Head Trauma in the UK'.

An American lawyer, Heather Kirkwood, who had worked with Dr Waney Squier, recognised Welsh's name, and attended his session, scribbling down notes as fast as she could. She was a former senior attorney at the Federal Trade Commission, who had worked on mergers and represented the US government in international meetings.

Kirkwood later signed an affidavit swearing that her notes were an accurate, although not verbatim, record of what was said. 'Shortly into the talk, I realised that the "national coordinated approach" referenced in the title of the talk was essentially a description of the joint efforts of New Scotland Yard, prosecution counsel, and prosecution medical experts to prevent Dr Squier and Dr [Marta] Cohen from testifying,' she wrote.

Welsh told delegates that the prosecution of shaken baby cases in the UK was now in 'dire straits' after the Geddes report. He blamed the downturn of successful convictions on the 'same handful of experts showing up at trial', whose role was to confuse the jury with the complexity of science. As a response,

Welsh told delegates, the police would 'question everything, qualifications, employment history, testimony, research papers presented by these experts, go to their bodies [illegible word] to see if we can turn up anything'.

In over thirty years of legal practice, Heather Kirkwood said, she had never attended a professional meeting like it. She claimed that much of the conference was devoted to 'personal attacks on academic researchers and defence experts'. 'These attacks included direct and indirect accusations of untruthfulness, accompanied by the videos of Pinocchio and singalongs to the same effect,' she said.

At the start of 2010, a colleague, a neurosurgeon in Oxford, warned Dr Squier that there was 'a movement to get you reported to the GMC'. 'I just thought: "Why?" All I was trying to do was the best I could as a scientist,' Dr Squier told me. She was receiving heavy criticism in the courts, including the Court of Appeal, for the Ben Butler case.* Butler had been jailed for nineteen months for assaulting his daughter, Ellie, in 2007, when she was seven weeks old. But the conviction was overturned in 2010 following a judge's assessment of new scientific research on Shaken Baby Syndrome.

In 2016, Butler was convicted of murdering Ellie after she

---

* In one case (*Re S* [2009] EWHC 2115), the court noted that she and Dr Marta Cohen were outside mainstream thinking. It considered a paper by Jennian Geddes (*Geddes III*) and argued that the triad could be caused by severe hypoxia (lack of oxygen in the tissues) which led to brain swelling. The judge quoted one consultant neuropathologist who said that there were 'forty to forty-four' neuropathologists in the UK, but only one believing that hypoxia could cause subdural haemorrhages (Squier). The view was shared by two or three other people working in different specialities, including Cohen. 'They come in all the defence cases, so you do not realise that they are in such a minority,' he said. Squier and Cohen were criticised for being 'disingenuous' and betraying a 'scientific prejudice'.

suffered injuries reported to be similar to those inflicted in a high-speed car accident. When lawyer William Bache said that the innocence of most parents in cases of sudden infant death 'shines through', he qualified his remark by saying that there were exceptions. Bache was thinking of the horrific Butler case.

In June 2010, barrister Michael Turner QC rang Dr Squier in her Oxford office and demanded to know why she had not told him she would be facing a General Medical Council hearing. That was the first Dr Squier had heard of the hearing. She later learned that a previous report had been made in April. The same year, Dr Squier was reported to the Human Tissue Authority for retaining human tissue, which, if true, was a criminal offence. The accusation was later revealed to be without foundation.

In April 2012, the BBC crime drama *Silent Witness* featured a two-part episode about a 'Dr Helen Karamides', a Shaken Baby Syndrome sceptic who made wrong diagnoses, became an alcoholic and took her own life. The character was investigated by the Human Tissue Authority for illegally harvesting dead infants' brains for research.

'It was clearly meant to be me,' Dr Squier told me. The doctor claimed to have been rung up by the BBC's pronunciation unit eighteen months earlier, to check her name and that of another Shaken Baby Syndrome sceptic, Dr Irene Scheimberg. Apparently, a character in *Silent Witness* was going to mention their two names, so as to avoid any inference that the fictional Dr Karamides was a representation of either doctor.

Dr Squier complained to the BBC, saying that the portrayal of Karamides was 'professionally damaging' and harmed her reputation, 'casting doubt on my integrity as well as reflecting badly on my profession as a whole'. The suicide of the main character was 'disturbing to me and my friends', Dr Squier said, and was 'extremely painful and distressing' to her daughters.

• • •

In March 2016, Dr Waney Squier, one of the few experts prepared to question the existence of Shaken Baby Syndrome in court, was banned from practising. In a determination by the Medical Practitioners Tribunal, the GMC's disciplinary arm, she was adjudged to have lied and misled the courts.

More than 250 doctors, academics and lawyers had urged the regulator to rethink its decision to strike off Squier. In an open letter to the *British Medical Journal*, the signatories, led by the paediatric pathologist Dr Irene Scheimberg, argued that 'the GMC's decision was depriving patients of Squier's "invaluable contribution" to developmental neuropathology'. In a letter to *The Guardian*, leading human rights lawyers, including Michael Mansfield and Clive Stafford Smith, accused the regulator of conducting itself like a '21st-century inquisition'.

Later that year, Dr Squier received a Champion of Justice award at the annual Innocence Network conference in San Antonio, Texas. 'Her influence has been felt around the world, as she has written reports and/or testified in more than 160 cases in Canada, Germany, Hong Kong, Iceland, Ireland, Israel, the Netherlands, New Zealand, Sweden, Switzerland, the United Kingdom and the United States,' read the citation. 'Her work had contributed to at least 19 exonerations in the United States.'

The GMC has insisted that the allegations it brought against Dr Squier were not about 'the validity of her scientific theory', but related to 'her competence and conduct in presenting her evidence to the courts'.

One very senior lawyer involved in the GMC's proceedings, Michael Birnbaum QC, was so moved by the perceived unfairness of the panel's slight five-page ruling that he wrote a sixty-six-page analysis. 'In my forty-three years of practice at the Bar, I have rarely read a judgment of an English court, or tribunal, so deeply flawed and unfair as this,' his analysis began.

Birnbaum described the judgment as being 'largely formulaic and frequently illogical'. He was not a disinterested party. Birnbaum had given evidence before the tribunal on behalf of Dr Squier; for his trouble, he had been described as being 'somewhat vague' and lacking 'some credibility'.

The distinguished QC took issue with the suggestion that he was dishonest, calling it 'outrageous', but he insisted that he was not motivated by personal criticism. 'Given this bizarre combination of the apparently one-sided and the obviously inept, I cannot make up my mind whether the tribunal was actually biased in the sense of being actively prejudiced against Dr Squier, or whether it was just not up to its task,' he wrote.

A number of distinguished experts who lined up to speak up for Squier were given short shrift by a three-member panel headed up by a former RAF wing commander, and supported by an ex-police officer and a dementia expert.

• • •

Eight months after being struck off, Dr Waney Squier had her licence reinstated; she was cleared of dishonesty, having successfully appealed. In November 2016, Mr Justice Mitting in the High Court found 'serious irregularity' on the part of the GMC's tribunal. But he also said that the GMC was entitled to find that Dr Squier had 'failed to work within the limits of her competence and to be objective and unbiased'.

The judge was highly critical of the tribunal's 'flawed proceedings' and deemed its finding that Dr Squier had committed perjury 'unjust'.

Mr Justice Mitting also noted that the tribunal was 'less favourably impressed' by the evidence of those supporting Dr Squier. In a letter to the tribunal chair, Judge David Pearl, Jennian Geddes, the only one of five medical experts to give evidence for Squier who was not criticised by the panel, described its dismissive treatment of the other witnesses as 'deplorable'. They were 'distinguished experts in their respective fields who have been gratuitously defamed', she wrote.

Mitting's ruling was a damning assessment of the competence of the GMC tribunal.* As a concluding observation, the judge noted that there was nothing in the GMC's rules to prevent a lawyer with judicial experience from being appointed to chair such a complex case. 'It would, in hindsight, have been better if that power had been exercised in this case,' he added.

Dr Waney Squier is still prevented from giving expert

---

* Mr Justice Mitting ruled a number of the tribunal's conclusions about the witnesses 'untenable' with the 'most egregious example' being their finding that Michael Birnbaum 'lacked some credibility'. 'There was no foundation for such a statement,' the judge said, adding that it was 'the first of a number of unsustainable findings of greater significance'.

evidence in court: the ban lasts for three years. 'It's an absolutely huge loss,' William Bache told me. 'Not only have we lost her, but we have lost other people who have been prepared to say the sort of things she does.'

• • •

The travails of Dr Waney Squier have been followed closely in the US, where she also appeared in the courts. An American journalist, Susan Goldsmith, made a film about the attempts to silence critics of the triad. In a letter to *The Guardian*, Goldsmith wrote that the GMC ruling 'sent a message to all who dare question this dogma: speak up and we will ruin your career. The world is watching.'

Goldsmith has won numerous awards for her campaigning journalism. Her reporting at the Portland daily newspaper, *The Oregonian*, resulted in Oregon's state legislature passing laws to protect children in foster care. 'My newspaper would not let me do the story. They said it was too controversial,' Goldsmith told me. Her film was self-funded.

Challenging the mainstream consensus on either side of the Atlantic is a risky business. 'Nobody will touch us with a ten-foot pole. We are radioactive,' Goldsmith said. Her film was turned down by a number of film festivals, including Sundance, after threats of legal action.

The journalist claims to have established a link between three physicians who pioneered Shaken Baby Syndrome and the mass hysteria that infected the US justice system with zero evidential base back in the 1980s. That saga began with the McMartin child abuse case.

The panic began with a single allegation of abuse by a mother, whose child attended the McMartin Preschool near Los Angeles in 1983, and led to hundreds of allegations of satanic abuse and the longest criminal case in US history. After six years of lurid, bizarre and false allegations – flying witches, baby sacrifices, children drinking blood etc. – all charges were dropped.

'Doctors were going into court, testifying that there was medical evidence of abuse, and a science was born to make that look credible,' Goldsmith said. 'They developed a literature and an entire scientific edifice for this bullshit which looked very credible.'

Goldsmith sees parallels between the way the two phenomena gained traction in the courts and beyond. The so-called satanic panic scare kicked off with the McMartin case. Similarly, Shaken Baby Syndrome staged its high-profile US 'debut' before the global media in the trial of Louise Woodward. In 1997, the British au pair was released by the trial judge despite her conviction for the involuntary manslaughter of eight-month-old Matthew Eappen in Massachusetts. Woodward had been charged with murdering Matthew.

In Shaken Baby Syndrome, Susan Goldsmith argued that they have created a much more seemingly robust literature for propping up the triad. 'They have created a fake science. The hysteria has convinced the courts and juries that it is a legitimate science.'

When I interviewed Goldsmith, I asked her if her documentary wasn't simply stoking an already overheated debate, and wasn't there a case for a more nuanced approach? 'I'm not saying you shouldn't be fair and balanced but, you know, up to a point,' she replied.

It is like covering satanic panic and saying: 'Well, there is something to be said about Satan and day-care centres'. There really was nothing there. Look, it might well be there are people who abuse their kids, who get away with it and say: 'It was a fall.' But in many, many of these cases, the courts have gotten innocent people. We have a big nightmare on our hands.

• • •

The evening before I spoke to Carla Andrews and Craig Stillwell, their daughter Effie had another fit. 'Every time it happens she has a seizure, it's scary. It is a panic. She has come around every time on her own,' Andrews told me. 'She has not had to have a doctor's intervention to bring her around, but it is still terrifying to watch because we know every seizure that she is having is damaging her brain.'

The previous week, the parents had been at a meeting at Stoke Mandeville Hospital, with staff including the doctor who had reported the couple to social services. The hospital staff have told them that Effie has an 'unlimited open door' to see doctors. 'We don't trust them. It feels like they're looking at us,' Stillwell said. Andrews added: 'It makes us feel paranoid.'

'The doctor who accused us was there. We asked her to be there. They did not apologise, or rather they apologised through a third party,' Stillwell said. 'I said to them: "Who knows their child better than a parent?" We took Effie in seventeen times, saying something was seriously wrong with our child, and all they checked was blood pressure and the heart rate. They would tell us she was fine and send us away.

Clearly, she was not fine, she had a seizure and she had a bleed on the brain.'

How would the couple describe Effie? 'Even though she has been through so much, she is bubbly. She always dances when she hears music and she laughs all the time. The problem with EDS is that the kids look well on the outside but the smallest knock can kill them.'

CHAPTER NINE

MAKING A MURDERER

Timothy Stubbs was admitted to Horton Green General Hospital, Banbury in Oxfordshire on the afternoon of Thursday 5 February 2004. The 42-year-old had been sufficiently fit to drive himself to the hospital but arrived complaining of abdominal pains. By 7.30 p.m., he was fighting for breath and put on a life support machine.

The anaesthetist on duty, Dr Kirsten May, was puzzled: how had his condition deteriorated so dramatically? It was only when two drugs were discovered in his urine that the penny dropped. Neither had been prescribed. Someone must have given Thomas Stubbs not one but two unauthorised injections.

It was the second time that day that a patient appeared to suffer an unexpected respiratory arrest shortly after arriving at the hospital. After Stubbs stopped breathing, physicians and anaesthetists at the hospital were instantly suspicious; staff had already noticed an unexplained spike in the need for patients requiring resuscitation that winter.

The following morning, a Friday, they reported their concerns to the director of the hospital and a serious incident investigation was immediately launched. A couple of doctors already had a theory; it seemed that staff nurse Ben Geen would always be present whenever a patient stopped breathing.

'Once Dr May told me about her suspicions it was like all the pieces of a jigsaw falling into place,' Dr Graham Walker was to say later. 'The last thing we as doctors expect is foul play, but once the genie was out of the bottle, it was clear that all these cases fitted a general pattern.'

When an ambulance arrived at A&E, more likely than not Ben Geen was there to greet it. As the only male nurse in A&E, the 25-year-old stood out. A lieutenant in the Territorial Army, he aspired to a career in the military and was considered by colleagues as being 'a bit gung-ho'.

Ben Geen lived in hospital digs with his girlfriend and fellow nurse, Megan Crabbe. The day after Thomas Stubbs was admitted, Geen called in sick. The hospital's management agreed that, with their suspect off duty now until Monday, the patients were safe. Senior staff called in doctors from nearby John Radcliffe Hospital in Oxford and they spent the weekend going through case notes. By the end of the weekend, the team identified eighteen patients as having suffered an unexplained respiratory arrest or hypoglycaemia or both. In all cases, one or more of the following symptoms were noted: the patient's breathing had become increasingly shallow, blood sugars had fallen rapidly, and some exhibited sounds similar to an opiate (drug) overdose.

They were all linked by a common factor. On each occasion Ben Geen had been on duty. Dr Walker recalled going into the weekend meeting hoping that he would leave it 'looking like a fool – like the boy who cried wolf'. 'It was very distressing to come out of it having reached the conclusion that foul play had gone on,' he said.

The doctors handed over the case notes of twenty-five patients who had been in the emergency department in a 64-day period between December 2003 and the end of the first week of February the following year to the police.

The following Monday, Ben Geen was arrested. As he arrived for his night shift, he was called into a meeting. He had a syringe in his pocket. In a panic, the nurse discharged its contents into the pocket of his fleece jacket.

• • •

On 10 May 2006, Ben Geen received a prison sentence of a minimum term of thirty-eight years. He was found guilty on two counts of murder and causing grievous bodily harm to fifteen other patients.

'It seems that you relished the excitement of that feeling of taking control, but you must have known quite well that you were playing with their lives,' Mr Justice Crane told Geen as he passed sentence. 'This was a terrible betrayal. You betrayed your nursing and medical colleagues and the vital profession of which you have been a member. Most of all you betrayed the trust of the patients. They were in your care and you intentionally caused them huge damage.'

To the press, Ben Geen became 'the nurse who killed for kicks'. The prosecutor Michael Austin-Smith QC accused him of treating patients as 'just bits of flesh' that provided him with the opportunity to practise his 'skills and satisfy your lust for excitement'. A team of forty detectives worked on the case. Detective Superintendent Andy Taylor of Thames Valley Police told one reporter that Geen was 'almost narcissistic' in his 'desperate desire to be noticed'.

One broadsheet talked of a 'perverse need' to be at the centre of the action on the busy A&E ward. 'Like an arsonist who sparks a blaze and is then transfixed as the firefighters arrive, Geen would make his patients collapse and then join the adrenalin-charged frenzy as doctors and nurses battled to save them,' it said.

Ben Geen had become an angel of death, a medic who abuses their position of trust for their own twisted pleasure. Six years earlier, a jury found Britain's most prolific serial killer, Harold Shipman, guilty of murdering fifteen patients in his care. The GP was sentenced to life imprisonment with the recommendation that he never be released. A year before Geen was sentenced, the Shipman inquiry's final report identified 218 victims and estimated that the GP could have killed 250 patients. It also concluded that Shipman's killing spree may have begun when he was as young as twenty-five. Weeks before Geen came under suspicion, Harold Shipman was found hanging in his cell.

The nurse Beverley Allitt was given thirteen life sentences in 1993 for murdering four children, attempting to murder another three and causing grievous bodily harm with intent to a further six at Grantham and Kesteven Hospital in Lincolnshire. Some of the nurses had already nicknamed Geen 'Bev Allitt'.

• • •

At Ben Geen's trial the prosecution alleged that eighteen patients stopped breathing, suffering unexplained respiratory arrests while he was on duty at Horton Green General Hospital between December 2003 and February 2004; two of whom died: Anthony Bateman, sixty-six, and David Onley, seventy-five. There was only evidence of drugs being administered in two of those eighteen cases, including the case of Timothy Stubbs (the muscle relaxant vecuronium and an anaesthetic midazolam).

At a three-month trial which began in February 2006, it was alleged that incidents of respiratory arrest in A&E were extremely rare and unheard of without a cause. The Crown's lawyers argued that 'an unusual pattern' had emerged.

The prosecutor, Michael Austin-Smith, called the syringe discovered in his fleece pocket the 'smoking gun'. When the lining of Ben Geen's jacket was analysed, it tested positive for vecuronium and midazolam. The syringe, it was said, was old and worn from repeated use. Ben Geen was caught red-handed: a serial killer.

• • •

Ben Geen is currently in HMP Long Lartin prison in Worcestershire. Barrister Mark McDonald is not only convinced that Ben Geen is an innocent man, he takes the view no crime was ever committed.

Before Mark McDonald came to the Bar at thirty-three years of age, he himself worked in A&E as an anaesthetist's assistant and for fourteen years worked in operating theatres before become a barrister.* He spent time at University Hospital Coventry and Birmingham Accident Hospital as well as the Queen Elizabeth, St Thomas, St Bartholomew and Hammersmith in London. 'I did Ben's job. I know all the drugs he administered. I know the language,' he said.

The barrister believes that senior hospital staff convinced themselves in the wake of the Shipman hysteria that there was 'a maniac on the loose' (as prosecutor Austin-Smith put it). He believes that the medics misread an innocent statistical blip as evidence of a serial killer. Once they decided on their suspect, the investigation became a self-fulfilling prophecy. They went through the suspect's case notes to identify evidence that supported their hypothesis and ignored the rest. Then they handed over 'the evidence' to the police.

Mark McDonald has an analogy for the way that the doctors conducted their investigation and unknowingly rigged the evidence. 'Imagine we are both looking at the side of a shed,' he told me.

> I say: 'I bet you £20 I can get ten bullets into the centre of a target from a distance of 200 yards using my machine gun.' You say: 'No way.' So, I fire my machine gun into the side of the shed releasing 100 bullets. They're all over the place. I walk up to the shed and draw a circle around ten of the bullets and place a target over it. That's effectively what they did. They selectively put the target round ten patients. That's why I say no crime is committed here.

---

* In 2007, Mark McDonald set up the London Innocence Project, a non-profit legal clinic, to investigate possible miscarriages of justice.

The argument that no crime had been committed was one that Geen's lawyers attempted to run before the Court of Appeal in November 2009. In a report prepared ahead of the appeal, a medical statistician, Professor Jane Hutton, wrote:

> The evidence of an unusual pattern of sudden collapses given in the summing up was of no value in supporting a conclusion that there was an unusual pattern, nor a conclusion that any unusual pattern was not a chance event. Opinions given by expert or other witnesses which are based on anecdotal evidence are very likely to be misleading.

Professor Hutton pointed out that, according to an external review, there were five incidents of respiratory arrest in December 2002 and six incidents the following year. All six incidents in 2003 were pinned on Ben Geen, who hadn't been working at the hospital in 2002. According to Professor Hutton, based on the five natural cases (i.e., where there is no sinister explanation) in December 2002, the probability of there being no natural cases in the same month the following year was less than 1 per cent.

The court refused to hear her evidence. 'We are satisfied the jury was entitled to, and perfectly capable of, drawing proper inferences from the evidence that this pattern of events was as a result of deliberate action rather than mere chance,' said Lady Justice Hallett, giving judgment.

In 2005, the year that Heather Hallett presided over the Omar Benguit case, Hallett became the fifth woman to join the Court of Appeal. The daughter of a policeman and a secretary, she had forged a stellar career in the law without the benefit of the privileged background of many of her peers. She graduated from grammar school in the New Forest, before going on to attend Oxford. Fiercely ambitious, she achieved her success at the Bar in the face of often unpleasant discrimination. 'When I was a young woman, there were men in every walk of life who believed they had the right to make sexual advances to anyone they chose,' she once said.*

In 2009, Lady Justice Hallett was selected to act as coroner in the inquest of the fifty-two victims of the 7/7 bombings. 'It was a textbook example of how it should be done. Victims' relatives thought she was great,' observed one lawyer who has followed her career. He was less impressed by her performance in the Court of Appeal. 'No one can remember a single groundbreaking judgment she has given,' he told me. 'Her judgments are timid and simple. She just finds reasons to back the trial judge.' She is like a machine, he said. 'The only test is "What would help the prosecution?" She would not be interested in considering the justice of a case.' Fair or not, Hallett gave short shrift to Ben Geen's lawyers.

However, the critical significance of a challenge to the prosecution's assertion that respiratory arrests were in fact rare only dawned on his lawyers at the last minute. Professor Jane Hutton had been called after another of their experts, a clinical physiologist, noted in passing that the evidence about 'unusual

---

* 'Horrific' was how Lady Justice Hallett described one particularly nasty incident in her early years at the Bar. 'I was offered a position about which I was proud and a senior male judge said: "Are you pleased to have got that particular position?" I said: "I'm thrilled", and he then made it plain how I could thank him,"' she recalled in an interview with the *Evening Standard* on 7 November 2011.

patterns' was 'clearly a statistical issue'. He commented that, without a proper statistical basis, opinion evidence was 'valueless and misleading'. Lady Justice Hallett had disagreed, saying that it was 'a straightforward argument of the kind often put before a jury' without the need for any input from statisticians.

• • •

Lucia de Berk, a paediatric nurse, was found guilty of seven murders and three attempted murders of children in her care at Juliana Children's Hospital in The Hague in 2003. She was reckoned to be the Netherlands' most prolific serial killer. At least she was until she was exonerated in 2010. Now her case is recognised as one of the country's gravest miscarriages of justice.

The court heard that more children died on her shifts than could possibly be explained away by coincidence. The odds of her having been present by chance was reckoned to be one in 342 million. The alleged murders and attempted murders were claimed to have taken place at three hospitals between 1997 and 2001. They came to light after police began investigating the death of a baby girl named Amber. Her conviction was based on two deaths, including that of Amber, which toxicology reports suggested could have been a result of poisoning.

Statistics drove the case from start to end, according to British-born statistician Richard Gill, emeritus professor of mathematical statistics at the University of Leiden in the Netherlands. Gill campaigned for de Berk's conviction to be overturned. 'Why do we know beyond reasonable doubt that Lucia is innocent? Because an independent multidisciplinary scientific team of medical specialists, toxicologists were finally allowed complete access to complete medical dossiers of key cases,' Gill told me. 'They discovered that the alleged incident in each of those cases was entirely natural – though in each case there was a heap of medical errors and all kinds of important information had earlier been withheld from the courts.'

Just like the de Berk case, Geen's began with the hospital handing over the murderer to the police. Typically, murder investigations begin with 'an evidently murdered person' (Dr Gill's words) and the police are called in to find the perpetrator. However, in these cases that principle has been inverted; the police go with the story as told by the medics. 'As we know, "medical collegiality" means that that story will be very consistent,' he said. 'No one will break ranks and tell a different story.'

Dr Gill argued that the fact of Geen's presence came to be what defined an incident as an 'incident'. Again, that is what happened in the de Berk case. The two cases highlight the difference between the British adversarial legal system and the Continental inquisitorial system. In the Netherlands, the court can appoint a scientist to lead an investigation, which means that the judge and jury do not have to depend on the expert witnesses called by the prosecution and defence.

In Dr Gill's view, Ben Geen was convicted simply because the prosecution had the more persuasive experts. 'Unfortunately, Ben will never get a fair trial until medical experts start speaking out on his behalf. I am afraid that their ranks are closed,' he said. 'Lucia got a fair retrial because there was a medical whistleblower, well placed in society and with inside knowledge who fought for seven years.'

• • •

Sally Clark was a successful solicitor whose two sons, Christopher and Harry, sadly died in infancy – she was then accused of their double murder. Her conviction largely hinged on a statistic provided by expert witness Professor Sir Roy Meadows, who claimed that the probability of both of Clark's boys dying of cot death was one in 73 million. Meadows asserted that, as the likelihood of a child suffering cot death was reckoned to be one in 8,500, it would therefore logically follow that the chance of two unrelated incidents occurring in a single family would be one in 8,500 multiplied by 8,500, thus coming to the figure of one in 73 million.

The reasoning, which might seem plausible if you put to one side the immediate thought that the deaths could be the result of a genetic factor, is fundamentally flawed. It relies on a mistake so widespread in our courts that it is known as 'the prosecutor's fallacy'.

The prosecutor's fallacy is usually expressed as confusing the probability of finding the evidence on an innocent person with the probability that a person on whom the evidence is found is innocent. An illustration of this, attributed to John Maynard Keynes, envisages playing poker against the Archbishop of Canterbury.*

On the first hand, the Archbishop deals himself a straight flush. So what is the probability of the Archbishop dealing

---

* This is the example cited in a guide called 'Statistics and probability for advocates', produced by the Royal Statistical Society and the Inns of Court College of Advocacy in 2017.

himself a straight flush (the evidence) if he were playing honestly (i.e. he is innocent)? What is the probability that the Archbishop is playing honestly (i.e. he is innocent), given that he has dealt himself a straight flush (the evidence)?

There are 2,598,960 five-card hands that can be dealt from a pack of fifty-two cards including thirty-six hands that would be a straight flush. The answer to the first question is thirty-six in 2,598,960, or about one in 72,000. For the second question, most people would assess the probability of the Archbishop of Canterbury's honesty as being extremely high. The prosecutor's fallacy would be to argue that the probability of the Archbishop having played honestly, considering he has handed himself a straight flush, is thirty-six in 2,598,960.*

• • •

In the case of Ben Geen, an application to the Criminal Cases Review Commission was backed by a distinguished array of experts: Professor David Hand, emeritus professor of mathematics at Imperial College; Sheila Bird OBE, the Royal Statistical Society's vice-president for external affairs; Sir David Spiegelhalter, professor for the public understanding of risk and professor of biostatistics at the University of Cambridge; Professor Norman Fenton, professor in the school of electronic engineering and computer science at Queen Mary University of London; and Professor Stephen Senn, professor of statistics at CRP-Santé.

---

* In the Eddie Gilfoyle case, the same mistake might be to confuse the odds of an eight-and-a-half-month pregnant woman taking her life by suicide with the likelihood of the husband being the murderer.

Sir David Spiegelhalter describes himself as an expert in assessing the 'unusualness' of events. 'I would consider myself a professional coincidence investigator,' he told me.

> I study coincidences. The first thing I know is that I don't trust my own intuition one inch. I have to sit down with a piece of paper and find as much evidence as I can get and try to work out how likely an event of this type really is. In other words, the likelihood of any similar event occurring over a fixed period of time in any area. That is the crucial insight. You cannot work anything out by looking at the chance of the specific event itself. All events are completely improbable.

In a report for the Ben Geen case, Sir David cited an example of three major plane crashes taking place in an eight-day period in July 2014. While striking in itself, he argued that according to detailed calculations, there was 'a 60 per cent chance' of such a cluster happening over a ten-year period. 'People do win the lottery twice. It does not necessarily mean they are criminals,' he told me. 'It is an extremely tempting psychological trait to say this event is so unusual and therefore to say that there must be a reason. No, unusual things happen all the time.'

In preparation for Ben Geen's appeal, Freedom of Information requests were made for data relating to respiratory arrests at hospitals. The data suggested that, for a small hospital like Horton General, it was not unusual for there to be several incidents a month. Professor Fenton's report also supported the notion that a cluster of respiratory arrests at the hospital – eighteen in two months, where the same nurse was present – was not at all unusual. The probability that in any four-year period there would be a two-month sequence in which at least eighteen respiratory attacks occur purely by chance in a given hospital would be very rare. But there are around 2,300 hospitals in the UK. 'In any four-year period in the UK it is almost certain that there will be several instances of exactly this kind of 'abnormally high' sequence of respiratory events,' Fenton wrote. 'It is actually very likely that, purely by chance, in at least one case there will be a nurse present at each event.'

Once the idea of an 'unusual event' had been established in people's minds, there is a well-known phenomenon of 'selecting historical data to fit the "coincidence"', noted Spiegelhalter, who gave evidence to the Shipman inquiry.

An inquiry was set up in 1998 to investigate the deaths of twenty-nine babies who underwent heart surgery at the Bristol Royal Infirmary in the late 1980s and early 1990s. Sir David Spiegelhalter led the statistical team in the Bristol inquiry. The 'unusualness' of the spike in the number of deaths was clear. Spiegelhalter looked at how rare the incidence was across twelve hospitals and it turned out that Bristol was, indeed, an outlier.

'I am very surprised that a sequence of events has been labelled as unusual without any formal analysis of what "unusual" means,' Sir David said of the events at Horton Green. 'This is a very subtle area in which human intuition is remarkably fallible.'

One of the reasons why the Ben Geen case has attracted such support amongst such eminent statisticians is that they share a concern about the way that the courts deal with probability.

'I am very doubtful of the capacity of advocates, even the judiciary and certainly the jury, to assess these coincidences in a reasonable way,' Sir David told me. 'The courts like either incontrovertible numerical facts, or overall expert opinions. But statisticians deal with a delicate combination of data and judgement that gives rise to rough numbers, and these don't seem to fit well with the legal process.'

While misunderstanding the probability of an outcome can kick-start a criminal investigation, that initial motivating factor often becomes lost. 'If you look at the way these cases are prosecuted, the statistics by no means dominate,' Dr Fenton told me. 'It's all about the medical evidence. It doesn't look like it has anything to do with a problem to do with statistics. But it is the statistics that initially drive the case.'

• • •

Mark McDonald contacted Richard Gill in 2013, as Geen's legal team prepared to make an application to the CCRC. The statistician saw numerous alarming parallels with the Lucia de Berk case, and was left rather stunned that no one had spotted the similarities sooner.

In one year, the year in which de Berk was accused of going on a killing spree, nine incidents occurred in the ward she worked in. Almost no incidents were reported in the two preceding years and the year that followed. According to Dr Gill, this information, which was provided by the hospital, while correct, was fatally misleading. The ward had been renamed immediately before those two incident-free years and, previously, nine incidents a year was the norm and had been recorded several times before.

Gill pointed to the irony that in the de Berk case the prosecution argued that respiratory arrest was normal and cardiac arrest was unusual. Of course, in Ben Geen's case it was the other way around. 'In one of the key events, the crucial question for deciding whether a baby had died of poisoning or naturally was whether heart failure took place before or after lung failure,' he said.

If someone is terminally ill, the body becomes exhausted, the lungs and then the heart fail in that order. On the other hand, 'unexpected' heart failure, which is when the lungs naturally fail, could indicate poisoning. 'I don't suppose how terminally ill people die in the Netherlands is terribly different from how they do it in the UK,' he said.

It was as a result of Gill's involvement that Freedom of Information requests were submitted to thirty hospitals in England and Wales, roughly similar in size to Horton General. Drawing on that research, Dr Gill observed that respiratory arrest, while certainly less common than cardio-respiratory arrest (where there is heart failure coupled with respiratory failure; the former having triggered the latter), was not 'rare'. He reckoned that respiratory arrests in emergency departments were about four times less frequent than cardio-respiratory arrests, which were 'extremely frequent'.

The data produced by the Freedom of Information request was rough and ready. A consultant in anaesthesia and pain medicine, Dr A. G. Lakhen, was commissioned to evaluate Gill's work. Lakhen concluded that the data was not strong enough, but he concluded that there was evidence from 'more robust studies' to demonstrate that cardiac arrest from respiratory compromise in the emergency department was not rare.*

Professor Jane Hutton was 'surprised and disappointed' not to be called to give evidence in the Court of Appeal. 'I felt it was rather arrogant and the court simply didn't take the point,' she told me. According to the academic, there were 'some fundamental misunderstandings' in the Court of Appeal judgment. 'The court is effectively saying that everybody agreed that respiratory arrests were rare. That completely misses the point that came up in the Sally Clark case. It is not how rarely events occur but what are the competing explanations.'

. . .

The eminent statisticians do not comment on Ben Geen's guilt or innocence. They all agree that there was no evidential basis for the prosecution claim of an 'unusual pattern', and that such a claim was misleading. The exception is Richard Gill. He is convinced of the nurse's innocence.

What about the 'smoking gun'? The syringe that Ben Geen deliberately emptied into his jacket pocket just before he was arrested? Richard Gill readily concedes that when he talks to people about the Geen case, some don't get beyond that striking fact.

---

* One 2003 American study in the Lakhen report looked at 14,720 cardiac arrests and found that almost four out of ten patients were recorded as having respiratory compromise prior to cardiac arrest. A 2008 paper collecting data of acute respiratory compromise preceding cardiac arrest in hospital patients found that 11 per cent of patients were in the emergency department and of these 14 per cent suffered a cardiac arrest due to respiratory causes.

Dr Gill believes that the nurse's suspicious behaviour actually points more to his innocence than his guilt. Gill has discussed what happened with Geen's ex-girlfriend, who told him to return the syringe and properly dispose of it at the hospital. 'I think that was a really stupid thing to do,' he said. 'But the point is that a serious serial killer who knows that the hospital is already suspicious of him – he knew people were gossiping – to walk into hospital with a syringe-ful of poison that he could have chucked in the rubbish somewhere? For me, that doesn't fit with guilty behaviour.'

The barrister Mark McDonald has represented Ben Geen on a pro bono basis for the past ten years.

He draws on his own experience in A&E. 'I used to walk backwards and forwards with a load of rubbish in my pockets, including syringes, and I use to throw them away at home – just as he did. His girlfriend told him to put it back in the "sharps" bin – and so he took it back.'

What about the discharging of the syringe? 'It could be that he just knew he should not have been carrying it,' McDonald said. The notion that the syringe was worn through repeated use was always a red herring, the barrister said. 'If you want to get hold of a syringe, you do not have to carry around the same one,' McDonald said. 'Nurses go through syringes like we go through pencils.'

• • •

It is unlikely that Ben Geen is going to be leaving prison any time soon. Since his incarceration, Geen has completed two diplomas through the Open University. 'He's doing very well. He likes to immerse himself in his studies,' his father, Mick Geen, told me.

Ben Geen recently finished a Master's in English that took three years, as well as a course in prison law. 'By far the biggest cost for us is his education,' said father Mick. 'We can send in second-hand books now, but before they had to come new through Amazon. It can cost us £2,000 a year but, if it's for his education, we don't mind. Thankfully, educational charities have helped towards the costs.'

Geen is currently planning to complete a PhD on prison libraries and the role of reading in the rehabilitation of prisoners. 'It's almost impossible to do a PhD in prison,' his father told me. The family has found two academics at universities willing to supervise his studies.

Mick and his wife, Erica, who is a nurse with thirty-four years of experience, were obviously devastated by what happened to their son. They are, and always were, convinced of his innocence. Mick and Erica visit their son every week and are often joined by his brothers and sisters. Ben Geen is the eldest of four children. During Geen's trial, his sister was involved in a car crash that left her with nineteen fractures; his parents spent all day in court and all night in hospital.

Mick Geen, a former paratrooper who left the army in 1986 to work on a newspaper printing press, is an unlikely prison reformer. He regularly turns up at meetings about miscarriages of justice and prisoners' rights.

In his son's case, there was only evidence of drugs being administered in two of the eighteen cases. If there were real concerns before Timothy Stubbs was admitted, Geen Sr argues doctors would have ordered specific blood and urine tests to be taken. 'There was no evidence of this,' he told me. 'For those other sixteen "suspicious" incidents, there was no specific toxicology tests requested. For the other two, it was most probable that they were given the drugs as part of their emergency treatment in the highly charged A&E environment, and that they were not recorded accurately.'

He reckoned that in one case, in which a patient was suffering from a suspected Lithium overdose, drugs with anaesthetic properties had been noted on the patient's chart and signed for by a doctor, but this was subsequently crossed out. 'Even the prosecution expert gave evidence that it was possible that these drugs could have been given as part of a treatment to prevent the patient moving when being taken for a CT scan,' Mick Geen said.

It is his view that many of the allegations can be explained by poor patient recordkeeping and drug recording in the A&E department. 'There was no direct evidence,' said the father. 'Nobody at any point saw Ben do anything wrong.'

According to Mick Geen, some patients' conditions were misdiagnosed by doctors and nurses; others were seriously ill and their deterioration was explained by their presenting conditions. He believes that his son was convicted at trial because the hospital trust chose to look only at patients that had suffered complications when his son was on shift, and the prosecution then went on to cherry-pick unauthorised drugs to fit the individual circumstances. If a patient recovered quicker than expected as a result of the drugs claimed to have been injected, then the prosecution argued Geen must have given the patient a smaller dose of a drug. Conversely, if the patient was out cold for a longer period, it was alleged that Geen had administered a larger dose of a drug or a more potent cocktail of drugs.

'You cannot present evidence like this in court under other circumstances. The prosecution couldn't say you might have hit him with a chair, a baseball bat or a bit of two-by-four. The court would say that's not evidence.'

Ben Geen had no criminal convictions. He appeared to be doing well in his job. There were a couple of minor, work-related issues which Mick Geen believes were blown out of proportion by the prosecution lawyers, who were trying to portray his son as a 'maniac on the loose'. For example, it was claimed that Geen had been telling people that he was a qualified nurse when in actual fact he wasn't. Before becoming a qualified nurse, Geen had been temporally employed by the A&E department as a health care assistant. According to his father, Geen's new position as a nurse was not immediately made official, as he had to resubmit an assignment. While waiting for his assignment to be assessed, Geen wore his new staff nurse uniform and badge as issued to him by a senior member of staff. Later, Geen was asked to put tape over the epaulettes and name badge, which he did. It was also suggested he applied a plaster case without being authorised to do so. Ben Geen has always maintained that he doesn't remember the incident. 'There was a great deal of locker-room talk,' Geen Sr said.

> Ben was pretty forthright at work. He would always be willing to put himself on the frontline in demanding situations. This is not unusual for people who work in the emergency services or

the military. Some people didn't like that that aspect of Ben. But that suspicion was put in their minds retrospectively by staff.

Geen had aspirations to join the regular army.

He was planning to get another two or three years under his belt in the hospital environment first. They used his army past to suggest that he was a glory hunter. Throughout the trial there was never a clear motive established. The only thing they could come up with was that he did it for the hell of it; for the thrill of it. There is no other motive or any propensity at all to commit the crimes he has been convicted of.

• • •

In October 2015, the CCRC rejected an application on behalf of Ben Geen's family. The family challenged the commission by way of judicial review. In April 2016, the miscarriage of justice watchdog agreed to take another look at the case.

It has now become fairly routine for lawyers who specialise in miscarriages of justice cases to challenge the CCRC when they reject a case through judicial review (this happened in Eddie Gilfoyle's case). According to the CCRC's 2016/17 annual report, there were thirty-four challenges to its decisions last year. The watchdog claims to have only lost one judicial review in its twenty years, but it does concede that it would 'rather spend its resources reviewing cases than contesting expensive litigation but on the few occasions when it is necessary we will fight judicial reviews all the way through the Admin Court process'.

The watchdog found Dr Richard Gill's report of 'extremely limited value'. The fact that the statistician had publicly stated that he believed Geen was 'clearly completely innocent' did not help. Such a comment was 'at the very least, somewhat surprising' coming from someone being put forward as an independent expert whose duty was to the court and 'even more so' as his report went 'no way to establishing such innocence or to addressing the other aspects of the case against Mr Geen over and above the issue of "unusual pattern".'

The watchdog countered that the issue at the heart of the prosecution case was not the rarity of respiratory arrest but the rarity of respiratory arrest with no explanation. For Dr Gill, that is a somewhat meaningless distinction. According to the academic, there is no data on medically unexplained respiratory arrests. 'And anyway, all the respiratory arrests in Ben's case can be explained if you believe the defence experts – it is a very subjective judgement,' he said. 'The person who said this case or that case is "unexplained" was the same guy who knew all the cases were suspected of having been murdered by a serial killer nurse.'

CHAPTER TEN

CAUGHT IN THE DRAGNET

At the start of court business on 14 June 2017, court four in the Royal Courts of Justice was packed. Londoners had woken up to the unfolding horror of the fire at Grenfell Tower that was to claim the lives of seventy-one residents of the 24-storey block. As people arrived late to court, held up by the ensuing chaos, they struggled to squeeze onto the public benches.

Two young men joined the proceedings via video link: Janhelle Grant-Murray, in grey sweatshirt, from HMP Leicester; and Alex Henry, wearing suit and tie, from HMP Whitemoor in Cambridgeshire.

On 13 March 2014, the pair had been found guilty at the Old Bailey of murdering Taqui Khezihi and wounding his brother Bourhane. Henry, just twenty years old at the time of the murder, was sentenced to life imprisonment with a minimum term of nineteen years.

To secure a murder conviction, the prosecution usually must prove that the defendant intended to kill or commit serious injury. In this case, a third man and one of a group of four friends present on the day, Cameron Ferguson, had stabbed both Khezihi brothers. Midway through the six-week trial, Ferguson changed his plea to guilty and admitted to the stabbing.

It is under the ancient common law doctrine of joint enterprise that the prosecution can seek a murder conviction if it can prove that a secondary defendant (i.e., someone other than the person wielding the knife) foresaw the 'possibility' that death might occur.

The stakes could not have been higher for Henry and Grant-Murray, but they couldn't have looked more bored. On the grainy screen, the court watched as the pair fidgeted, yawned, rolled their eyes and stretched. Grant-Murray occasionally rested his forehead on the desk in front of him in that universal gesture of profound boredom familiar to teachers up and down the country.

The Lord Chief Justice, Lord Thomas, was flanked by Lady Justice Hallett and Mr Justice Goss. They were considering two joined applications in what was billed as a critical test case on the application of joint enterprise to the very young and very vulnerable. The cases involved young men from west London, barely out of their teens; and, in the second case, boys from Liverpool barely in their teens.

On Wednesday 6 August 2013, Henry and Grant-Murray had been shopping with an old friend, Younis Tayyib. The three had known each other for years. Grant-Murray and Tayyib walked back to the latter's house when they were confronted by four older boys: the brothers Bourhane and Taqui Khezihi, and two other friends, Dapo Tajani and Leon Thompson.

What followed was random and unplanned: a moment of madness that left one young person dead and ruined the lives of countless others. The events took place in forty-seven seconds.

The facts are disputed.

The stand-off began like countless other fights between young men. Grant-Murray thought Taqui Khezihi had looked at him in a disrespectful way. He was followed by the brothers and their friends. So he walked into a local Costcutter, grabbed the first bottle he saw from a shelf, and returned holding a bottle of rosé by its neck.

All of this was caught on CCTV. Tayyib is clearly shown trying to calm down the situation, physically intervening between his friend and the brothers. According to Alex Henry's account, he claimed to have seen his friend in trouble as he walked down the road with Cameron Ferguson. Grant-Murray is reported to have then shouted: 'You're fucked now.'

As Henry approached, he claimed to have picked up Grant-Murray's dropped mobile phone, panicked and thrown it at one of his friend's attackers. He then threw a punch at one of the other gang, which, he said, was in self-defence. On his account, that was the extent of his involvement. Bourhane claimed 'the white boy' (Henry) had 'a shiny object' in his hand. Tajani told the police it was a knife.

Cameron Ferguson joined in. He grabbed a knife from inside his bag and stabbed Taqui and Bourhane. Everyone fled. Taqui's injury proved fatal. Henry claimed that it was only hours later, when they regrouped in a local park, that they realised that Ferguson had 'poked' the brothers with a knife.

The case is shocking but at the same time, sadly, mundane. It happens all the time. On every day in 2016, three people were killed or seriously injured in stabbings on London's streets. According to the Metropolitan Police, sixty people were stabbed to death, 1,159 sustained serious injuries and 21,365 were victims of knife crime.

The utter futility of the death of the 21-year-old Taqui Khezihi is underlined by the fact that neither set of boys actually knew each other.

• • •

The second case before the appeal court judges was even more disturbing. Joseph James McGill, Andrew James Hewitt, and Corey Hewitt were just thirteen and fourteen when they took part in the gang killing of Sean McHugh.

They were members of the Laneheads gang from the Townsend Lane area of Anfield and cornered their prey in the back room of a launderette. McHugh had gone to wash his girlfriend's clothes and happened to be on their 'turf'. He was a member of the Walton Village Heads, who had been fighting the Laneheads.

The terrified nineteen-year-old barricaded himself in the back room. The gang came armed with knives, a broom handle and what was described as a 'walking cane sword', an antique-type martial arts weapon. The attack was captured on the launderette's CCTV. 'These were feral youths who didn't intend to kill, but set out to cause harm and now they must pay the penalty,' said Detective Chief Inspector Andy O'Connor, of Merseyside Police.

• • •

Joint enterprise has delivered a number of notable convictions. It famously enabled the killers of black teenager Stephen

Lawrence to be brought to justice. There was no way of establishing which of the six men involved in the racially motivated attack in south-east London stabbed eighteen-year-old Stephen. However, in 2011, eighteen years after the attack, Gary Dobson and David Norris were jailed thanks to a legal doctrine that has its origins in a rather different form of knife crime.

The 300-year-old doctrine was originally used to help stop aristocrats from duelling by making their surgeons and 'seconds' liable for murder. Times have changed, but the law has proved versatile. It is now reckoned to be a key weapon in the fight against gang culture and, in particular, knife crime.

In 2016, almost four out of ten homicides in the UK (213 in total) involved a knife. According to the Crime Survey for England and Wales, a knife was used in 6 per cent of all incidents of violence experienced by adults. In the same year, hospitals recorded 4,119 admissions as a result of stabbings.

Joint enterprise put the three killers of Ben Kinsella behind bars. The sixteen-year-old student was stabbed eleven times in five seconds when he was out celebrating the end of his GCSEs in June 2008 with friends in Islington, north London. The fight started when one boy turned to another and said: 'What are you staring at?' After his death, hundreds of people attended a candlelit vigil demanding an end to knife crime.

'The message that the law is sending out is that we are very willing to see people convicted if they are a part of gang violence – and that violence ends in somebody's death,' the former Lord Chancellor, Lord Charlie Falconer, said in 2010.

Is it unfair? Well, what you've got to decide is not 'does the system lead to people being wrongly convicted?' I think the real question is 'do you want a law as draconian as our law is, which says juries can convict even if you are quite a peripheral member of the gang which killed?' And I think, broadly, the view of reasonable people is that you probably do need a quite draconian law in that respect.

In the west London case, all four defendants, including Alex Henry, had previous convictions related to the owning of knives. Weeks before the murder, Grant-Murray was stabbed in Sylvester's barbers in Ealing in the neck, chest and arm. Henry was with his friend at the time. Grant-Murray has always claimed not to know why he was attacked.

Critics of joint enterprise argue that the law has become 'a dragnet', hoovering up urban youth, disproportionately black and often vulnerable, in its wake. It indiscriminately pulls those on the periphery, and sometimes not involved in serious criminal acts, into the justice system.

Up to half of those convicted under joint enterprise were from black, Asian and minority ethnic (BAME) backgrounds, according to a 2017 review of the criminal justice system by Labour MP David Lammy. The review revealed that almost nine out of ten of the 3,621 names on the Metropolitan Police's database of gang suspects were BAME.

• • •

Dr Sally Halsall always worried about her son. From the age of sixteen months, Alex Henry would scream and throw such explosive tantrums that nurseries refused to take in the toddler. When he was three, he was still having meltdowns, and even at the age of ten he would throw what she called 'all-nighters'.

By then, Dr Halsall had separated from Henry's father. 'When I look back on the marriage, we were under so much strain because we knew there was something wrong with Henry. Both his father and I thought that,' she told me. 'We also felt that we weren't believed. We felt that people were thinking there was something wrong with us as parents.' She recalled taking a screaming Henry to a GP, who referred her to A&E and handed her a sealed letter.

> I opened the letter. It read: 'Mrs Henry is now a well-adjusted mother [she had suffered post-natal depression with Henry's sister] and has returned to education. I truly believe that there is something wrong with this child. I myself witnessed his projectile vomiting in my consultation room.' I was horrified.

Alex Henry was eight years old when his parents split up. After a short period of dividing the week between parents, Henry went to live with his father, while Charlotte, Henry's sister, stayed with her mother. 'Living with Mum, you come home and dinner is on the table. You sit down and do your homework and bed time is a set time,' Charlotte told me. She said their father was an alcoholic. 'Instead of verbally telling you off, it would be more physical,' she said. 'You would come home and there would be nothing in the fridge. But it was a fun household at Dad's. You could hang out with your friends until whatever time you wanted. But there was no structure and Alex needed structure.'

Henry had a short school career. He was badly bullied at primary school and then moved to a private school where he was soon expelled. He was initially refused a place at Charlotte's secondary school but his parents successfully appealed against this decision. However, after a couple of months there, Henry dropped out at the age of eleven.

Over the next few years, Henry was assessed by many agencies. The year after his parents split up, he was referred to CAMHS, the child and adolescent mental health service, for the first time because of his disruptive behaviour, and then referred again the following year, when he was deemed to be suffering with anxiety and overwhelmed by his parents' divorce. His mother felt Henry's father was not providing the discipline her wayward son needed.

When Alex Henry was fourteen years old, he saw a family therapist and was assessed by a senior social worker later that year, who observed that proper boundaries were not being imposed at home. It was noted that Henry avoided eye contact, struggled to sit still and used babyish language.

In 2005, Dr Halsall completed her PhD in psychology researching the implications of bullying in schools. 'One of the reasons why I did it was because I wanted to get to the bottom of what was wrong with Alex,' she told me. The mother raised a possible diagnosis of attention deficit hyperactivity disorder. A clinical psychologist agreed.

Following a minor assault in 2007, a youth offending panel assessment recorded his father's concerns that Henry was running with the MDP gang (as in 'Money Drugs Power'). It wasn't all bad. Henry was considered to be academically bright, good at maths and chess, albeit slow at reading. The next year the local youth offending team, concerned about his involvement with the gang, noted that Henry was a bright, charismatic and articulate fifteen-year-old. The MDP gang members were typically in their late teens and early twenties and, according to Charlotte Henry, they briefly adopted her brother as a sort of 'kiddy mascot'. He left after a few months. One day, in a parting gesture by a gang member, Henry was punched in the face and knocked out as he walked down the street.

Following a serious bullying incident committed with nine others, a psychologist wrote a report for Acton youth court. It noted that there was not enough evidence to support a diagnosis of conduct disorder, a condition defined by persistent problems from aggressive and destructive behaviour, to lying and stealing, carrying weapons or staying out all night. However, the psychologist reckoned that Henry exhibited some symptoms of ADHD.

In April 2009, Alex Henry was charged in relation to threatening behaviour. The youth offender panel report recorded that he had a large group of friends with whom he was 'besotted'. He was on the receiving end of an antisocial behaviour order (ASBO) preventing him from seeing friends, including Janhelle Grant-Murray, and visiting certain streets.

Charlotte Henry had wanted to be a lawyer from an early age. 'Ever since I watched *Legally Blonde*,' as she put it. 'When I was eighteen years old, Henry was getting arrested on a regular basis for smoking cannabis, breaching the ASBO etc. I was always the appropriate adult for him. Mum works and Dad drinks, so I was the one who went to the police station.' She is now training to be a lawyer and working for a government watchdog body.

Alex Henry constantly breached his ASBO and ended up in prison a number of times, including one four-month stretch. 'Alex's behaviour was consistently bad until he was seventeen years old,' recalled Charlotte. After his ASBO came to an end, things calmed down. 'It was so sad for Alex,' said his mother. 'He never had an education. He was never given a chance. He was thrown into prison at every opportunity.'

At no point was Alex Henry diagnosed with autism. Nor was this suggested at his trial.

• • •

Shortly after the trial, Dr Sally Halsall was working at the Institute of Psychiatry when a woman emailed her after reading about her son's case. Had it ever occurred to her that her son might be autistic, the woman asked? Dr Halsall started reading up on autism and wrote to a number of experts, including Professor Simon Baron-Cohen, director of the Autism Research Centre at Cambridge University, asking him to meet her son.

The professor met Henry twice, in June and December 2014, at his category A prison. He recorded the interview. 'I didn't start the fight, and I didn't stab anyone,' Henry told Professor Baron-Cohen. 'Cameron stabbed both of them. It was all over in fifty seconds. I have been accused of joint enterprise ... They say I'm guilty of encouraging it. I didn't know Cameron had a knife at the time. I didn't know he stabbed someone. He told me after.'

The fight was seen by numerous witnesses. No one saw

a knife. Bourhane had claimed that 'the white boy' had been holding a 'shiny object in his hand', but at the trial Bourhane acknowledged he could not see what the object was.

One of Bourhane's friends also gave a statement saying that Alex Henry was definitely holding a knife, although in court the friend admitted that he was 'not 100 per cent sure'. He also described the attacker as being a 'tall, fair-skinned guy, between black and white complexion... in the middle, kind of'. Cameron Ferguson matched this description. Alex Henry did not: he is white and only 5ft 2in. tall.

At the original trial, all four co-defendants pleaded not guilty to charges of murder and attempted murder. The prosecution's case was that each defendant played a part in a joint attack on the Khezihi brothers; each knew about the existence of the knife and that it was intended to be used – in other words, the killing was a joint enterprise.

Five days into the trial, Cameron Ferguson changed his plea to guilty. At that point, his barrister said that Ferguson claimed to be the only person who had wielded the knife and had been 'on a frolic of his own'.

Alex Henry told Professor Baron-Cohen of his past antics: when he was young he was 'proper naughty', he admitted. Henry told the doctor that he had always been conscious of being 'different'. 'I talk to people in the prison a bit randomly. I play snooker but I don't get involved in conversation. I like to do Sudoku and crosswords. I spend hours on those. If I'm alone in my cell I stay on computer games all night.'

· · ·

On the day of the Grenfell Tower fire, Professor Baron-Cohen was due to give evidence after a lunch break. As we waited for court proceedings to resume, we watched Alex Henry and Janhelle Grant-Murray via the video link.

The two friends monkeyed around as if they hadn't a care in the world, seemingly oblivious to the impression they were creating in court. It showed the pair in a poor light – immature and disrespectful to the solemnity of the proceedings. On the other hand, being stuck in front of a video camera in a cell-like office in prison while lawyers decided their fate and spoke an impenetrable language must have seemed a particularly cruel and unusual punishment.

Professor Baron-Cohen is Britain's leading expert on autism. On his autism spectrum quotient questionnaire, which aims to test whether adults have the condition, Alex Henry scores 'a very high' thirty-five out of fifty. The majority of males tend to score seventeen and the average score for females is fifteen. If someone scores over thirty-two, then this suggests that they may have Asperger's.*

With an air of calm deriving from a peerless command of his area of specialism, the psychiatrist proved a credible and persuasive witness. He was unfazed by a court that was clearly sceptical about a late diagnosis.

As he explained to the court, his clinic in Cambridge has diagnosed over 1,000 people with autism or Asperger Syndrome whose diagnosis also had been overlooked into early adulthood.

---

* According to Professor Baron-Cohen, about 80 per cent of people who end up with a diagnosis for Asperger's score above thirty-two. The spectrum is not a diagnostic instrument, Baron-Cohen told me. 'We would not claim you can diagnose on the basis of a questionnaire, but it is a useful screening instrument.'

The signs are subtle and for that reason, he explained, it was often described as an invisible disability.

Autism 'just doesn't start out of the blue', said Professor Baron-Cohen, it was there throughout early development. It manifested itself in difficulties socialising, interpreting emotional expressions as well as understanding jokes. The Crown's barrister later noted that Alex Henry had been 'quick to laugh at 2 p.m.'

'I see autism as a complex disability,' the psychologist told the court from the witness box. 'It affects many different functions, including the processing of information. People with autism struggle with situations where there is too much information to take in. It is a major piece of information that the jury needs to know. It is nobody's fault because the diagnosis hadn't been made yet.'

Autism was a diagnosis from which all sorts of consequences flowed in the kind of fast-moving situation that took place on 6 August 2013. The incident took less than fifty seconds. 'People with autism struggle to make rapid decisions under pressure,' the professor said. They also tended to have 'a very black-and-white morality – in this instance, he wanted to protect his friend'. Professor Baron-Cohen said autistic people also tended to be 'very rigid in the application of rules' and so, for example, would stick to a solicitor's edict to make 'no comment'.

Autistic people also made poor choices in friends because they could not read people's motives, easily became fixated and displayed 'tunnel vision', the professor went on. 'Someone with autism could be mistaken for showing very little remorse,' Professor Baron-Cohen told the court. This, the professor argued, might in some way account for Henry's guilty-looking behaviour in the aftermath of the murder. For three days he went on the run from police, and stayed with Ferguson at a friend's flat in Croydon – despite knowing that Ferguson had murdered Taqui Khezihi. The reason for this, according to Henry, was that he wanted to be present when his girlfriend had a pregnancy scan.

Under the law of joint enterprise, a jury can convict if it is proved that the secondary defendant foresaw the 'possibility' that death might occur. That is exactly the kind of subjective judgement an autistic person might well struggle with. As Professor Baron-Cohen made clear, if a typical person had known that Cameron had a knife, they might well have assumed he would use that knife intentionally to kill. Henry's autism meant that no such assumption could be made. This, the psychiatrist pointed out, was because in people with autism, 'common-sense' inferences were not automatically drawn.

• • •

The message from the Metropolitan Police is that the law on joint enterprise is 'clear and unforgiving' – as the force says in its 'Drop the Weapons' campaign. It delivers, as Lord Falconer noted in 2010, a simple message. The force has a video explaining joint enterprise to schools in London as part of its crackdown on gang crime.

Metropolitan Police Detective Chief Inspector John McFarlane has spoken about the value of joint enterprise as a 'deterrent' to young people who might otherwise think they would not go to prison 'just because they did not deliver the fatal blow'.* It is certainly 'unforgiving' but it is also not always clear.

The Met has even sent letters to those it suspects are gang members or else up to no good, warning them they could be sent to prison for 'just being present when a serious crime is committed' thanks to joint enterprise. 'Information indicates that you have or are associated to a gang that is involved with crime,' read the letter. 'If you are involved with crime and do not stop you may be targeted by the police and partner agencies. Under a piece of legislation called joint enterprise, you may be convicted of a crime and sent to prison for just being present when a serious crime is committed.' If you want to avoid the attentions of the Metropolitan Police, the letter warns, 'you need to change your behaviour'.

Obviously, it is not an offence simply to be present when a crime is committed, serious or otherwise. I interviewed 'Sean', a 22-year-old who had such a letter posted through his door. He had convictions for drugs offences but had never been a gang member or carried a knife. He was, in his view, an undeserving victim of police harassment and was unfairly stopped and searched. 'It's frightening to think police are watching you like this,' he told me.

According to the defence lawyer Simon Natas, who has specialised in joint enterprise cases, placing people under this kind of scrutiny ('in a way that is threatening to them') was likely to have completely the opposite effect to that intended. 'You could've scared them and got the law accurate. The law is scary,'

---

* He was speaking after the sentencing of the killers of fifteen-year-old Zac Olumegbon in 2011.

he said. 'But if they are going to send out these letters, at the very least they could get the law right.'

Dr Ben Crewe, from Cambridge University, is unconvinced about the deterrent effect as seemingly endorsed by the Metropolitan Police. In evidence he gave to a 2015 House of Commons' Justice Committee investigation into joint enterprise, Dr Crewe said that two conditions needed to be met for an effective deterrent. Young people must be aware of joint enterprise and, according to the research, very few people had any idea of what it was; and, if they had, they didn't understand it. The second condition was that it would have to have an impact on behaviour. Dr Crewe argued that the prospect of being caught was a greater deterrent than length of sentence or severity of any sentence.

The then chair of the Justice Committee, Sir Alan Beith, warned that there was a real danger in justifying joint enterprise on the basis that it sent 'a signal or delivers a wider social message', rather than it being necessary to ensure people were found guilty of offences in accordance with the law.

According to statistics obtained by the Bureau of Investigative Journalism under a Freedom of Information request, 1,853 people were prosecuted for homicides involving four or more defendants between 2005 and 2013 which almost certainly relied upon joint enterprise – and 4,590 for homicides involving two or more people.

More than one in five of all Court of Appeal rulings in 2013 related to joint enterprise cases (22 per cent). That was, according to the legal academic Dr Matthew Dyson, a 'terrifying statistic and evidence of the constant appeals against this doctrine'.

It was also revealed in the 2015 justice committee investigation that some 145 applications had been made to the Criminal Cases Review Commission since 2004 from people convicted under the doctrine. The group explained that there were likely to have been many more applications, but they had not been labelled joint enterprise.

The Bureau of Investigative Journalism, which looked at over 800 published Court of Appeal rulings in its 2014 report, reckoned that the rate at which joint enterprise cases were brought to appeal doubled between 2008 and 2013. In 2008, just over one in ten of Court of Appeal rulings (11 per cent) dealt with convictions where there had been some element of joint enterprise. In 2013, the rate had doubled and accounted for forty-three out of 194 rulings.

In one case, cited by the Bureau of Investigative Journalism, a fifteen-year-old was sentenced to a minimum term of twelve years for murder after the jury decided that his presence at the scene of a stabbing meant he was guilty of murder. He was 120 yards away when the stabbing took place, but the jury decided the teenager had gone to the scene knowing a fight might take place. His solicitor, Greg Stewart, told the Bureau of Investigative Journalism that joint enterprise covered such a range of behaviour and intent that it became 'a lottery if you are convicted or not'.*

---

* On 2 October 2007, a 26-year-old Polish care worker, Magda Pniewska, walked home from the nursing home where she worked in south London. As she was talking to her sister on her mobile phone, she was struck in the head by a single bullet and died instantly. The man who fired the fatal shot was never prosecuted. Known only as 'bandana-man', he escaped. The other gunman, Armel Gnango, seventeen, was convicted of her murder in 2008. The ruling was upheld by the Supreme Court in 2011.

At the time of the justice committee investigation, the CCRC had made seven referrals in joint enterprise cases since 2004, but only one conviction was quashed. This compared to its average 70 per cent success rate. The CCRC identified three 'obstacles' for joint enterprise applicants: the difficulty of finding the new evidence required for an appeal in light of conflicting testimonies from various defendants; the difficulty of that evidence impacting on *mens rea* (in other words, intention or foresight); and, finally, joint enterprise cases often arose 'on the spur of the moment'.

• • •

At Alex Henry's appeal there was the usual large turnout of women in red T-shirts as worn by JENGbA (Joint Enterprise Not Guilty by Association) campaigners. The group runs a formidable grassroots campaign and is composed largely of working-class women with loved ones in prison.

I met one of the group's leading lights, Gloria Morrison, in the group's office in a large council estate just off Ladbroke Grove, west London. She and two other volunteers – mothers of black sons serving twenty-four and twenty-eight years respectively – were busy stuffing 543 envelopes with their monthly newsletter. Two years later, JENGbA reckons that they are in touch with 1,000 joint enterprise prisoners.

'I instinctively knew that joint enterprise was all about racism,' Morrison told me. She became involved in the campaign as a result of the experience of her son's best friend. In 2007, Kenneth Alexander was found guilty of murder and given a life sentence as a result of his part in the April 2005 stabbing of Michael Campbell. Alexander had been hit on the back of the head and was semi-conscious when Campbell was killed, Morrison said. 'It was Alexander's role in ringing friends to call in reinforcements for a possible confrontation that provided the prosecution with his joint enterprise,' she said. 'That he knew some of his mates carried knives, even though he never did, was also a factor in his conviction.'

'It could have been my son,' Morrison said. 'The boys all went to the same Catholic school in west London. All the boys were black. My son is white. They all came from affluent backgrounds. Ken's mother is a psychologist. The boy who did do the stabbing was the son of a deputy head teacher.'

Every week new families contact JENGbA. The day before I spoke to Morrison she had been at a meeting in Birmingham. 'Five people contacted us. Almost every single name was Asian,' she said.

'I had never even heard of joint enterprise until it happened to me,' Barbara, one of the JENGbA volunteers, told me. Her son was only nineteen years old when he was sentenced to twenty-four years last March. He was in HMP High Down, Surrey as a result of his part in a fatal stabbing after an altercation with a Somalian gang. She readily admitted her son was involved in the fight that led to the killing. 'I am not saying he is innocent, but he's not guilty of murder,' she said.

After her son was sentenced, Barbara's other son was attacked by the gang and other members of the family were threatened with having acid thrown in their faces. Barbara ended up being housed temporarily in a safe house with her daughter for a year and has now moved out of Kentish Town.

According to Barbara, her son is holding up.

> He knows we are here outside fighting for him. My son always says: 'I would never change my plea. I am not pleading guilty for something I didn't do.' There was no evidence to say that my son had a knife. A boy pleaded guilty on the first day of the trial. The judge sentenced my son and a co-defendant to longer than the kid who actually did it. They didn't have any weapons on them. Sentence them to the part that they played – but not to murder. I just don't understand it.

Gloria Morrison says that she and her colleagues don't sit 'as judge and jury' when someone rings up. 'I say to them: "You do not have to prove it to me what their involvement was, if any." They have already been tried once in a court of law which I do not trust any more. If the courts are using this kind of charge, they don't have any credibility.'

• • •

'The courts took a wrong turn in 1984,' said Lord Neuberger, President of the Supreme Court, in February 2016. 'This court is always very cautious before departing from a previous decision. It is the responsibility of this court to put the law right.'

JENGbA campaigners and their lawyers hugged each other. The Criminal Bar Association issued a press release declaring the ruling 'a masterpiece of modern legal reasoning' that 'significantly enhanced our justice system and will be widely welcomed'.

There was not universal approval. Commentators predicted 'hundreds of convicted killers' would be walking free, including the killers of Stephen Lawrence. The appeal concerned the case of Ameen Jogee. It was another difficult case. Paul Fyfe was stabbed to death in the hallway of his girlfriend's home in the early hours of the morning in June 2011 by Mohammed Hirsi, who pleaded guilty to murder. Jogee and Hirsi spent the night getting high on a cocktail of drink and drugs before they arrived at the home of Fyfe's girlfriend close to midnight. The girlfriend told them to leave and that she was expecting Fyfe to return. Hirsi entered the house and there was an angry confrontation between him and Fyfe. Jogee was outside with a bottle, egging Hirsi on to do something to Fyfe. At one stage Jogee came to the door and threatened to smash his bottle over Fyfe's head. The fatal stabbing was done by Hirsi with a knife taken from the kitchen.

The Sun spoke to Paul Fyfe's widow, Tracey. 'I think [joint enterprise] is a very important law and it think it would be quite devastating for the victims' families like us, which would mean that criminals like Ameen Jogee would literally be getting away with murder,' she said.

The Supreme Court sought to restore the pre-1984 position – and so for a secondary defendant to be found guilty of a crime they would need to have 'intentionally assisted or encouraged' the crime committed rather than merely having had some 'foresight' that the crime might take place. 'The correct rule is that foresight is simply evidence, albeit sometimes strong evidence, of intent to assist or encourage, which is the proper mental element for establishing secondary liability,' Lord Neuberger said.

Six months after the landmark ruling in *Jogee*, the Court of Appeal looked at the first wave of appeals sent back. Where an appeal is brought outside of the normal 28-day limit, the appellant must seek exceptional leave to appeal to the Court of Appeal. Under the *Jogee* ruling, permission to appeal would be granted only if 'substantial injustice' had been caused and not simply because the law was wrong.

Dr Sally Halsall and Charlotte Henry were in the Supreme Court. 'We thought if you have been convicted of murder, and you might not have been convicted of murder but convicted of manslaughter, then obviously that is a "substantial injustice",' Charlotte explained. 'The mandatory minimum term is life imprisonment plus the stigma of being labelled a murderer. It's common sense.'

Sitting alone and looking out at the women in their red T-shirts, the Lord Chief Justice, Lord Thomas, read out a short statement denying leave to appeal to all thirteen defendants in six cases. He reached the end of the judgment to sounds of a woman sobbing in the corridor. Shouts of 'No justice, no peace' rang out as the judge walked out of the courtroom.

• • •

The following year, Lord Thomas read out the judgment in the cases of Alex Henry, Janhelle Grant-Murray and three Liverpool boys. One of the boys, Joseph McGill, just thirteen years old at the time of Khezihi's murder, was diagnosed with ADHD and, in terms of his cognitive ability, was reckoned to be in the bottom 5 per cent for children of his age. Corey Hewitt, also thirteen at the time, was in the bottom 2 per cent and had an IQ of sixty-nine. All five relied upon the *Jogee* ruling.

It was another wipeout in the Court of Appeal.

The bench had little sympathy for Professor Baron-Cohen's insight into Alex Henry. 'It seems to us, having regard to all the evidence, that it can have had no effect on the issue of Henry's thinking process at the time of the murder in the respects identified by Professor Baron-Cohen,' they said. At worst, they ruled Henry suffered from 'mild mental illness that was immaterial to his culpability for murder'.

Some six months after the Court of Appeal hearing, I interviewed Professor Baron-Cohen. I asked him what impression his day in court had made on him. 'It felt as though the prosecution had ambushed me and also that I hadn't been adequately briefed by the defence team,' he told me. As an expert, he understood his role was 'to be there to serve the court rather than either side'. 'Frankly, that wasn't what it felt like,' he said.

The doctor felt that the prosecuting counsel's interrogation of him was 'bordering on the offensive'. 'I had to be quite restrained in how I replied,' he said. In particular, he resented the suggestion that Henry's mother, Dr Sally Halsall, might have tried to dupe him. He pointed out that he visited Henry a second time in prison, after receiving an anonymous letter suggesting he was having the wool pulled over his eyes.

Professor Baron-Cohen accepted the court's offer to examine all of the reports on Alex Henry and submitted a second report on that basis after the hearing. 'It didn't change my diagnosis. If anything, it bolstered it,' he said.

Why, I asked, did he agree to see Alex Henry in the first place? He said it was because of his concerns about joint enterprise. 'It's the potential for miscarriages of justice,' he told me.

That someone is guilty by association for being in the wrong place at the wrong time. Even if there was no evidence that they did anything to hurt somebody. The idea that any of us will be able to make a level-headed decision in such a short period of time, less than fifty seconds in this case, would be challenging, but for somebody with autism that would be even harder. If expert witness evidence is dismissed so readily, this is a very worrying sign of how the courts take into account disabilities such as autism.

CHAPTER ELEVEN

INNOCENT – BUT NOT INNOCENT ENOUGH

On Thursday 16 May 2012, Sam Hallam emerged from the Court of Appeal and walked out onto a busy Strand a free man. The 24-year-old had spent seven years in prison for a gang-related murder he had always denied involvement in.

Pictures of Hallam appeared on news bulletins that evening and in the national newspapers next morning. They captured a seemingly joyful moment: a shyly smiling Hallam, one arm firmly gripped by mother Wendy, walking down the court steps and being doused with champagne by an army of well-wishers.

A miscarriage of justice, as confirmed by our courts, is a rare event indeed. There are only about twelve people every year released from prison in the manner of Sam Hallam. A 'miscarriage of justice' is, you might think, hardly a complicated concept to grasp. However, what *we* understand it to be might not necessarily accord with what the courts, lawyers and the Ministry of Justice understand it to mean.

Sam Hallam, who spent seven years in prison for a crime he didn't commit, is an innocent man. But our courts and the Ministry of Justice are reluctant to say so.

• • •

While the photographs suggested otherwise, Hallam's predominant emotions as he left the Royal Courts of Justice that day were fear and uncertainty. 'It was just overwhelming. I was in shock. I was scared,' he told me in 2015.

Earlier that day, as business resumed after lunch in court eight, David Hatton QC, for the Crown, had announced: 'We have given this anxious consideration for a long time, and again today, and we are not in a position to oppose the appeal.'

Lady Justice Hallett gently asked Hallam if he understood what was happening and if he was OK to carry on. 'Yes,' he replied shakily. Then there was pandemonium as the penny dropped. Family and supporters hugged each other, there were tears and shouts of 'Justice'. Heather Hallett switched back to stern judicial mode. 'I will not have my courtroom turned into a circus,' she warned from the bench.

When a conviction is quashed, the wrongly convicted person often walks out with no notice and little preparation. It is shocking, but nonetheless true, that there is less state support for the victims of miscarriages of justice than for other prisoners.* There is only one source of help specifically available to this tiny subset of prisoners: the Royal Court of Justice's miscarriage of justice support service, which is run by Citizens Advice. In

---

* This is the finding of an academic study conducted by the London School of Economics in 2015 and commissioned by the London housing charity Commonweal. 'The startling lack of statutory support available to victims [of miscarriages of justice] can mean many who deserve to receive social housing are rejected,' the charity said. 'Some fail a local connection test owing to their imprisonment, while others, in a particularly Kafkaesque twist, are even deemed to have caused their own homelessness.'

2011, it reckoned that one third of its clients found themselves homeless after being freed.

Thankfully, this was not true for Sam Hallam. He was supported by family and friends. They had been there every step of the way. The north London community came out in force to help him clear his name: there were packed campaign meetings, charity fundraisers, parachute jumps and numerous gigs in support of one of their own. MPs were lobbied, sympathetic press articles were written and the actor Ray Winstone fronted a documentary on ITV's *Tonight with Trevor McDonald*. Winstone is the uncle of Hallam's best friend.

On his twenty-first birthday, Hallam's family and supporters hired an open-top double-decker bus, drove from north London to Aylesbury prison in Buckinghamshire, then held an impromptu party outside the prison gates. Megaphones were brought to make sure Hallam knew they were there.

His release had been eagerly anticipated. Yet Sam Hallam was unprepared for what was about to happen at the Royal Courts of Justice. A few hours before he was released, he had left HMP Pentonville in a prison van; he had been transferred from HMP Bullingdon in Oxfordshire the previous day. He was told to prepare himself for 'an overnight stay' and was only allowed a bar of soap and a few essentials. 'As we were leaving court, I asked my mum if there were going to be people outside. She said: "Oh, no." The whole day was a blur.'

• • •

On 11 October 2004, about fifty youths gathered on the St Luke's housing estate in Islington, north London in the early evening.

Most came from neighbouring Hoxton in east London, not the 'Hoxton' of hipsters but part of a long-established working-class community. Some came equipped with baseball bats. But most were simply there because it was a Monday night and there wasn't much else to do. They had no idea what was about to happen.

Three nights earlier, on the previous Friday, there had been a stand-off between some of the boys and a twenty-year-old called Louis Colley outside the Toffee Park Youth Club on the St Luke's estate. The boys came back seeking revenge. Word quickly spread that a fight was about to kick off. The reason for the bad feeling was predictable enough. According to Colley, he caught the eye of a fifteen-year-old who he didn't know. The boy said words to the effect of 'Who are you looking at?'

Now, three nights later, this slight was going to be avenged. Colley was confronted by Bullabeck Ring-Biong and another male. A third man went to punch Colley, who hit back. Colley was then quickly surrounded and set upon by a number of the group with fists, feet and weapons. Witnesses described baseball bats being wielded and at least one knife was seen. One witness, Bilel Khelfa, who would later testify against Sam Hallam, described seeing a baseball bat with a screw, possibly a nail, protruding from its end.

Essayas Kassahun, a trainee chef, went to his friend Colley's help and, tragically, paid the price. Kassahun was struck on the head with a sharp, thin object which penetrated his skull. Colley fled, seeking refuge in a local Somerfield store. The attackers rapidly made their escape, some of them fleeing on BMX bikes.

Kassahun, bleeding heavily, was helped across Old Street to

a nearby Shell garage. The police and ambulance soon arrived but he had already lost consciousness. He never came around. His time of death was recorded at the Royal London Hospital as 11 a.m. on Wednesday 13 October.

Lady Justice Hallett described the death of Essayas Kassahun as 'yet another tragic example of gang violence'. It was one more senseless killing which came about, predictably enough, due to perceived disrespect between groups of young men who scarcely knew each other.

As the judge put it: 'A fight that began for little reason and lasted less than five minutes left one young man dying in the street and several other young men incarcerated for many years.' Sam Hallam was seventeen years old at the time of his arrest. He was working as a kitchen fitter with his father, Terry. He had no criminal record.

He told the police that he had not been present at St Luke's estate when the violence erupted. There was no forensic evidence linking Hallam to the killing and no CCTV footage. He was the only person to stand trial who claimed not to have been present on the night. None of his co-accused attempted to implicate Hallam, nor did they suggest that he had been at St Luke's estate.

Of eight people charged with murder, only Sam Hallam and Bullabek Ring-Biong were convicted.

So how was Hallam convicted?

It was a busy murder scene. Two witnesses placed him there: Phoebe Henville and Bilel Khelfa, the witness who claimed he had seen the customised baseball bat.

The evidence of these two witnesses was weak from the

start. In their initial statements to the police, neither witness said anything to indicate that they had recognised Sam Hallam or anyone who looked like him at the scene of the crime. Khelfa's identification was prompted by Phoebe Henville's identification, which was made in a second statement to the police. Khelfa even disavowed his own testimony at the trial.

In the wake of the killing, rumours were flying around that a 'Sam' had been one of the attackers. Seventeen-year-old Phoebe Henville, who told the police she was the victim's girlfriend, had heard the rumours. Shortly after she had been told that Kassahun had died, she was walking down the street with a friend and bumped into Sam Hallam. Phoebe Henville's friend shouted at Hallam: 'Are you happy now he's dead?' Henville then confronted Hallam and accused him of taking part in the attack. After this encounter, she contacted the police.

Henville then made her second statement identifying Sam Hallam as one of the attackers. Khelfa then made a second statement. At the trial, he explained that he identified Hallam because Henville had told him Hallam's name. He now thought he had made a mistake. In light of his unhelpful testimony, the prosecution applied for him to be treated as a hostile witness.

During the course of the trial, Henville said: 'If it wasn't him [Sam Hallam], I saw someone who looked like him.' She was asked: 'So the position is it may not have been him but someone who looked like him?' 'Yes,' she replied.

Under cross-examination, Henville was asked whether she had any doubts that Hallam was the person she had seen at the incident. She replied: 'No, I was just looking for someone to blame on the spot really.'

The subsequent appeal laid bare a woeful police investigation and another shocking failure to disclose. Hallam had two phones taken from him after being arrested. He had one at the interview. That phone contained several photographs, taken at 6.41 p.m. on the night of the murder, that showed Hallam and his father in the George & Vulture pub a couple of miles from the scene of the killing.

The phone also contained a photograph of Hallam with a friend, Tim Harrington. Hallam had originally claimed he was playing football with Harrington at the time of the attack. However, Harrington said that he had not seen his friend all week. Hallam's failure to recall where he was on the fatal night was claimed by the prosecution as evidence that he had invented a false alibi. 'Given the attachment of young people and the more mature to their mobile phones, we can't understand why someone, either from the investigating team or the defence team, did not think to examine the phones attributable to the appellant,' noted Lady Justice Hallett.

The Metropolitan Police originally claimed that they didn't have the in-house technology to examine the phones. However, Hallett noted that even a cursory check would have produced 'some interesting results'.

The Criminal Cases Review Commission used its Section 19 powers under the Criminal Appeal Act 1995 to instruct an outside police force to investigate the case.*

Thames Valley Police spoke to thirty-seven witnesses who

---

* It is a power that had been invoked by the CCRC on seventy occasions since 1997. More than one third of Section 19 investigations have led to cases then being referred to the Court of Appeal.

were at St Luke's estate on the night of the killing. Not one of them placed Sam Hallam at the scene. Thames Valley officers also spoke to Khelfa, who confirmed '200 per cent' that Hallam had not been present that night. As regards his second statement identifying Hallam, Khelfa told the officers to 'wipe it … 'Cos it's not true.' 'Phoebe come over and told me: "Yeah, it's Sam Hallam." I go and tell everyone: "Yeah, it's Sam Hallam." That's dumb, isn't it? Really and truly, I should go to jail…'

Phoebe Henville refused to be interviewed.

The CCRC's chairman damned the Metropolitan Police for conducting a 'poor-quality investigation' and said the record-keeping was 'just a disaster'. Superintendent Mick Broster, the detective in charge of the case, was reported to be leading a further fourteen major inquiries, most of them murders. According to the Thames Valley Police report, every witness statement, interview or other inquiry document came with a front 'control sheet' meant to be signed off by the senior investigating officer or his junior. In the Hallam file, there were more than 800 such control sheets, not one of which was signed by Broster or his deputy. 'There was simply no control over this investigation, not because of dishonesty, but poor management and staff shortages,' a CCRC commissioner told the media.

• • •

Sam Hallam was one of the youngest victims of a UK miscarriage of justice. He was convicted when he was just seventeen years old and spent seven years in prison before his conviction was quashed. I interviewed him in May 2015, three years after his release. At the time friends and family were concerned about how the then 27-year-old was coping with life on the outside.

Patrick Maguire had a unique insight into the kind of damage likely to have been done to Hallam. He was thirteen years old when he was arrested at his home in west London along with his mother, Anne Maguire, her husband Paddy and four other members of his family in December 1974. He was the youngest of the Maguire Seven, wrongly convicted for an IRA bombing campaign in the 1970s.

Patrick Maguire visited Hallam in prison in 2006 and, convinced of Hallam's innocence, campaigned for his release. 'My biggest sentence started when I was released – and Sam will have to go through this too,' Maguire said when Hallam was freed. 'What it's done to him mentally, I honestly don't know.' Maguire is now in his mid-fifties and is still going to counselling.

When I met Sam Hallam he was living with girlfriend Renee in her flat in Stoke Newington, north London. Although just a few miles from the tight-knit Hoxton community the couple had grown up in, they talked as though they had moved to a different city. As Hallam put it: 'It is like a whole new life to me.'

'I used to get really angry. But now, I say to people I feel more angry than I did then,' Hallam told me. He found prison hard. 'When I first went there, I just hated it,' he said. 'But you can't do time as long as I did without in some way making it normal. You can't spend every day just dwelling on it, dreading the next day.' He recalled his twenty-first birthday party and the double-decker bus. He didn't hear his family and friends 'but I knew they were there'.

It was not an easy interview to conduct. Hallam, like many

young men, is not someone who finds it easy to discuss his emotions with a stranger. Instead, his bright and concerned girlfriend, Renee, talked about the impact of the lost years. 'Sam's doing a lot better than he was,' she told me. Starting a family had apparently helped. The couple, who had an eleven-month-old baby, had known each other since childhood. 'Sam's really, really great with Thierry. That's because he's a big kid – technically, they're the same age,' Renee teased.

Hallam had not worked since his release, other than brief stints on a building site and in Marks & Spencer. When I asked what his ideal job would be, he replied: 'I don't know. I know I should know, but I don't have a clue. These things take time. It will happen when it happens.'

Baby Thierry took his name from Thierry Henry – Hallam is a keen Arsenal fan – but it was also a tribute to Hallam's own father, Terry, who hanged himself from a balcony in a block of flats in October 2010 because, as Hallam's mother put it, he 'couldn't take it any more'. Sam Hallam had yet to come to come to terms with that tragedy and hadn't visited his father's grave. 'It will happen when it happens,' he told me.

• • •

In the early 1990s, Dr Adrian Grounds, a forensic psychiatrist and honorary fellow at Cambridge University, was asked to assess five men from the Birmingham Six and Guildford Four. He did not anticipate finding evidence of what he called 'psychiatric morbidity' because none of the men had had any history of psychiatric illness before being incarcerated.

'What emerged from the interviews was wholly unexpected,' Dr Grounds wrote in a 2005 paper.* His assessments revealed a pattern of 'disabling symptoms and psychological problems' that were severe, similar in all the cases but unfamiliar to the psychiatrist. The extent of the men's suffering was 'profound', the psychiatrist wrote.

Dr Grounds later assessed thirteen more men released on appeal, including ten who were wrongfully convicted of non-terrorist murders. Like Sam Hallam, the men struggled talking about their experiences. Some of their most severe psychological problems, such as the loss of feelings of closeness to their families who had supported them, made them feel guilty and ashamed.

All but four of the thirteen had undergone a personality change consistent with a diagnosis of 'enduring personality change after catastrophic experience'. Characteristics not previously seen included 'a hostile or mistrustful attitude towards the world, social withdrawal, feelings of emptiness or hopelessness, a chronic feeling of threat, and estrangement'.

A dozen of the men met the diagnostic criteria for post-traumatic stress disorder, with symptoms that usually related to events involving extreme threats of violence following arrest or in prison. In seven cases, the men reported suffering terror that they would be killed following their arrest. Of the other five men, one reported assaults by the police and four experienced terror of being assaulted or killed in prison.

Ten of the men suffered from depression after being released

---

* 'Understanding the Effects of Wrongful Imprisonment', Adrian Grounds from prison, four exhibited symptoms of paranoia, three were drug addicts and two alcoholics. 'Those who misused drugs or alcohol after release appear to be using to try and blot out depression and PTSD [post-traumatic stress disorder] symptoms,' Grounds noted.

All of the men in his report had been released suddenly, without preparation or support from statutory services that were usually available for long-term prisoners. The psychiatrist observed that after being in maximum-security prison for years, the prisoners were 'typically taken to the Court of Appeal, the decision was given, and then they were released with a small amount of money and a bag of possessions to their waiting families and the media.'*

. . .

Victor Nealon left HMP Wakefield in December 2013 with just three hours' notice, £46 in his pocket and a train ticket to Shrewsbury. The former postman had been convicted in January 1997 for the attempted rape of a woman leaving a night club in Redditch, Worcestershire. His conviction was quashed after new DNA evidence pointed to another man being the likely attacker.

Nealon spent seventeen years in prison. He could have been

---

* Michael Hickey was convicted of the murder of thirteen-year-old Carl Bridgewater in 1978. Hickey, sixteen at the time, and three other men were sentenced to life for the shooting. He spent eighteen years in prison. He was delivered from the cells to the Royal Courts of Justice barefoot in 1997 because, as his barrister Henry Blaxland QC explained, 'He had just been taken from his cell not knowing what was going to happen. He never recovered from his experiences.'

released after seven years, but was rejected for parole because he refused to accept guilt or undergo rehabilitation to address his 'crime'. 'It is one thing to lose your freedom, family, friends, job and money; but it's quite another thing to be told in prison that, unless you confess to the crime, you'll never ever be released,' he told me in 2015. 'I was told I had no prospect for release. I continued to maintain my innocence for seventeen years.'

It was widely, but inaccurately, reported that Victor Nealon spent his first night of freedom sleeping on the streets. What happened was that the newly released Nealon was driven by the deputy prison governor to Wakefield railway station. He then made his way to Shrewsbury to meet a friend he knew from prison. Unfortunately, and unbeknownst to Victor Nealon, his pal had travelled to the Royal Courts of Justice in London to meet him.

Nealon was forced to spend his £46 discharge grant on a room at a local bed and breakfast. The next morning he was approached by BBC journalists who (in his words) 'agreed to accommodate me temporarily in a cheap hotel if I gave them an interview'. I asked if he had been comfortable with the deal. 'It was better than being on the streets but, no, I wasn't,' he said. 'It was expedient. I had absolutely no idea what to do. I was living from hour to hour.' His friend later put him in touch with Birmingham Yardley MP John Hemming. Nealon then stayed in a flat above the MP's constituency office.

In an interview that he gave to the *Mail on Sunday* upon his release, Victor Nealon told the journalist that he was 'a greater person for prison'. 'All experiences are valuable,' he said. 'Like Nelson Mandela said, there is no easy walk to freedom.' He later regretted making this comment. 'My mind was so overloaded at the time,' he explained to me. 'I was overwhelmed by the fact that I was released and that there were people around me listening to me.' Any post-release euphoria swiftly evaporated.

Prison had been traumatic. 'The most damaging aspect of the system isn't being with violent people but the state ideology that says if you don't conform you are never going to be released,' he said. 'That was what was so damaging. If I had not overturned my conviction I would still be classified as "a denier".'

• • •

Victor Nealon and Sam Hallam have little in common, quite possibly nothing other than their shared experience of being locked up for crimes they did not commit. The government has rejected their claims for compensation and their two cases are now joined in a test case challenging the new scheme that is due to be heard in the Supreme Court in 2018. The new scheme reflects a run of cases where the courts have increasingly narrowed the definition of 'miscarriage of justice'.

When a conviction is quashed, the Court of Appeal does not reinstate the presumption of innocence. In fact, the court almost never offers an unequivocal declaration of innocence. In one study of the Criminal Cases Review Commission database of 133 Court of Appeal judgments, there was only one such judgment.*

Victor Nealon's conviction was quashed in December 2012

---

* According to Carolyn Hoyle in her chapter 'Compensating Injustice' from *The Integrity of Criminal Process* (Oxford: Hart, 2016). The case was Peter Fell.

after DNA pointed to another man as the perpetrator ('the unknown male'). The appeal court noted that 'the jury may reasonably have reached the conclusion, based on the DNA evidence, that it was a real possibility that the "unknown male" – and not the appellant – was the attacker'.*

In the case of Sam Hallam, the appeal court expressed sympathy (quite rightly) to the brother and family of Essayas Kassahun. 'By all accounts he was a charming young man with a great deal to offer. They have had to cope with their grief at the death of Essayas, the original investigation, the trial, a reopening of the investigation, and now these proceedings,' Lady Justice Hallett said. 'We hope that they understand that we must all do our job according to law.'

There was no sympathy expressed for Sam Hallam. In fact, there was more than a suggestion that the then seventeen-year-old was the architect of his own fate. 'We now know there is the real possibility that the appellant's failed alibi was consistent with faulty recollection and a dysfunctional lifestyle, and that it was not a deliberate lie,' Lady Justice Hallett said.

The judge also noted that 'for whatever reason, be it distress or well-intentioned legal advice', Sam Hallam did not help himself during interviews or in the witness box. 'This was not a

---

* Victor Nealon had volunteered for a DNA test at his very first police interview. He made two earlier applications to the CCRC in 1999 and 2002. On both occasions, the group agreed to investigate his case and, on both occasions, Nealon called for the watchdog to carry out a DNA test. In its 2002 decision not to refer the case, the CCRC said that it was not its policy to carry out 'speculative tests'. Nealon blames the group for him spending an additional ten years in prison because (in his words) it 'accepted at face value evidence given by the police that examinations had been carried out in respect of forensic evidence'. Richard Foster, chairman of the CCRC, wrote to Nealon in June 2014 acknowledging that the group 'could and should have identified there were forensic opportunities that had not been explored'.

case therefore, in our judgement, in which either the prosecutor or the trial judge could conclude that there was no evidence against him,' she said. 'There was evidence of his involvement for the jury to consider, whatever criticisms could be made of it. The criticisms went to the credibility and reliability of witnesses.'

Despite the clear failures of the police investigation, no criticism was made of officers involved or the CPS. In 2014, the Ministry of Justice introduced the new arrangements for compensation. It has rejected Sam Hallam's compensation claim, as well as that of Victor Nealon.

The two men find themselves caught in a bind: no doubt innocent but, as they cannot categorically demonstrate their innocence, the state does not recognise them as the victims of 'miscarriages of justice' and worthy of compensation.

• • •

Paddy Hill and Robert Brown first met thirty years ago in Wormwood Scrubs. It was around the time of the Birmingham Six's first appeal in 1988. Brown had been in prison for ten years for the murder of Annie Walsh. 'We heard about each other through the grapevine when we were being shifted from jail to jail,' Hill told me. 'What did you hear?' I asked him. 'That he was innocent and that he had been fighting his case for years, and when I get out I said I would do something,' Hill replied. 'Of course, it took another ten fucking years.'

In 1991, the Birmingham Six finally had their convictions overturned for the 1974 pub bombings that killed twenty-one people. Robert Brown spent twenty-five years in jail before his conviction was overturned in 2002. Brown had been living in Hulme, Manchester in 1977 when Annie Walsh was bludgeoned to death in her flat. The police had beaten a confession out of the nineteen-year-old Roberts after interviewing him for thirty-two hours without any lawyer being present.

I met Paddy Hill and Robert Brown at the end of 2017 to talk about their campaign to highlight the lack of support available to wrongly convicted people after they are released.* The main idea for the campaign is to ensure that the kind of services available to guilty prisoners on release is also available to those who are wrongly convicted. They also want a public announcement on behalf of the wrongly convicted of innocence to be made automatically on release.

Robert Brown, one of the longest-serving victims of a miscarriage of justice, inevitably did time with all of the Birmingham Six over the years. Pointing to Hill, he said: 'What this guy has done for miscarriages of justice and their families, he deserves a fucking knighthood. If he was doing it for the system, he'd get the recognition.' Without missing a beat, Brown added: 'I have no doubt he would tell them to shove it.'

Paddy Hill was once described by the psychiatrist Professor Gordon Turnbull, who had counselled the Beirut hostages Terry Waite and John McCarthy as well as survivors from the Gulf wars, as one of the most traumatised people he has ever come across. As well as the knowledge that he was innocent, Hill and the other Irish prisoners were terrorised by the prison

---

* The pair had been to the European Parliament, the Irish Parliament and Westminster with film-maker Mark McLoughlin. They were showing politicians a 2017 BBC documentary called *Fallout* which featured their stories. The "Say I'm Innocent" campaign has a website: www.sayiminnocent.com.

officers and prisoners alike because of the fury over the IRA's bombing campaign. Hill lost count of the number of times he was beaten up by the 'screws'.

Hill was one of the eighteen men whom Dr Adrian Grounds originally assessed in the early 1990s. He assessed Hill a second time in December 2001. The most striking observation was that there had been no substantial improvement in his condition. 'He continues to suffer from a chronic mood disorder and post-traumatic stress disorder,' Grounds wrote. 'The changes in his personality and his estrangement from others remain, and he has not been able to sustain intimate and close relationships.'

When I interviewed Paddy Hill in 2016, on the twenty-fifth anniversary of the release of the Birmingham Six Irishmen, he told me: 'I still break down and cry even now. It is like a big black cloud descends on you. I don't even know what I'm crying about. Sometimes I pull the shutters down, and stare at the walls for days.'

Paddy Hill and Robert Brown remain damaged people. They are the first to admit it. A 2017 BBC documentary juxtaposed the experiences of Hill and Brown, wired and raging, with those of two other prisoners, Peter Pringle and Sunny Jacobs, who collectively spent thirty-two years on death row for crimes they did not commit. Pringle and Jacobs seemed to have achieved some kind of hard-won serenity in their idyllic home in Connemara in the west of Ireland.

Peter Pringle spent fifteen years in Ireland's 'Death Cell' awaiting execution after being wrongfully convicted of killing two Irish police officers in 1980. In the BBC documentary, he spoke almost poetically about his first day of freedom, reflecting on a 'big, twisted, gnarled and very beautiful' apple tree at the bottom of the garden where he was staying. 'All the time I had spent in prison, all the difficulties I had been through, all the machinations and hustle and bustle and this tree was doing its thing untouched by the injustices of the justice system,' he said. 'I put my arms around the trunk of the tree and I wept.'

Pringle quickly added that post-release euphoria was short-lived. Dr Adrian Grounds spent three days with the Irishman. He explained to Pringle about grief and how, at some point, he would be forced to mourn for the life he might have had. The psychologist advised Pringle not to look for that moment but to be prepared to deal with its inevitable pain. The moment arrived four years after Pringle's release. His housemate returned home to hear a sound like 'an animal in pain'. He discovered Pringle in a box-room upstairs, lying in a foetal position and screaming.

I spoke to Robert Brown about the peace of mind finally achieved by Pringle and Jacobs. 'Did you really buy that?' Brown retorted. 'I can't convey the pain I feel,' he said. 'I feel like walking out into the street with a sawn-off shotgun and just blasting cops. That's how I get to sleep every night, fantasising about that. They have made me like this.'

Brown recalled his old self as an 'innocent kid of nineteen years'. 'The system made me violent. You have to be violent to survive,' he said. 'You have to come out of your cell with a knife every day because you do not know who is going to attack you. It is an environment that produces psychoses in people. It produces hate, anger and jealousy. A lot of men in jail are little boys. They become stunted. They never grow up.'

The damage is ingrained. One of the punishments meted out

to difficult prisoners was to deprive them of privileges. This included the removal of beds between seven in the morning and eight in the evening. As an act of defiance, Brown refused to sleep on his bed at night; instead he would lie down on the cold cell floor, with his coat pulled over him. To this day he sleeps on the floor despite having a double bed. 'Prison is a harmful environment – the longer you serve the more harm it does,' he said.

Adrian Grounds's research shows that a proportion of miscarriage of justice victims succumb to drink and drugs in an attempt to deal with their lives. Robert Brown freely admitted that he is one of them. 'I take drugs every day to get through this,' he said. 'People use hard drugs and drink to blast themselves into oblivion, to numb the nightmares that they see and hear every night; to deal with recurring memories and the pain.'

Paddy Hill can make a frankly alarming impression on people. 'I was described by a number of people who interviewed me as the angriest person they have ever interviewed. I think I have got a fucking right to be angry,' Hill said. 'I walked into a police station of my own free will to be eliminated from enquiries. It took me sixteen and a half fucking years to get out. I was happily married with six kids. I lost everything.'

One of the saddest aspects of Adrian Grounds's research was the 'profound estrangement' it showed between the men and their families, who spent years campaigning and waiting for their release. One of the interviewee's daughters told the psychiatrist that at the time of her father's release, everyone assumed the closeness would return immediately. 'But no one realised how distant we would be,' she said. 'Everyone thought we could slot into a happy family routine, and it's been a great shock to everyone concerned that it has not worked out like that. Nowhere near.'

When I first interviewed Hill in 1999, the father of six told me that he no longer had feelings for his children. It was a shocking statement. I asked him how he now felt, eighteen years after our first interview. 'I spent more time here with you today than I have spent with my kids in the last five years,' he replied. 'It is not because I don't want to: I can't.' Hill has tirelessly campaigned for other innocent men and women in prison through his Glasgow-based Miscarriage of Justice Organisation. 'When I got out, I promised the guys in jail the first year of my life campaigning for them highlighting miscarriages of justice; then I got involved with families, it made me realise this is what my family went through. I have been doing it ever since. My anger level has actually gone up – for these people.'

• • •

When Robert Brown left prison it was Paddy Hill who was there to meet him. Bizarrely, this arrangement was at the suggestion of the Lord Chief Justice's office. Hill received a phone call three weeks before he was released and he was asked if he could travel to HMP Kirkham to pick up Brown and (as Hill puts it) 'he was released into my custody'. 'The only stipulation was that I would bring him to the Court of Appeal at 10 a.m. on the day of the appeal,' he says.*

---

* Apparently, the same arrangement was made in other miscarriage of justice cases including Patrick Nicholls and John Kamara.

Brown has always insisted on his innocence and refused to recognise the parole system. 'I was going to leave prison one of two ways: innocent or dead,' he said. He had been given a fifteen-year tariff. 'They tried to offer me release on licence after thirteen years if I admitted I was guilty,' he recalled. So, as he puts it, 'like Morgan Freeman in *Shawshank Redemption*' he went before the parole board every twelve months to say: 'I do not recognise the system. I am an innocent man.'

Six weeks before his successful appeal, Brown discovered his mother had cancer and had been given six months to live. He was advised to apply for bail. Paddy Hill took his friend's dying mother to court for the bail application. 'They sat in the front row of the court,' Brown recalled. 'The judge didn't even look at me. Bail denied. There was no compassion whatsoever.'

Paddy Hill would visit Brown's sick mother. Robert Brown was given compassionate leave for a day. 'They brought him up to the house on a fucking dog chain,' Hill recalled.

When Robert Brown left prison, all he had was the £46 grant and a train ticket to Glasgow where his dying mother lived. 'They threw me out with next to no money. All I had was a black bag for my possessions.' He remains indebted to Hill. 'He picked me up outside the jail. This man has dedicated his life since he was released to expose the injustice in the British justice system.'

• • •

When Eddie Gilfoyle left prison in 2010 after seventeen years, there was talk of him living with Paddy Hill. Gilfoyle often stays with Hill at his home in Scotland. Both Hill and Brown served time with him. When I met Brown and Hill at the end of 2017 they were both angry at the Criminal Cases Review Commission's refusal to refer the Gilfoyle case back to the Court of Appeal. 'Sad and bewildering,' said Brown, shaking his head.

Hill gave the following bitter assessment. 'The Court of Appeal never looks at the full picture. They look at the bits and pieces. That is no way to view a case. You need to look at all the evidence. They are there to uphold the conviction and uphold the so-called integrity of British judicial system. The system is supposed to the fairest in the world – it's not the system, it is the people that administer it. They don't live in the same world. They live in their ivory towers.'

Two weeks after my interview with Hill and Brown, I travelled to Paul and Sue Caddick's house. Eddie Gilfoyle has lived with his sister and brother-in-law since his release from prison. It can't be easy.

Eddie Gilfoyle is instantly recognisable as the same man in the smiling wedding photographs taken all those years ago at Moreton Presbyterian Church – he still has the same heavy moustache – but he now looks alarming frail; his features are taut, his hair grey. He is in his fifties but looks much older. He is unsteady on his feet and prone to falling. Paul and Sue do most of the talking. Occasionally Eddie interjects, and when he does this Paul often qualifies a statement and puts him right on the detail. Eddie Gilfoyle looks a shattered and beaten man. The house is tucked away off a quiet country road in a remote and picturesque setting. Gilfoyle never leaves the house alone.

All three of them are devastated by the latest setback, which has seen the Criminal Cases Review Commission refuse to refer the Gilfoyle case back to the Court of Appeal. 'What do we do now?' Sue Caddick asks, as we sit down. 'We have fought so long. But what is the point?'

Someone from the CCRC once told me that they have found Eddie Gilfoyle a disturbing presence at conferences. Gilfoyle didn't try to speak to this person; it was the intensity of his stare that made the person feel uncomfortable. But today the fight has gone out of Eddie Gilfoyle. No doubt it will return.

• • •

Paddy Hill and Robert Brown are driven by seemingly endless reserves of fury. Their anger is not just aimed at the police who fitted them up, or the prison staff that beat them up. It is also directed at the shameful way that the justice system conspired to cover up the original wrongs and refused to recognise their innocence.

The main reason for Paddy Hill's 'chronic anger', as Dr Grounds put it in his report, was the absence of any official apology for his wrongful imprisonment. 'In my experience, among those who have been wrongfully imprisoned, the need to have an apology, an official response of regret and acknowledgment that they were wronged, is of the greatest psychological importance,' the psychiatrist wrote. 'Commonly, they feel this to be more important than money, and the absence of such responses maintains intense bitterness.'

• • •

A generation of politicians cut their campaigning teeth calling for the release of the Birmingham Six and Guildford Four in the 1980s and 1990s; but they turned their backs on the other victims of miscarriages of justice.

The political mood music changed when 'New' Labour came to power in 1997 with its famous 'tough on crime, tough on the causes of crime' electoral promise. Five years into Tony Blair's government, a new theme emerged in the criminal justice discourse: the criminal justice system was to be 'rebalanced'. The scales of justice were to be tipped in the direction of the rights of victims and away from the rights of defendants.

At the 2002 Labour Party conference, Tony Blair sought to redefine what was commonly understood by the phrase 'miscarriage of justice'. 'It's a miscarriage of justice when delays and time-wasting deny victims justice for months on end,' the PM told the party faithful. 'It's a miscarriage of justice when the police see their hard work and bravery thrown away by courts, who let a mugger out on bail for the seventh or eighth time to offend again, or when courts don't have the secure places to put people. And it's perhaps the biggest miscarriage of justice in today's system when the guilty walk away unpunished.'

Labour's Baroness Helena Kennedy once said that Blair's words were 'a complete reversal' of the approach to justice that every mature democracy took.

Tony Blair's notion of 'rebalancing' the justice system has set the tone for how successive generations of politicians have talked about criminal justice. The PM, with his sharp ear for the popular mood, unhelpfully linked the rights of defendants to those of victims. It takes a brave politician to champion the rights of suspects if those rights are at the expense of victims. There are no votes in prisoners, even innocent ones.

In 2006, Home Secretary Charles Clarke offered the following one-sided caricature of the relatively tiny number of defence lawyers willing to take on notoriously difficult cases: 'A massive industry for the legal profession that has been giving away large amounts of money to individuals who do not deserve it.'

Clarke decided, without any consultation, to scrap an *ex gratia* scheme to compensate the victims of miscarriages of justice in what was, he suggested, part of his efforts to rebalance the justice system. He reckoned that the scheme was costing over £2 million a year to run and benefited between five and ten applicants a year.* Professor John Spencer QC, of Cambridge University, denounced the move as 'monstrous'. In an open letter, the academic argued that scrapping the scheme hit not only those whose convictions were quashed in circumstances that left their factual guilt or innocence in doubt ('a group for whom some people's sympathy, understandably, is limited') but also those whose innocence is absolutely clear. He cited the example of Colin Stagg, who was wrongly accused of the murder of Rachel Nickell on Wimbledon Common.† Stagg received compensation of over £700,000

---

* Charles Clarke also wanted to introduce the Scottish verdict of 'not proven', which effectively leaves a stain on someone's reputation. Paddy Hill, released in 1991, was offered compensation of more than £960,000 – less £50,000 for 'bed and board'.

† Fourteen years after Colin Stagg was acquitted in 1994, the real killer was found: Robert Napper, a paranoid schizophrenic.

under the old scheme but would now, Spencer pointed out, receive nothing.*

Thanks to Charles Clarke's intervention, compensation has now been limited to those who have a statutory right under the Criminal Justice Act 1988, Section 133. Professor Spencer described such provisions as 'very mean' and only enacted to put the UK in line with minimal international obligations.

That was not to be the end of the sorry saga. The uncertain territory between guilt and non-guilt had also been troubling the courts. 'Innocence as such is not a concept known to our criminal justice system,' said Lady Hale in 2011, as the Supreme Court tussled with the meaning of 'a miscarriage of justice'. 'We distinguish between the "guilty" and the "not guilty". A person is only guilty if the state can prove his guilt beyond reasonable doubt.'†

Government ministers did not find the lawyerly distinction terribly helpful. The coalition government sought to clarify and limit the meaning even further. Its Anti-Social Behaviour, Crime and Policing Act 2014 amended the section 133 scheme so that compensation payments were restricted to those few people who could demonstrate their innocence 'beyond reasonable doubt'.

---

* The academic paraphrased Clarke's position. 'None of these people are really innocent – otherwise they wouldn't have attracted the attention of the police,' he said. 'They're not victims of miscarriages of justice, they're just lucky. Too bad they didn't get the punishment that they deserved; a good thing they had to spend at least some time in prison; and no way should we add to their undeserved good luck by handing them out compensation: except in those cases where, to our regret, our international obligations make it compulsory.'

† In R (Adams) v. Secretary of State for Justice, the Supreme Court in a majority ruling (five to four) held that a miscarriage of justice had occurred when 'a new or newly discovered fact' showed conclusively that the 'evidence against a defendant has been so undermined that no conviction could possibly be based upon it'.

So much for the presumption of innocence. To ask people to prove their innocence beyond reasonable doubt was 'an affront to our system of law', said Baroness Helena Kennedy in a debate as the legislation was going through the House of Lords. 'It is very difficult for people to prove that they are innocent beyond reasonable doubt: "Prove that you didn't kill your baby; prove that you didn't leave a bomb in the pub."'*

The Labour peer and barrister cited her own experience of representing the Guildford Four, as well as the case of Mary Druhan, convicted of arson when she was in her fifties.

Mary Druhan arrived in England from Ireland to work as a private nurse. She started drinking when her husband died, her alcoholism spiralled out of control and she lost her home. In 1989, she was convicted of murdering two alcoholics by causing a fire in a squat at Kingston. Her conviction was overturned when it was argued that one of the prosecution witnesses had subsequently been linked to two other fires in derelict houses.

According to Baroness Kennedy, Mary Druhan 'came blinking out into the light' after eleven years in jail, 'totally institutionalised, unable to negotiate public transport and incapable of rebuilding her life without considerable help'. Her daughter had committed suicide while she was in prison. 'Systems go wrong,' Kennedy said. 'It is one measure of a society's values that it is able to put right what has gone wrong.'

In his 2005 research, Dr Adrian Grounds said that the prospect of financial compensation was 'not a strong motivating factor' for

---

* Both Suzanne Holdsworth and Lorraine Harris (see Chapter 8) were denied compensation by the Ministry of Justice under Section 133. The Court of Appeal rejected Harris's claim that she was a miscarriage of justice victim.

the eighteen men he interviewed. 'The men were much more preoccupied with a desire for apology, exoneration and exposure of those they held to blame for the miscarriage of justice,' he wrote.

At Sam Hallam's appeal, when the prosecution counsel David Hatton QC told the court that he was 'not in a position to oppose the appeal', Hallam's lawyer Matt Foot recalled 'the most almighty roar' from the public gallery. 'It was an expression of relief from the Hoxton community that something they knew to be wrong for so long had finally come to an end,' he told me.

The lawyer recalled the 'same roar' being heard twice more: when Sam Hallam was given bail at the end of the day, and the following day when the judgment was read aloud, confirming the conviction had been quashed. 'I remember people clapping the legal team as we walked from the cells. I regret we didn't stop and clap them for getting the case to the court,' Foot said.

However, there was a nagging fear on the part of the lawyers that the court had closed off Sam Hallam's chances of a successful compensation claim under the new scheme. They were well aware of the fact that the Ministry of Justice was likely to reject any claim unless there was an unambiguous statement of innocence from the court. Hallam's barrister, Henry Blaxland QC, invited the court to make such a declaration. But Lady Justice Hallett did not oblige. 'This is not a court of compensation,' she warned him.

As Matt Foot put it: 'In my view, she criticised a seventeen-year-old arrested for murder, placed in custody away from his family for the first time in his life, for basic failures of the police, who had failed to review one of his phones which they had seized as an exhibit.'

The lawyer points out that that court had evidence from the Thames Valley Police report that fourteen witnesses, who had no reason to lie, had said that Sam Hallam was not present at the murder scene. The intended victim of the murder, Louis Colley, was amongst those who vouched for Hallam. Apart from the unreliable and discredited identification evidence, there was nothing at all to place Sam Hallam at the scene.

When I met Sam Hallam, I asked him what 'compensation' might mean to him. 'Money cannot make up for what happened. It is more about recognising the harm done,' he told me. As his girlfriend Renee put it: 'There has to be some recognition of what happened. Everyone just shrugged their shoulders and said, "Well, you're out now. You should just be happy."'

• • •

A miscarriage of justice is not a one-off event. The correct analogy is not so much a car crash, but a serial motorway pile-up.

First, they are failed by the criminal justice system – in itself, often a serial failure involving police, prosecution, courts and their own lawyers – with devastating consequences for not only their lives but the lives of their loved ones as well. Then they are further failed by a penal system that uses the denial of privileges and parole to punish them for maintaining their innocence. Then, after all the wasted years, their trauma (and it is almost always traumatic) is compounded by the extreme reluctance of the courts to correct the original wrong.

Finally, if their conviction is overturned then, like Sam Hallam, they are undoubtedly innocent – and yet not innocent enough.

ACKNOWLEDGEMENTS

I want to pay tribute to the courage and determination of those fighting to clear their names, as well as to their families and loved ones.

Miscarriages of justice are stories with heroes as well as villains. All too often, the villains get away with it and the heroes – the campaigners, lawyers, academics and journalists who champion these most difficult of cases – go unsung. Hopefully, this book goes some way to redressing the balance.

I want to take this opportunity to thank everyone who has written for or supported the Justice Gap (www.thejusticegap.com) since we launched in 2011. The site has become a forum for discussion about miscarriages of justice and, more generally, the limits of our justice system at a time when press interest in these difficult issues appears to have waned.

A number of regular contributors have been campaigning in this area for well over twenty years in the wake of scandals such as the Guildford Four and the Birmingham Six.

We are still fighting the same fights. Their support for the site has had a huge influence on me and has been a major motivation for writing this book.

Michael Mansfield QC has acted in many of these cases. It means a great deal that he has written the foreword.

A special mention for Will Bordell. Will was a researcher on *Guilty Until Proven Innocent*. He helped me with the analysis of original documents, including the trial manuscript in the Eddie Gilfoyle case and what remains of the paperwork in the Omar Benguit case. He first wrote about Carla Andrews and Craig Stillwell's case in an article for the Justice Gap. His contribution was always insightful and valuable. Will reviewed the first draft of the manuscript, suggested countless improvements and (tactfully) picked up many typos.

Thanks also to the Justice Gap team of reporters and editors. It is an ever-changing cast of volunteer reporters which currently includes Will, Caterina Franchi, Miranda Grell, Calum McCrae, Charlotte Hughes, Elle Sheerin and Hannah Wilson.

I am grateful to Rod Hayler and David Osborne of Old Bailey Solicitors. Without their support, this project would never have got off the ground. Thanks to Kim Evans, a friend of the Justice Gap from day one, for introducing us.

Other old friends of the Justice Gap include Brian Thornton, senior journalism lecturer at Winchester University; and Professor Julie Price, head of pro bono at Cardiff Law School and who runs their Innocence Project. Julie and Brian have supported the Justice Gap and, in particular, made our new print magazine, *Proof*, happen.

Finally, thanks to my parents, Chris and Margaret, for their unstinting support and love.

ACKNOWLEDGEMENTS

This book is dedicated to Juliet, Bea and Eve – in memory of lunch in Mallorca.

Jon Robins
May 2018

ABOUT THE AUTHOR

Jon Robins is an award-winning journalist and author. He has written about law and justice for twenty years. His work has appeared in *The Times, The Observer, The Guardian, The Independent,* the *Financial Times* and the *Mail on Sunday.*

His books include *The First Miscarriage of Justice: The Unreported and Amazing Case of Tony Stock, The Justice Gap: Whatever Happened to Legal Aid?* and *People Power: How to Run a Campaign and Make a Difference in Your Community.*

Jon is a lecturer in the journalism department at Winchester University. He is also a visiting senior fellow in access to justice at the University of Lincoln, a patron of Hackney Community Law Centre and on the advisory committee for the Centre for Criminal Appeals.

Jon has won the Bar Council's legal journalist of the year award twice (2015 and 2005). He won the Halsbury Legal Journalism award in 2013 and was shortlisted for last year's Criminal Justice Alliance awards.

INDEX

Abdullah, Yusef 54
Alexander, Kenneth 288–9
Allan, Liam viii–ix, xv–xvi, 195–7
Allitt, Beverley 250
Andrews, Carla 221–3, 226–9, 244–5
Andrews, Molly 81
Anti-Social Behaviour, Crime and Policing Act (2014) 321
Aspinall, James xviii–xix
Aspinall, Margaret xviii–xix
Austin-Smith, Michael 249–50, 251, 252
Avery, Steven xxiv

Bache, William 229, 230, 231, 238, 242
Bailey, Simon 156–7, 199
Baines, Chief Inspector 15, 25–6
Barlow, Mark 216
Barnett, Heather 90–91, 92, 103
Baron-Cohen, Simon 280, 281, 282–4, 293–4
Barrington, Ralph 124, 125–6, 127
Bateman, Anthony 251
BB
    interview on *Jeremy Kyle Show* 73–6
    inconsistencies in testimony 76–7, 89, 91–2, 101–3, 106
    at Omar Benguit's trial and retrials 78, 81–7
Beale, Jemma 197–8
Beck, Adolph 24
Beith, Sir Alan 286

Beldam, Lord Justice 33, 34
Bell, Mary 32
Benefield, Samuel
    at Court of Appeal in Tony Stock case 107, 110, 114–19, 121–2, 123
    turns supergrass 112–13
Benguit, Amie 93–5, 96, 97, 98, 100–101, 103, 104
Benguit, Omar
    and BB's testimony 76, 77, 78, 81–7, 101–3
    trials and retrials of 78–87
    and Innocence Project 89
    and CCRC 90, 91, 128
    at Court of Appeal 91–3
    arrest of 93–4
    early life of 94–5
    and Portsmouth University criminal justice clinic 96–7, 98–100
    seeks legal advice 97–8
    life in prison 100–101, 106
    and evidence disclosure 104–5
de Berk, Lucia 255–6, 261–2
Bird, Sheila 258
Birmingham Six ix
    effect on judicial system xvi–xvii
    background to 5–6
    and Runciman Commission 6–7
    represented by Michael Mansfield 28
    effect of life in prison 304–6
Birnbaum, Michael 240

Blair, Tony xv, 319–20
Blaxland, Henry 306
Bobrow, Clive 120
Bramall, Lord 148, 155, 158
Bridgewater, Carl 306
British Medical Journal 239
Brittan, Leon 148, 155
Brown, Robert 310–12, 313–14, 315–16
Bryant, David 208–13, 216–17, 218–19
Bryant, Lynn 216–19
Bryn Estyn abuse allegations 168
Buckley, Christine 50
Bureau of Investigative Journalism 287
Burns, James 19–20, 36
Burns-Williamson, Mark 42
Butler, Ben 237–8
Butler, Rupert 210, 211–13, 216, 218

Caddick, Paul 1, 3–4, 22–3, 28, 30, 48, 67–71, 136, 139–40, 317
Caddick, Sue 60–61, 69, 70, 136, 317, 318
Callaghan, Hugh xvi, 5
Callaghan, Mark 106
Cameron, David vii–viii
Campbell, Michael 288–9
Cannings, Angela 229–30
Canter, Professor 60–61
Cardiff Three 24, 54–6
Carter of Coles, Lord 88
Castree, Ronald 29
Chainsaw Gang 112, 117, 119
Claps, Elisa 90, 91, 92
Clark, Sally 230, 257, 263
Clarke, Charles 320–21
Colley, Louis 298
Commonweal 296
compensation payments 320–24
Conan Doyle, Sir Arthur 24
Cooper, Sarah 80
Court of Appeal
    and CCRC xix–xx, 123–4, 130, 133, 137, 17
    and Runciman Commission 24–5
    and Eddie Gilfoyle 38
    and Danny Major 58–9
    and Omar Benguit 91–3

and Tony Stock 107, 110, 114–21, 123–6, 134–5
and Ben Geen 253–5
Justice Heather Hallett joins 253–4
and joint enterprise cases 286–7, 292
and Alex Henry 292–4
and Sam Hallam 295, 309, 310
declarations of innocence from 308
and Victor Nealon 308–10
Crabbe, Megan 248
Crabtree, Justice 170
Crane, Mr Justice 249
Cranston, Mr Justice 91
Crawford, Sir Frederick 122
Crewe, Ben 286
Crime Survey for England and Wales 275
Criminal Bar Association 196
Criminal Cases Review Commission (CCRC)
    current state of xix–xx, 128–33
    and Court of Appeal xix–xx, 123–4, 130, 133, 137, 171
    creation of 24, 28
    and Eddie Gilfoyle 38, 62–3, 128, 133–40
    and Danny Major 56, 127
    and JUSTICE 88
    and lawyer-supported applications 88
    and Omar Benguit 90, 91, 128
    and university projects 97
    and Tony Stock 121–4, 125–6, 127, 132
    and Ben Geen 258–64, 268–9
    and joint enterprise cases 287, 288
    and Sam Hallam 301–2
    and Victor Nealon 309
Crown Court Record Retention and Disposition Schedules 105
Crown Prosecution Service Inspectorate 54
Curtis-Thomas, Claire 170
Cutting, John 81

Daily Echo 89, 210
Daily Express 15
Daily Mail 113
Daily Post 15, 25–6

INDEX

Daily Telegraph 167–8
Davies, Sandra 12–13, 14, 21, 26
Day, Danny 208–13
Debelle, Geoff 225–6, 230
Demos, Moira xxiv
Denning, Lord 6–7
Dobson, Gary 275
Dreyfus affair 63
Druhan, Mary 322
Dyson, Matthew 286

Eappen, Matthew 243
Earle, Rachel 216
Edalji, George 24
Elks, Laurie 135
European Convention on Human Rights 166
European Court of Human Rights 120
evidence disclosure
   and Liam Allan viii–ix, xv–xvi, 195–7
   Alison Saunders on ix, xvi
   collapse in prosecutions xvi, 197
   and Elgan Varney xvi
   and Danny Major 44, 46–7, 56–9
   and Judith Ward 52–3
   rules on 53, 105–6
   quality of 54
   and Cardiff Three 54–6
   and Eddie Gilfoyle 63–4
   and Omar Benguit 104–5
   and Geoffrey Long 216
Exaro 157, 158
Exposure: The Other Side of Jimmy Savile (TV programme) 145

Falconer, Charlie 275–6, 284
Fell, Peter 308
Fenton, Norman 258, 259–60, 261
Ferguson, Cameron 271–2, 273, 280, 281, 284
File on 4 (radio programme) 127
Finkelstein, Daniel 63, 166
First Miscarriage of Justice, The: The Unreported and Amazing Case of Tony Stock (Robins) 126
Fisher, Kyle 234–6

Flannigan, Sarah 64
Foot, Matt 47–9, 62, 64, 66, 116, 134, 136–7, 323–4
Foot, Paul 116, 124
forensic science ix
   and Birmingham Six 6
   and Judith Ward 52–3
   and Cardiff Three 54
Foster, Richard xx, 127, 130, 132, 309
Fyfe, Paul 291
Fyfe, Tracey 291

Gafoor, Jeffery 54
Gallan, Patricia 158
Gambaccini, Paul 160–63, 174–5
Garsden, Peter 173–4
Gbadamosi, Nick 78, 79–80, 82, 83–4, 85, 86, 101–3
Geddes, Jennian 232, 236, 241
Geen, Ben
   suspicions over hospital deaths 248–9
   arrest and trial 249–51, 256
   press coverage of 249–50
   and Mark McDonald 251–2, 261, 264
   at Court of Appeal 253–4
   and CCRC 258–64, 268–9
   continuing campaign for 264–8
Geen, Erica 265
Geen, Mike 265, 266, 267–8
Gilfoyle, Eddie
   and death of wife 1–5
   murder investigation 7–10, 29–31, 45
   marriage difficulties 10–15
   arrest 15–16
   press coverage 15–16, 25–7, 61–2
   trial of 16–23
   1995 appeal 28–34
   and *Trial and Error* 34–7, 62, 129
   life in prison 37–8
   and CCRC 38, 62–3, 128, 133–40
   review of unused material 47–51
   campaign to overturn conviction 59–66
   evidence disclosure in 63–4
   persecution of Paul Caddick 67–71
   last appeal rejected 133–6
   release from prison 316–18

Gilfoyle, Norman 1, 3, 8, 16, 138
Gilfoyle, Paula
  death of 1–5, 137–8
  murder investigation 7–10, 29–31, 45, 137–40
  marriage difficulties 10–15
  press coverage 15–16, 25–7
  trial of husband 16–23
  likelihood of suicide 26–8, 134, 135–6, 258
  1995 appeal 28–34
  and *Trial and Error* 34–7
  review of unused material 47–51
Gill, Richard 255–6, 261–4, 269
Glidewell, Lord Justice 53
Glover, Margaret 7, 49
Glover, Peter 8, 22–3, 51
Goldsmith, Peter 225
Goldsmith, Susan 242–4
Gooch, Graham 31, 36
Goodman, Dennis 208, 209
Goodyear-Smith, Felicity 199–200
Goss, Mr Justice 272
Gove, Michael xiv
Grant, Linda 169
Grant-Murray, Janhelle 271–3, 276, 279, 282, 292
Great Parliamentary Scandals (Parris) 148
Green, Michael 43
Gregory, Nick 211
Grounds, Adrian 304, 305, 306, 312, 313, 314, 318, 322–3
Guardian, The 146, 169, 198, 242
Guildford Four 7, 28, 304–6
Gunn, Ben 172

Hale, Lady 321
Halford, Alison 60, 68
Hallam, Sam
  at Court of Appeal 295–7, 309, 310
  background to arrest 297–9
  trial of 299–300
  and CCRC 301–2
  effect of life in prison 302–4
  compensation for 323–4

Hallam, Terry 299
Hallam, Wendy 295
Hallett, Justice Heather 78–9, 80, 81, 84, 253–4, 255, 272, 296, 299
Halsall, Sally
  and childhood of Alex Henry 276–8
  and Alex Henry's autism 280, 281
  at Alex Henry's appeal 292, 293
Hands, David 258
Hanson, Ian 43
Harris, Lorraine 233–4, 322
Hatton, David 296, 323
Hayes, Jerry 195–6
Hazell, Stuart 106
Heath, Sir Edward 155, 164–8
Henneberg, Marika 96, 98–9, 104
Henriques, Sir Richard 156, 157–8, 175, 199
Henry, Alex
  on trial 271–2
  at scene of crime 272–4
  previous convictions 276
  behaviour as child 276–8
  early brushes with law 278–80
  diagnosis of autism 280–84
  at Court of Appeal 292–4
Henry, Charlotte 277, 278, 279, 280, 292
Henville, Phoebe 299, 300
Her Majesty's Inspectorate of Constabulary 54
Hewitt, Andrew James 274
Hewitt, Corey 274, 293
Hickey, Michael 306
Hill, Paddy xvi, 5, 6, 310–12, 314, 315, 316–18, 320
Hillsborough disaster xviii–xix
Hirsi, Mohammed 291
Hogan-Howe, Sir Bernard 145, 158–9, 160, 175
Holdsworth, Suzanne 234–6, 322
Horwell, Richard 54–6
Hoyle, Carolyn 308
Humphreys, Detective Superintendent 29–30
Hunt, David (Lord Hunt of Wirral) 60, 165

INDEX

Hunter, Gerry xvi, 5
Hutton, Jane 253, 254–5, 263

Independent Inquiry into Child Sexual Abuse 147
Innocence Network UK 96, 97
Innocence Project 89, 96
Inside Time (newspaper) 174

Jacobs, Sunny 312
Janner, Lord 155, 211–12
Jeremy Kyle Show 73–6, 87
Jessel, David 34, 36, 129
Jogee, Ameen 291–2
joint enterprise
  and Lammy Review viii, 276
  and Alex Henry 271–4, 275–84, 288, 292–4
  and Stephen Lawrence murder 274
  and knife crime 275
  and Ben Kinsella murder 275
  deterrent effect of 284–6
  statistics on 286–8
  JENGbA campaign against 288–90
  and Ameen Jogee 291–2
Jones, Brian 4–5, 34
Jong-Ok Shin (Oki)
  murder of 73–4
  and BB's testimony 73–7
  trails for murder of 78–87
  Danilo Restivo becomes suspect 90–91
  and Danilo Restivo 92
Judge, Lord Justice Igor 115–16, 118
JUSTICE 88, 110, 113–14, 129, 130–31

Kassahun, Essays 298–9
Kennedy, Dominic 59
Kennedy, Helena 319, 322
Kennedy, Ludovic 114
Keynes, John Maynard 257–8
Khelfa, Bilel 298, 299–300
Khezihi, Bourhane 271, 273, 281
Khezihi, Taqui 271, 272–3, 274, 281, 284, 292z
Kinsella, Ben 275
Kirkwood, Heather 236, 237

Kiszko, Stefan 24, 29
Klevan, Rodney 69
Knight, Bernard 32–3, 36–7
Knox, Peter 216
Kray twins 117

Lakhaen, A. G. 262–3
Lammy Review vii–viii, 276
Latham, Lord Justice 124–5
Lawrence, Stephen viii, 274–5
legal aid
  cuts in xiv
  scrapped for accident claims 174
Leveson, Lord Justice 208
Linsell, Izzy 98
Liverpool Echo 15, 16
London Innocence Project 252
London School of Economics 296
Long, Geoffrey
  trials for sexual abuse allegations 203–5, 214–16, 219
  in prison 206–7
  evidence disclosure in 216
Long, James 206, 208
Long, Louise 203, 204–5, 208, 214, 215–16, 219
Loraine-Smith, Nicholas 197–8
Love, Paul Gambaccini (Gambaccini) 160, 162–3
Loveday, Barry 89, 96
Lynöe, Niels 224

McCullough, Mr Justice 16, 17–18, 20, 22
MacDonald, Ken 165
McDonald, Kenny 144, 146–7
McDonald, Mark 251–2, 261, 264
McFarlane, John 284–5
McGill, Joseph James 274, 292
McGregor, Brian 99–100
McHugh, Sean 274
McIlkenny, Richard xvi, 5
McIntosh, Steve 80
McMartin child abuse case 242–3
Macpherson Report viii
Maddocks, Glyn 126, 132
Maguire, Anne 303

Maguire, Paddy 303
Maguire, Patrick 303
Maguire Seven 7
Mail on Sunday 166, 307
Major, Bernadette 127
Major, Danny
   accusation of attack on Sean
      Rimington 39, 40–41
   failings in initial investigation 42–7
   and evidence disclosure 44, 46–7, 56–9
   and CCRC 56, 127
   retrial of 58–9
   as police officer 66
   effect of accusation on 66–7, 70
Major, Eric 127
Making a Murderer (documentary) xxiv
Malone, Campbell 28–9, 235
Mansfield, Michael
   and 1995 Eddie Gilfoyle appeal 28, 31
   and Judith Ward 52
   and Tony Stock 115
Mather, John 108–9, 111, 121, 124
May, Kirsten 247, 248
May, Lord Justice 123
May, Paul 132–3
May, Theresa xiv, viii
Meadows, Sir Roy 229–30, 257
Memory, Sean 166–7
Miller, Stephen 54
Miscarriage of Justice Organisation 315
Mitting, Mr Justice 241
Molseed, Lesley 29
Moody, Jimmy 117
Morgan, Rhodri 169
Morrison, Gloria 288–9, 290

Naish, Peter 190–92
Napper, Robert 320
Natas, Simon 285
Naughtie, James 150
Naughton, Michael 96–7
Nealon, Victor 306–10
Neuberger, Lord 290, 291
New Scientist 224
Newby, Mark 180, 204, 216
Newcomen, Nigel 207

Newsnight (TV programme) 234
Nickell, Rachel 320
Norris, David 275
NSPCC 147

Observer, The 130, 170, 196–7
O'Connor, Andy 274
Office for National Statistics 147
Oldham Evening Chronicle 27
Olumegbob, Zac 285
O'Mara, Anna 193–4
Onley, David 251
Operation Conifer 164–8
Operation Hydrant 156, 199
Operation Lamp 42–7, 57, 59, 66, 127
Operation Midland 147, 156, 175, 199
Operation Yewtree 160

Paddick, Brian 161
Paget, Reginald 24
Panorama (TV programme) 223–4
Paris, Tony 54
Parris, Matthew 148–9
Pearl, Judge David 241
Piper, Maureen 31–2, 33, 45
Police Complaints Authority 31
Police and Criminal Evidence Act (1984)
   111
Portsmouth University 96–7, 98–100, 104
Power, Billy xvi, 5, 6
press coverage
   of Eddie Gilfoyle 5–16, 25–7, 61–2
   of Harvey Proctor 148–9, 158
   of Elgan Varney 181
   of Ben Geen 249–50
Pringle, Peter 312–13
prison experiences
   Sam Hallam 302–4
   Birmingham Six 304–6
   Guildford Four 304–6
   Victor Nealon 306–8
   Paddy Hill 310–12, 314, 315–18
   Robert Brown 310–12, 313–14, 315–16
   Peter Pringle 312–13
   effect on families 314–15
   Eddie Gilfoyle 316–18

INDEX

Private Eye 116, 124, 163
Proctor, Harvey
    fall of 143–4
    background to abuse accusation 144–8
    home searched 147–8
    press coverage 148–9, 158
    reacts to abuse accusations 150–51, 154, 158, 159
    abuse allegations against 151–4, 155
    sexuality of 163–4
    receives apology 175

Rafferty, Lady Justice 91–2
Rainey, Carolaine 27
Rainey, John 27
Restivo, Danilo 90–91, 92, 103, 106
Ricciardi, Laura xxiv
Richard, Cliff 158
Richardson, Charlie 117
Richardson, Eddie 117
Righton, Peter 145
Rimington, Sean
    arrest of 39–41
    background to hospitalisation 41–2
    failings in initial investigation 42–7
Ring-Biong, Bullabeck 298, 299
Roberts, Mark 49–51, 134
Roberts, Steve 80, 82, 85
Rose, David 129, 169–70, 171
Rossan, Sheila 27
Rough Justice ((TV programme) 118
Runciman Commission 5–7, 24–5, 128, 129
Runciman, Lord Garry 24
Russell Jones & Walker 62

Saltrese, Chris 170
Sands, Bobby 11
Sargant, Thomas 88
    and Tony Stock 110–112, 113–14
    and reform of criminal justice system 129
    analysis of Court of Appeal 130
Saunders, Alison ix, xvi
Savile, Jimmy 145
SBU 224

Scallywag (magazine) 145
Scheimberg, Irene 238, 239
Scotch Sammy 112
Scott, Roger 41, 46, 58
Secret of Bryn Estyn, The (Webster) 168
Senn, Stephen 258
Serial (podcast) xxiv
sexual abuse
    and Harvey Proctor 143–4, 147–54, 158, 159
    start of investigations into 144–7
    growth in reports of 147
    and Sir Edward Heath 155, 164–8
    review of investigations into 156–9
    and Paul Gambaccini 160–63, 174–5
    view of abuse as endemic 168–9
    House of Commons committee review 169–71, 173
    and Ben Gunn 172
    and Peter Garsden 173–4
    and Geoffrey Long 203–8, 214–16, 219
    false accusations of 205–6
    and David Bryant 208–13, 216–17, 218–19
sexual assault
    and Elgan Varney 177–8, 179–94, 200–201
    police and CPS reactions to reports 178–9
    and Liam Allen 195–7
    and Jemma Beale 197–8
    false allegations of 197–200
Shaken Baby Syndrome
    and Carla Andrews and Craig Stillwell 221–3, 226–9, 230, 244–5
    research into 223–6
    and expert witnesses 229–30
    and Waney Squier 231–4, 236, 237–42
    and Lorraine Harris 233–4
    and Suzanne Holdsworth 234–6
    and Colin Welsh 236–7
    and Ben Butler 237–8
    fear of challenging consensus on 242–4
Shipman, Harold 250, 252
Silent Witness (TV drama) 238–9
Singh, Mr Justice 211

Skuse, Frank 6, 52
Spencer, John 320, 321
Spencer, Lee 234, 235
Spielgelhalter, Sir David 258, 259, 260, 261
Squier, Waney 224, 226, 231–4, 237–42
Stagg, Colin 320–21
Stanbury, Matt 194
Stanley, Alex 218–19
Stanley, Simon 218
Starmer, Keir 178
di Stefano, Giovanni 97–8
Stewart, Greg 287
Stewart, Mr Justice 9
Stillwell, Craig 221–3, 226–9, 244–5
Stock, Alan 126
Stock, Anne 119
Stock, Anthony 140, 141
Stock, Antoinette ('Twinnie') 140, 141
Stock, Brenda 109, 110, 140
Stock, Charlene 140
Stock, James 118, 119, 120
Stock, Mary 112
Stock, Stephen 140–41
Stock, Tony
    at Court of Appeal 107, 110, 114–21, 123–6, 134–5
    arrest and trial 108–9
    and Tom Sargant 110–112
    refused pardon 113–14
    and CCRC 121–4, 125–6, 127, 132
    death of 126
    effect on family 140–41
Stubbs, Hannah
    makes sexual assault accusation 177–8, 185–8, 193–4
    deteriorating relationship with Elgan Varney 179–80
    relationship with Elgan Varney 181–5
    death of 189–92
Stubbs, Timothy 247–8, 249, 266
Sun, The 60, 291
Sunday Mirror 26
Sunday People 148
Sunday Times 31
Sutton, June 79–80
Sweeney, John 234

Syed, Adnan xxiv

Tajani, Dapo 272
Taylor, Andy 250
Taylor, Lord Justice 122
Tayyib, Younis 272
Thomas, Des 99, 100
Thomas, Lord 272
Thompson, Leon 272
Times, The 59, 61–6, 132, 166
Today (radio programme) 150
Tottenham (Broadwater Farm) Three 24
Trial and Error (TV programme) 34–7, 62, 129
Tuerkheimer, Deborah 223, 224
Tully, Gillian ix
Turnbull, Gordon 311
Turner, Michael 238

university projects 96–7

Varney, Elgan
    and evidence disclosure xvi
    accusation of sexual assault 177–8, 179, 185–8
    deteriorating relationship with Hannah Stubbs 179–80
    press coverage of 181
    relationship with Hannah Stubbs 181–5
    inquest into Hannah Stubbs's death 189–92
    interview by police 189
    charged with sexual assault 193–4
    effect of charge on 200–201
Veale, Mike 165–6
Venables, Karen 228
victims' rights xv, 319–20
Vine, Helen 80–81
'Violence against Women and Girls Report' (CPS) 178–9

Walker, Graham 248–9
Walker, Johnny xvi, 5
Walsh, Annie 310, 311
Ward, Judith ix, 24
    evidence disclosure in 52–3

Watson, Tom 145–6
Watts, Mark 146
Webster, Richard 168, 170
West, Fred 32
West, Rosemary 32
White, Chris 209, 211
White, Lynette 54
Whitelaw, Willie 113, 114
Williams, Zoe 198
Wilson, A. N. xvii
Wilson, Stewart 108, 109, 122–3, 124
Winstone, Ray 297
Woodward, Louise 243
Woolry, Delroy 78, 83, 85, 86
World in Action (TV programme) 6, 113, 118
World at One (radio programme) 169

Yorkshire Post 112

Zander, Michael 133
Zellick, Graham 132

ALSO AVAILABLE FROM BITEBACK PUBLISHING

448PP HARDBACK, £20

Paul Gambaccini was arrested in the dead of night in October 2013. Possessions confiscated, smeared in the press and rendered unemployable, Gambaccini was forced to pay tens of thousands of pounds in legal fees without an income.

For a year he was repeatedly bailed and rebailed, often learning of new developments in his case from the media furore that surrounded him.

Finally, inevitably, he was exonerated and added to the ever-growing list of celebrities falsely accused of historical sexual abuse.

Love, Paul Gambaccini is the full, unflinching story of the witch-hunt Gambaccini endured during those twelve horrific months as part of Operation Yewtree. Drawing strength from family and friends, he vowed to keep a journal during his ordeal, writing every day until his case was dismissed. The result is not only a searing account of how it felt to have the full weight of the state brought to bear on him; it is also an urgent, rallying call to arms to all those who care about the quest for justice.

— AVAILABLE FROM ALL GOOD BOOKSHOPS —

WWW.BITEBACKPUBLISHING.COM

ALSO AVAILABLE FROM BITEBACK PUBLISHING

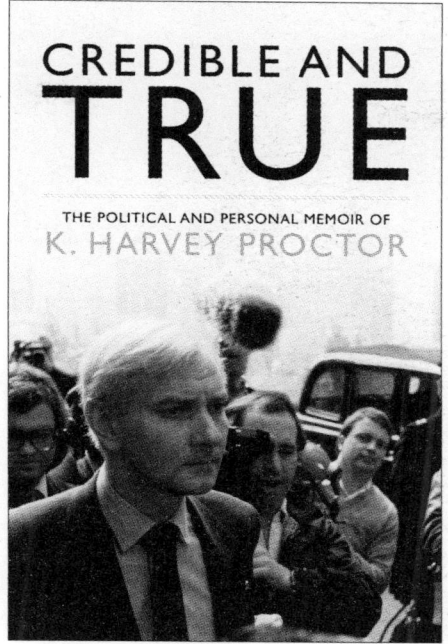

496PP HARDBACK, £20

Early in the morning of 4 March 2015, a fierce knock at the door heralded the start of a new chapter in Harvey Proctor's almost continuous relationship with the police and media, when officers from the Metropolitan Police raided his home in connection with Operation Midland, Scotland Yard's investigation into allegations of a historical Westminster paedophile ring.

In *Credible and True* – words famously used by the police to describe the allegations of Proctor's traducer – the former Conservative MP talks frankly about his life in and out of Parliament, from the struggles and controversy surrounding his resignation in 1987 to the numerous homophobic attacks endured since – one of which, revealed here in horrific detail for the first time, was a very nearly successful attempt on his life.

Finally, he speaks candidly about his most recent embroilment in Operation Midland, of being the victim of a 'homosexual witch-hunt' that has all but destroyed his reputation, adding to the topical debate about police lack of due process in the post-Savile world of 'guilty until proven innocent'.

— AVAILABLE FROM ALL GOOD BOOKSHOPS —

WWW.BITEBACKPUBLISHING.COM

ALSO AVAILABLE FROM BITEBACK PUBLISHING

336PP HARDBACK, £20

On Wednesday 15 April 1998, Detective Sergeant Gurpal Singh Virdi was arrested and accused of sending racist hate mail to himself and ethnic minority colleagues. Dismissed from the Metropolitan Police Service, his reputation in ruins, Virdi took his case to an employment tribunal, which judged that he had been a victim of racial discrimination. Completely vindicated, Virdi was reinstated to the job he loved – but his travails were far from over. Constantly overlooked for promotion, he realised that by challenging the Met he had effectively ended his career.

Following his retirement from the force and keen to serve his local community, Virdi decided to run for election as a Labour councillor – but, prior to the election, he was arrested a second time. The allegations levelled against him were horrifying: he stood accused of sexually assaulting an underage prisoner nearly thirty years earlier. Yet, when the case went to trial, a jury took less than fifty minutes to clear Virdi of all charges, with the judge noting the likelihood of a conspiracy behind the case. But the damage had been done.

Behind the Blue Line is Virdi's deeply shocking account of how one of Britain's biggest institutions brought the apparatus of the state to bear in a campaign to destroy the life of one of its own officers.

— AVAILABLE FROM ALL GOOD BOOKSHOPS —

WWW.BITEBACKPUBLISHING.COM

ALSO AVAILABLE FROM BITEBACK PUBLISHING

320PP HARDBACK, £20

On 18 December 2012, Simon Warr's life changed irrevocably. A respected boarding school teacher, described by his peers as 'one of the outstanding schoolmasters of his generation', Warr was arrested following an allegation of historical child abuse. The complainant was a former pupil at a school where Warr had taught over thirty years previously. Although horrified by the claim, Warr was confident that without conclusive evidence the case would be dropped immediately. Instead, he spent an agonising 672 days on bail, waiting first to be charged and then for the case to go to trial.

It took a jury less than forty minutes to acquit Warr unanimously on all charges. But despite being exonerated by the court, the damage to his reputation was irreversible. And while he struggled to cope in the devastating aftermath of the false accusations levelled against him, his complainants walked away with impunity, under a permanent cloak of anonymity.

Presumed Guilty is a harrowing true story that examines our flawed justice system, and an impassioned plea for us to reconsider the way our police handle cases of alleged historical child abuse, to protect innocent people against further false claims.

— AVAILABLE FROM ALL GOOD BOOKSHOPS —

WWW.BITEBACKPUBLISHING.COM